"Und immer zügelloser
wird die Lust"

Beth V. Linklater

"Und immer zügelloser wird die Lust"

Constructions of sexuality in East German Literatures

With special reference to Irmtraud Morgner
and Gabriele Stötzer-Kachold

Peter Lang · Bern

Die Deutsche Bibliothek – CIP-Einheitsaufnahme

Linklater, Beth V.
"Und immer zügelloser wird die Lust" : constructions of sexuality
in East German literatures ; with special reference to Irmtraud Morgner
and Gabriele Stötzer-Kachold / Beth V. Linklater. – Bern : Lang, 1997
ISBN 3-906759-53-9

Cover illustration: *The Unicorn in Captivity*
Detail from the seventh tapestry
in the series *The Hunt of the Unicorn,* ca. 1500
The Metropolitan Museum of Art

ISBN 3-906759-53-9
US-ISBN 0-8204-3426-4

© Peter Lang AG, European Academic Publishers, Berne 1998

Printed in Germany

To Mum, Dad, Fay, and Stuart

Acknowledgements

I would particularly like to thank Tony for all his help, encouragement and support, without which this book would never have been written. Thanks too to Barry Russell for his expertise and humour, and to Birgit Dahlke, Elizabeth Boa, Margaret Ives, Mariam Fraser, Hans Hahn, Graham Bartram, Sally Johnson, Kath Cross, Annik Taylor and other colleagues for their invaluable help. Many friends have helped me to survive, above all Janine, Mike, Dara, Katrin, Jenny, Tilo and Kathrin. Thanks also to my Gran for buying me a computer. Finally, thanks to the British Academy and the DAAD for their generous support, to the Germanistik Abteilung at the MLU, and everyone whose research has inspired mine.

Table of Contents

Introduction

In 1992 Wolfgang Emmerich, the eminent GDR literary critic, advocated 'eine andere Wahrnehmung der DDR-Literatur: Neue Kontexte, neue Paradigmen, ein neuer Kanon'. 'Theoretische Reflexion und Methodendiskussion', he claimed, 'tun not' (1992, p. 9). In the midst of a *Literaturstreit* which pronounced judgement on artistic products according to the moral, political or *Stasi* standing of the author, it seemed imperative that Emmerich's call be answered. Art from the GDR could no longer be seen solely in terms of dissidence and deference. Five years later it is clear that Emmerich's words echoed much research that had been carried out prior to the *Wende*, and much that was continuing and begun beyond it. New canons and new literary histories have indeed been established. These are based on readings that transcend the limits of a criticism which ignored aesthetic quality, treating the literary text only as a social mirror. The term 'canon' itself has been exposed as a construct which relies upon value judgements open to question, rather than a supposed timelessly valid body of works and writers. A range of 'andere Wahrnehmung*en*' have been proposed and debated. It is within this new context that this book is set. In the attempt to create one more new perspective East German art is united with Western feminism – a unity which is founded in stories of sexuality.

Emmerich's call for a reassessment of literature from the GDR post-1989 echoed also the 'revisionary imperative' which characterises feminist readings of art. His use of the term 'Methodendiskussion' suggests that Western critical theories can be used to ask new questions of the works being studied. The range of theoretical reflexion with which the modern critic is faced is immense, she must of necessity be eclectic. This study adopts a feminist methodology centred on the position of the reader, whereby gender becomes the primary criterion which informs the research. 'A text', wrote Roland Barthes 'is not a line of words releasing a single 'theological' meaning (the 'message' of the Author-God) but a multi-dimensional space in which a variety of writings, none of them original, blend and clash' (1968, p. 146). The true focus of writing, he concludes, is thus reading – the 'death of the author' allows the 'birth of the reader'. Barthes' work has been appropriated by various schools of thought aiming to radically change the role of the literary critic. Hans Robert Jauß's 'Rezeptionsästhetik', for example, emphasises the historical factors at work in the reception of literature by the public. For, as he maintains, the literary work is not an immutable object offering the same message throughout the ages.

Every reading will produce a new meaning, an alternative rather than a definitive answer. With this in mind, feminism has foregrounded 'reading as a woman'.

The analyses presented cannot, however, offer a feminist authority, for in reading as a woman I am, as Jonathan Culler (1983, p. 64) recognises, 'reading as a woman reading as a woman'. Culler argues that the female reader does not rely on a fixed identity to provide her literary and social assumptions but rather, that she 'plays a role she constructs with reference to her identity as a woman, which is also a construct'. Each speaking position is itself constructed, both consciously and subconsciously. While it is impossibile to definitively fix this position, founded upon numerous experiences, the readings here are ultimately united by a political aim to understand and contest patriarchal relations.

If Roland Barthes polemically declares the author dead, Michel Foucault (1969, p. 200) shows that we are constantly at pains to resurrect this sacred authority. In asking 'what is an author?' he notes that: 'it is not enough [...] to repeat the empty affirmation that the author has disappeared'. His utopian question 'what difference does it make who is speaking?' is still, despite Barthes' declaration of authorial suicide, a relevant one. It is one that is especially relevant in patriarchal society, where the speaking position has for so long been occupied by men and where women have traditionally had limited access to the wider discursive field which constitutes gender. For a feminist reading, where 'woman' is to represent producer as well as product, the author's gender thus becomes a matter of vital importance, for 'einem großen und breiten Panoptikum imaginierter Frauenfiguren stehen nur wenige imaginierende Frauen gegenüber' (Bovenschen 1979, p. 12). With this consideration in mind, this study focuses not merely upon the female reader but also upon female authors.

If we are to redress the literary balance by making the female voice heard then we need also to pay heed to Elaine Showalter's 'gynocritical' approach. An interest in women writers is not, of course, a necessarily feminist interest. If gender is largely culturally produced then the gender of the writer, like that of the reader, cannot automatically endow women's representations with authority. Yet this interest can contribute not only to female literary, but also to female critical traditions, traditions which are, at present, obscured by gaps and silences. However, Showalter's assumption that 'women's culture forms a collective experience within the cultural whole' (1986b, p. 260) cannot be taken as a starting point. A concentration on individual writers rather than on groups is essential, for each woman will be influenced by different intersecting discourses. Analysing writing by women in complete isolation from that by men is also potentially reductive, in as far as it relies on a fixed 'female' experience.

In the GDR 'women writers' were constituted as a single category – by censors, critics and the writers themselves. East German officials exploited the Marxist maxim that social progress could be measured by the status of 'das schöne Geschlecht'. Women writers became symbolic of socialist progress towards emancipation, a view sustained also by the acclaim they found abroad. This literary category was even mentioned in official speeches. At the X *Schriftstellerkongreß* Hermann Kant (1988, p. 22) gives a long list of female authors and proclaims: 'Längst ist es ein vor dieser unvollständigen Liste verständlicher Brauch, den internationalen Rang der DDR-Literatur auch vom enormen Anteil schreibender Frauen herzuleiten'. Irmtraud Morgner and Gabriele Stötzer-Kachold are part of this 'Anteil schreibender Frauen', but beyond this they are individual writers in whose work the sexual figures in a variety of ways. In this respect their contribution to GDR literatures stands out, particularly when their oeuvre is compared with texts by other East German writers. At the same time the feminist tendencies in the work of Morgner and Stötzer-Kachold, though in many ways related, are also notably contrasting. They thus testify to the heterogeneity of feminist projects.

In order to answer Emmerich's call for a new perception it is not only the object of the debate which must be unsettled, but also the terms of that debate. Simone de Beauvoir notes, in *The Second Sex*, that:

> It is doubtless impossible to approach any human problem with a mind free from bias. [...] Rather than attempt to conceal principles more or less definitely implied, it is better to state them openly at the beginning (1949, p. 28).

This introduction will thus define terminology and introduce the main methodolgical and theoretical arguments that form the implicit basis of later analyses. Firstly, if canons are to be properly revised the term 'GDR literature' itself must be called into question. Helga Schütz (1991, p. 20) claims that 'die DDR-Literatur ist von Westmedien und DDR-Lesern gemacht worden', thereby effacing the role of the author. 'Made' by critics, readers and politicians, the concept was deployed to mark culturally a historical, political and geographical division which had been cemented in 1961:

> Die Konzeption einer eigenständigen DDR-Literatur entstand erst in den 60er Jahren, im Gefolge eines politischen Strategiewechsels. [...] Wie einst das Konzept der deutschen Nationalliteratur sollte die Konzeption der DDR-Literatur der Identitäts-bildung dienen (Rosenberg 1995, p. 9).

13

Whereas the political divisions disappeared in 1989/90, the idea of an homogenous national literature had already become problematic from the 1970s, when the range of aesthetic styles and themes accepted under the rubric of socialist art could no longer be easily defined. 'DDR-Literatur' and 'sozialistische Nationalliteratur' were clearly not synonomous. This literary development, too, can clearly be set within a changed political situation, where international recognition of the GDR made it easier for writers to broaden their interests.

The wave of artists leaving the GDR during the 1970s and the 1980s added to the difficulties of definition. Over one hundred East German writers lived in West Germany. The work of these writers was often coloured by their Eastern upbringing, yet was read and received primarily in the West. Thus it could be regarded as both East and West German. Other artists resident in the GDR produced work which was explicitly 'Western' rather than East German. Many novels and plays written and produced in the GDR were read and performed in the West, forming what appeared to be the basis for a common German litera-ture. In a world increasingly dominated by the threat of nuclear war or environ-mental disaster and by the rise of computer technology – issues which affect people globally – such breadth was especially appropriate. The theme of sexuality can be seen in this context.

The term 'DDR-Literatur' was, therefore, abandoned by some in favour of the all-embracing 'Deutsche' or 'deutschsprachige Literatur' reflecting a common language, a common literary heritage and common concerns. Fritz Raddatz (1972), who had proclaimed the existence of two separate German literatures in the 1970s, later conceded that he had been wrong (1987). Günter Grass (1980, p. 8), in advocating a single cultural nation, accorded unified literature a function beyond political borders:

> Als etwas Gesamtdeutsches läßt sich in beiden deutschen Staaten nur noch die Literatur nachweisen; sie hält sich nicht an die Grenze, so hemmend besonders ihr die Grenze ge-zogen wurde.

German literature thus embraced texts written and read in the FRG, Austria, Switzerland, the GDR, Brazil, Luxembourg, Romania and America. Others continued to defend, or at least work with the notion of 'GDR literature'. In interview with Jachimczak (1988, p. 358) Christoph Hein argues that the term had become more applicable since the 1970s than it was in earlier decades, for literature is always developed in the context of a specific society. Hein's own work is both Western- and GDR-specific, a fact which he relates to his biography. Positions between these two poles were also common, positions which expressed the dilemma faced by critics. Emmerich, in his widely-read *Literaturgeschichte* (1989, p. 449), concludes that: 'das Verhältnis von deutscher Literatur Ost und deutscher Literatur West ist heute eins von Konvergenz und Divergenz zugleich'. In his opinion it is more important to set GDR literature in an international literary context than to erect demarcation lines.

Literature is, however, manufactured, published and read within social contexts. The origin of the texts is not entirely irrelevant. The GDR did produce a specific literary system, not least because of the effect of censorship and the resulting 'self-' or 'inner' censorship. The artist needed constantly to be aware of his/her stance towards the state. This awareness exerted pressure on literary production. Yet writers in the East were not as dependent on the market forces of art as those in the West. Artists returning from exile after the War also contributed notably to the image of literature in the GDR, more so than they did in the FRG. The influence of these and other 'GDR' factors will have been decisive for some texts and unimportant for others. Similarly, the influence of certain texts will have been decisive for how the GDR itself was understood, both by its own citizens and abroad. Thus, as new works are published in which experiences of the GDR can be discovered, 'GDR Literature' can perhaps be said to live on beyond the collapse of the GDR.

The problems outlined indicate that generalising always means silencing contradiction. Ultimately the texts themselves are more important than a critique which remains focused on the GDR. Yet the term 'DDR-Literatur' and its English equivalent will remain problematic for some time to come. Within *Germanistik* the alternative concepts of 'Literatur in der DDR', 'Literatur aus der DDR' and 'Literatur der DDR' have been used. Here the broad concept of 'GDR literatures' has been adopted. The plural noun indicates the variety of possible artistic approaches taken in the GDR, particularly since the late 1960s. The reference to the GDR allows for a certain specificity of literature that has a different social, political and cultural background to that produced in the FRG, Austria or Switzerland.

The term 'GDR Literature' was augmented in the 1980s by its apparent opposite, 'alternative GDR Literature'. In German the terms used to describe this moment in literary history included *alternativ, unabhängig, inoffiziell, avantgarde, autonom, Ost-Moderne* and *underground.* The general label *Prenzlauer-Berg-Szene* emphasised merely one area where this art was produced and gave the false impression that a unified literary school was in the making. After the *Wende* this art, first championed as the only real East German art and then cast aside, tarnished by the *Stasi* associations of some of its foremost representatives, suffered the same fate as its 'official' counterpart and the shortcomings of the either/or categories became clear. Whilst recognising these problems, the difference in contexts of production between those texts published in the GDR with the open approval of the *Hauptverwaltung Verlage* and those published without this approval remains important. For the purposes of this study the terms 'official' and 'unoffical' are employed.

In terms of the plurality of GDR literatures Morgner and Stötzer-Kachold represent different generations and different forms of writing: 'official' and 'unofficial'. The older author began to write in the 1950s, the younger in the 1970s. Stötzer-Kachold's poetic prose is often ignored and therefore has not yet become part of the standard canon. Irmtraud Morgner's novels, on the other hand, were accepted classics of GDR art, at least in the West. The juxtaposition of two such authors can thus justify a scepticism towards the canon. Furthermore, both authors – using varying artistic techniques – invite their audience to productively engage with the text and create meanings, thus highlighting the role of the audience. Morgner's use of fantasy and operative montage relies upon an active reader.[1] The confusion of authorial positions present in the texts, including that identified as Morgner's own, further adds to the stress placed upon the act of reading as unifying source rather than that of writing. Stötzer-Kachold too disrupts classic realism, undoing unified character and narrator, time, place and fixed genre. The subject position from which she writes is divided, decentred, in crisis. Her constant questioning of language and the subject's relationship to language links her work with that of other representatives of the 'alternative' GDR literary scene and with poststructuralist art. Such art demands that the reader engage productively with the fragmented text, reforming her own narratives.

Neither Morgner nor Stötzer-Kachold attempts to impose a single 'right' interpretation upon their work. If Foucault's question 'What difference does it make who is speaking?' is important, then so too is the implicit correlation of this question: What difference does it make who is listening? Meanings are produced in a dialectical process of communication between writer and reader, a process which functions around a text and within competing ideologies. The critic can only provide some of these possible meanings. A new canon, such as that desired by Emmerich, must therefore aim to include by description rather than to exclude by prescription. The following study adds to this description as

---

1 The term 'operative montage' describes the technique favoured by Morgner, whereby extracts from sources as varied as scientific documents and sexual manuals are woven into her novels. The montage becomes operative in that it aims to use unusual texts in a new way, and also to allow the reader to make links between the texts.

far as constructions of sexuality in GDR literatures are concerned, specifically within the work of Irmtraud Morgner and Gabriele Stötzer-Kachold.

The use of plural forms and quotation marks makes clear that language is not fixed but is, rather, a site where meanings are produced, sustained renegotiated or created. Certain terms, understood in relation to one another, are fundamental to the hierarchical linguistic structures of patriarchy. These terms, challenged in feminist theories, form the second set of coordinates which structure this study. Concepts such as 'male', 'female', 'masculine', 'feminine', 'sex', 'sexuality' and 'gender' have been contested, exposed as signs rather than essences. Conventionally, the term 'sex' refers to one's biological sex, i.e. male or female. Gender is the cultural meaning attributed to biological sex, i.e. masculine or feminine. Recent debate has, however, unsettled the terms 'sex' and 'gender'. Such usage obscures differences within the opposing and mutually reliant categories of 'female' or 'male', which are made to appear 'natural', without any questioning of the term 'nature'. Judith Butler (1990, p. 7) has argued that sex and gender cannot be separated. In her opinion such a division is irrelevant and misleading:

> If the immutable character of sex is contested, perhaps this construct called 'sex' is as culturally constructed as gender; indeed, perhaps it was always already gender, with the consequence that the distinction between sex and gender turns out to be no distinction at all.

Butler understands sexual identities as permanent copies, as performance. She claims that sex can never remain outside of discursive production. Woman is a category which achieves meaning only in a heterosexual context. Whilst recognising Butler's important contribution to feminist debate, the sex/gender divide offers a useful tool with which to analyse the texts under consideration, mainly because the works themselves rely upon this division.

The notion of sexuality describes the whole area of personality connected with sexual behaviour and sexual desire. It is produced by discourses on 'sex'. The word 'erotic' is used in the sense of pertaining to the sexual or the amorous. For Morgner in particular the concept of the erotic is not merely concerned with sexual desire, but expresses a utopian and universal sensuality. This study concentrates on various representations of the body and of coitus, including homosexuality, rape, prostitution, orgasm and pornography, where pornography can be vaguely defined as 'possessive voyeurism inviting rape' (Pollock 1992, p. 142). The theme of love, traditionally regarded as, at least for women, linked to the sexual, romance, marriage and the family, is again ambivalent. For the authors studied here love is a utopian desire. It is not reduced to that emotion felt between two people in a sexual relationship, but has a wider social meaning. Yet within feminism love is often also regarded as a major factor in the way patriarchy trains women to conceive eroticism only in terms of heterosexual romance. Elements of this argument surface in the work of both Morgner and Stötzer-Kachold.

As used here, the term feminism designates the ideology of women's liberation. Intrinsic in all feminist argument is the belief that women suffer some form of injustice because of the gendered construction of their sex. As Eva Kaufmann puts it, feminism signifies:

> Geistige Bestrebungen und praktische Bewegungen, Haltungen und Politik von Frauen, die auf die Veränderung von Strukturen, Beziehungen, Denk- und Verhaltensweisen gerichtet sind, die Diskriminierung und Unterdrückung der Frau bedingen (1991, p. 109).

'Feminism', as Gayle Rubin (1992, p. 301) notes, 'has always been vitally interested in sex'. Indeed many feminist writings emphasise the sexual, in line with the famous slogan of second wave feminism, 'the personal is political'. As Vance (1992, p. 16) writes, 'sexuality poses a challenge to feminist enquiry, since it is an intersection of the political, social, economic, historical, personal and experimental, linking behavior and thought, fantasy and action'. Negative and oppressive constructions of female sexuality, where expressed in cultural artefacts, can be regarded as exemplary for the general privileging of the male within Western society.

Recent feminist enquiry into sexuality, aiming to expose examples of subordination, began by investigating 'images of women', images which were also 'images of sexuality'. Kate Millett's (1969) powerful attacks on writers such as Mailer, Miller and Lawrence emphasised the way in which woman is represented as sexual object and accorded portrayals of sexuality a political meaning. In a culture dominated by the visual image there will always be a need for this type of approach, not only to contest certain meanings attached to the signifier 'woman', but also to welcome change and resistance. Where applied with excessive dogmatism, however, it can achieve no more than to expose numerous examples of sexist ideologies. A specific authorial intention or an all-pervasive monolithic system of male power are often unproblematically accepted. Critics may tend to assume a common experience of sexual 'reality', failing to recognise the complex structure of fictional texts and positing art simply as a mirror or a vehicle for change. Griselda Pollock (1992, p. 136) therefore questions the term 'Images of Women' itself, which, she proposes:

'implies a juxtaposition of two separable elements – women as a gender or social group versus representations of women, or a real entity, women, opposed to falsified, distorted or male views of women'.

Ilse Braatz (1980, p. 165), in her investigations of both East and West German literatures in terms of sexual imagery, avoids the conflation of artist and text. She asks about the role that sexual relationships appear to play in the texts:

> Gibt es auf gesellschaftliche Verhältnisse gerichtete Widerstandsliteratur, bei der Liebesbeziehungen nicht belanglose Ergänzung bleiben, sondern entscheidend zur Motivation und zum Inhalt des Widerstands beitragen, insofern also neue Möglichkeiten der sexuellen Befreiung zeigen?

These are issues which are important in the following literary critiques, which question whether female characters are portrayed as sexual victim or sexual actor, whether sexual stereotypes are reinforced or questioned, and how female sexuality as a concept is constructed. If woman is, as John Berger (1972, p. 47) argues, 'an object of vision: a sight', then the questions of how, and by whom, she is seen, will always be important.

In analysing images of sexuality it is also necessary to question the vocabulary used in the coding of the image. With regard to naming both the anatomy and the sexual act, linguistic treatments are traditionally cold, clinical, crude or androcentric. At the opposite end of the scale there is emotional trivia and bathos, often centred around similes of nature as 'pure' or 'virginal'. No sign can be neutral, each word possesses a variety of ideological connotations, connotations which will be gendered, understood through the traditions of patriarchy. Medical terminology, for example, relies on 'a technology of health and pathology' (Foucault 1979, p. 44) and thus participates in the traditional forms of disciplinary power which aim to control the body. An author attempting to create erotic portrayals must take issue with these semantics if s/he is to effectively challenge sexual stereotypes. Even supposed 'alternatives' will always be read within existing ideological structures.

The method which takes images of women as a starting point and asks how texts relate to 'female experience' has consistently been adopted in analysing GDR writing by women. Curious Western commentators in particular were often concerned merely to show how a text presented the conflicts and contradictions of a woman's life under socialist rule, rather than to seriously take issue with aesthetic aspects of the writing. Much secondary literature thus begins by outlining the legal and political situation of the woman in the GDR, followed by the 'reflection' of this situation in the art works. Schmitz-Köster's

Trobadora und Kassandra und... Weibliches Schreiben in der DDR (1989), for example, devotes a chapter to 'Frauenalltag in der DDR'. Nancy Lukens and Dorothy Rosenberg's edition of English translations of writing by East German women (1993) also begins with an outline of the social and legal position of women in the GDR. Malcolm Humble (1992, p. 335) provides an illustrative example of this approach: 'women's writing', he states, 'developed in the former GDR to take account of the particular problems there'.

This emphasis on authentic realism was not the sole province of critics interested in feminism or women's writing in the GDR but was rather a characteristic of general GDR literary criticism. It meant that art was regarded, in some cases, as merely a substitute for political discussion, media debate or sociological study. Many commentators have, then, referred to the *Ersatz-funktion* (substitute role) of GDR art.[2] The GDR economic historian Jürgen Kuczynski, for example, argued in 1980 that future historians would find modern literature more useful than most academic texts. Irma Hanke (1986, p. 142) bemoans the lack of detailed sociological studies in the GDR and similarly directs the interested reader to 'die Schilderung der DDR-Gesellschaft in der schönen Literatur'. The sociologist Irene Dölling (1980) uses extracts from Maxie Wander's *Guten Morgen, du Schöne* as 'evidence' for her work. The state-controlled press in the GDR, 'to all intents and purposes the Party's mouthpiece' (Sandford 1984, p. 33), was characterised by uniformity and repetition.[3] Here too, there was little of sociological or historical value to be found. Whereas the newspapers concentrated on the success stories of socialism, literature dealt critically with problems regarded as 'real'.

Art in the GDR thus functioned as much more than a means of entertainment. It was, rather, a 'Vorreiter' and a 'Lückenbüßer für andere Disziplinen, für andere Medien' (Böck 1990a, p. 62), offering a forum where issues such as feminism could be discussed, (particularly in the absence of an East German women's movement other than the official DFD).[4] As David Bathrick (1991, p. 245) contends, fictive voices 'represented an important alternative discourse outside and in some cases *critical* of Marxism'. In this respect one can identify a specific East German literary system and there is thus some justification for the critical treatment of East German literature as *Ersatz*. Early Socialist Realist demands for art forms which optimistically reflect and influence 'reality' court

2   See, for example, Helmut Göhler 1990.
3   See also David Childs 1983.
4   Demokratischer Frauenbund Deutschlands. This organisation is concisely described by Schwarz (1990, p. 14) as a 'Transmissionsriemen für herrschende Parteipolitik'.

this type of response, as does the popularity of the *Protokolle* (interview or documentary literature) in the former GDR.

The *Ersatzfunktion* is, therefore, an aspect of GDR art which remains worthy of consideration with regard to constructions of the sexual. Where sexual topics were considered taboo it was, in some cases, writers, painters or film makers who challenged these taboos. There are, however, limitations as well as possibilities of this public potential of art. East German erotic literature did not develop solely in order to provide a space where sexual taboos could be discussed. To claim that it did would be to ignore the aesthetic achievements, and failures, of the texts under consideration. Often the erotic scenes depicted were not 'realistic' at all, but were utopian visions or dream sequences. Ultimately these were, in every case, fictional portrayals, even where they possess, or are invested with, social relevance. Critiques which focus merely on the relationship between the art work and GDR society are liable to become prescriptive, judgemental and dogmatic.

A broadly materialist approach to literary study, such as that adopted by Marxist feminists, is useful in as far as it highlights the fact that men and women create social conditions, rather than any metaphysical agency. These conditions influence how sexuality is viewed in society. The modes of literary production and consumption will also affect possible readings of erotic texts. Within modern Marxist thought work by Louis Althusser and Pierre Macherey has allowed a development away from Lukács' ideas towards 'methods of reading texts which are compatible with the post-structuralist realisation that literature is not simply the *reflection* of the world outside the text' (Pearce/Mills 1989, p. 190). Texts are said to reveal the workings of 'ideologies',[5] and function within Althusser's 'Ideological State Apparatuses' to 'interpellate' the reader, rather than to mirror life itself.[6] Sexuality then, as it is constructed in culture, is one of the 'attendant ideological agencies' (ibid, p. 195) of the family, together with concepts such as 'gender difference' and 'romantic love'. Thus cultural representations of the sexual can be analysed in order to understand more clearly some of the means by which women are oppressed, and how they conspire with or resist that oppression. Any attempt, however, to define a fixed, or 'natural', female sexuality, which art 'should' reflect, would confute the overall aim of this study.

---

5   Belsey and Moore (1989, p. 245) define the term as used by Althusser as 'the beliefs, meanings and practices which shape our thoughts and actions [...] ideology is the condition of our experience'.

6   Cf. Louis Althusser, 'Ideology and Ideological State Apparatuses, in Easthope/McGowan 1992, pp. 50-59.

Feminist approaches to sexuality in literature have, however, extended far beyond images of eroticism and their relationship to 'reality'. Of particular importance in varied theoretical writings has been the role of the body, as the site where overlaid meanings, commands and contradictions compete to form sexual subjectivity. As Kaja Silverman (1992, p. 324) recognises:

> While human bodies exist prior to discourse it is only through discourse that they arrive at the condition of being 'male' or 'female' [...] Discourse functions first to territorialise and then to map meaning onto bodies.

Identity begins with the corporeal, particularly for women, who are conditioned, as potential mothers, to see themselves primarily in terms of their biological function. The female body is on offer everywhere, a commodity used, and misused, by Western culture. Conversely, it can also represent the focal point for possibilities of change. In literature, the anatomy can be analysed both as a sexual motif and in terms of a specific feminine, or female, aesthetic. Sigrid Weigel (1987, p. 112), for example, reviews texts which represent both 'ein Schreiben *über* den Körper' and a 'Körper-Sprache' for '"Mit dem Körper schreiben" beziehungsweise "den Körper schreiben" ist eines der Motive, das in den Debatten über "weibliche Ästhetik" immer wieder zu hören ist'. Sexuality, in this sense, so it is claimed, can act as a structuring principle, as a positive source of creativity rather than Freudian absence or lack. Female desire is perceived of as able to disrupt phallogocentric discourse. The language of the unconscious is thus associated with the female; conscious, rational language with the male.

In this respect the work of French feminists such as Hélène Cixous and Luce Irigaray has been, and still is, highly influential. Cixous deconstructs the binary oppositions based around male/female that structure patriarchy, and emphasises writing rather than a speaking subject.[7] She asks what feminine '*sexual pleasure*' is and how this is inscribed within writing. Concentrating on this 'jouissance'[8], her 'écriture féminine' aims: 'to proclaim woman as the source of life, power and energy' (Moi 1985, p. 105). She equates feminine writing with women and with the female body and posits the category of the 'female text',

[7] Here she uses the work of Jacques Derrida, for whom no signifier has meaning in itself. Meaning is created only through open-ended play with other signifiers, present or absent. Centres of discourse (such as 'man' or 'phallus') are deconstructed.

[8] Marx and de Courtivron define 'jouissance' thus: 'Women's *jouissance* carries with it the notion of fluidity, diffusion, duration. It is a kind of potlatch in the world of orgasms, a giving, expending, dispensing of pleasure without concern about ends or closure.' They continue: 'One can easily see how the same imagery could be used to describe women's writing' (1981, pp. 36-37).

which is continuous and spacious, round rather than linear – an idea which has influenced the work of many writers, including Stötzer-Kachold. The form of 'parler femme' associated with the writing of Luce Irigaray also 'pursues the relationship between female sexuality and language to create a different symbolic order' (Millard 1989, p. 160). This radical theory is founded upon fluidity, multiple forms of pleasure, and an autoerotic sense of touch.[9] Celebrating the female anatomy, it aims to decisively challenge the theorisation of female sexuality within masculine parameters, for 'woman's desire most likely does not speak the same language as man's desire' (Irigaray 1977, p. 101). As Margaret Whitford (1991) rightly contends, it is a mistake to see Irigaray solely in terms of 'écriture féminine'. Such a judgement reduces a wide oeuvre to one simple formula. It is this formula, however, which has been widely adopted by both critics and artists interested in female aesthetics.

Elements of these ideas have certainly been crucial to feminist thinking on sexuality, encouraging new representations of female experiences beyond passive sexual object. Yet an awareness of the historically determined codes of femininity is also necessary. The projects of Cixous and Irigaray need to be used with care. They are finely balanced on that 'tightrope between subversion and reappropriation' which Pollock (1992, p. 140) claims is walked by feminists who attempt to 'decolonize the female body' from existing male forms of signification. Moreover, the notion of femininity as positive 'otherness' is not new. As Patricia Waugh (1992) notes, its roots are in Romanticism. Concentration on this space, somehow located outside the 'Law of the Father', can eclipse the material conditions of the lives of actual women, and deny their liberation. The emphasis on the female body is a 'reduction', which 'precludes considering the many other ways in which we experience our embodiedness' (Flax 1990, p. 53) and pretends that men did not have bodies also. If, with Foucault, one starts from the premise that sexuality does not exist as a natural 'essence', but is a concept constructed for specific ideological purposes, then any theory which, (even if only through analogy), posits sexuality as a source of meaning in itself, has to be closely questioned. Postmodern feminism has stressed that: 'all attempts to inscribe female difference within writing are a matter of inscribing women within fictions of one kind or another (whether literary, critical or psychoanalytic)' (Jacobus 1989, p. 62). Silvia Bovenschen (1979) convincingly shows in her study of 'Weiblichkeit' that the concept has no meaning in itself. It merely encodes the many images and ideologies that it has historically been made to represent. The

---

9   Eg: In *Spéculum de l'autre femme* (1974).

term 'weibliche Ästhetik', when linked to sexuality, thus remains problematic. There can, as Showalter (1986b, p. 252) warns, 'be no expression of the body which is unmediated by linguistic, social and literary structures'.

More recent feminist research therefore, such as that by Julia Kristeva, has, as Waugh (1992, p. 189) notes, 'developed a self-reflexive mode'. Kristeva's concept of the 'semiotic' is 'feminine' rather than female. Hers is a poetic resource open to men as well as women, for it foregrounds identification with the mother rather than anatomy: 'This recourse to the semiotic, the inscription of the archaic relation to the mother in language – it isn't the monopoly of women. [...] It's a question of subjectivity' (1989, p. 132). Similarly, post-modern feminism abandons the 'quest for an authentic women's language' as 'utterly misguided and fruitless' (Cameron 1985, p. 177), turning instead to the issues of power, identity and difference raised by writers such as Michel Foucault, issues which are foundational for sexual constructions.

The points of overlap between feminism and postmodernism have been documented extensively and continue to cause much discussion.[10] Undoing traditional boundaries, both movements question the Enlightenment concepts of truth, knowledge, power, reason, autonomy, language and self, and expose the discursive production of all meanings. Furthermore, both undo the fundamental male/female notion of opposition. Postmodern critiques make clear that the feminist construction of a sense of identity can become problematic if given cross cultural values or any specific content. For as Waugh (1992, p. 189) recognises, the gendered self for which women seek recognition 'has been constructed through the very culture and ideological formations which feminism seeks to challenge and dismantle'. However, the wholesale post-modern rejection of the category of gender leads ultimately to the decon-struction of feminism itself. As a utopian ideal this may be inspirational, and can be given concrete form through fiction. Yet if notions of historical progress and human agency are abandoned entirely, traditional feminist agendas are doomed to failure. Thus, at this moment in history, as Sandra Harding (1990, p.

---

[10] The boundaries between postmodernism and poststructuralism remain blurred, as does the relationship of Foucault's work to these two movements. A discussion of these issues is outside the scope of this thesis and, for my purposes here, I use the broad term postmodernism to suggest that: 'In applying and extending the modernist insistence on the essentially conventional nature of sociopolitical arrangements and their representations, postmodernism renders the conventional into the arbitrary and promotes a politics and theory of disbelief toward the language of rights, rationality, interests and autonomy as presumed characteristics of a humanistic self that was thought to provide the legitimizing foundation for modern social life' (de Stefano 1990, p. 63-64).

101) writes, 'our feminisms need both Enlightenment and postmodernist agendas'.

One such postmodern agenda is to be found in the work of Michel Foucault, which is useful in as much as it clearly shows how the concept of the sexual is overlaid with a number of significations. The modern age, as Foucault (1979, p. 11) describes it, has witnessed 'a veritable discursive explosion' of writings 'around and apropos of sex'. Of these writings, Foucault's own are amongst the most important. In *Histoire de la Sexualité 1: La volonté de savoir* the author sets sex within specific historical and social contexts: 'What is at issue, briefly, is the overall 'discursive fact', the way in which sex is put into discourse' (Foucault 1979, p. 11). Sexuality, Foucault (1979, p. 105) contends, 'must not be thought of as a kind of natural given which power tries to hold in check, or as an obscure domain which knowledge tries gradually to uncover. It is a name that can be given to a historical construct'. The text outlines a process that began with the Church and was taken up by the medical and legal professions, whereby sexuality became a secret to be simultaneously revealed and hidden, a focus for ideas of truth and falsehood and a path to self-understanding. Experts surveyed, studied, named, classified and administered a wide range of sexual 'cases', erecting a myriad of practices designed to control an individual's body. The two most important systems set up in society and in language for the regulation of sex were, Foucault summarises, the traditional family unit and the 'order of desires'. This latter represents the hierarchy that created 'normal' and 'perverse' sexual acts, based around a system of binary oppositions such as healthy/ill or sane/mad. Embedded within a structure based on a binary interplay of licit and illicit, sexuality is, therefore, anything but 'natural'.

The body is, then, not simply a biological entity, but is the site where discourses of power and knowledge meet. Foucault's notions of power are developed in contrast to ideologies based on what he calls the 'juridico-discursive' model, which sees power as being possessed and primarily prohibitive. Foucault analyses power as exercised rather than possessed and as primarily productive rather than repressive. He isolates power relations at the microlevel of society, for it is here that centralised forms of control are made possible. Discursive fields in which power is exercised require a speaking position and a spoken subject. Identity is formed within and by these dynamic relations and is unstable and polymorphous. An individual can merely choose between constantly varying subject roles. She does not constitute meanings herself which she then transcribes into discourse, but rather it is through discourse itself that she understands meaning. The humanist rational and revolutionary subject is thus redefined as a myth. Foucault's subject is neither entirely free nor completely enslaved.

Foucault's analyses of power inform 'genealogy' as a critical method. A 'genealogy' in Foucault's terms is a social and historical investigation to discover not who we 'really' are, but how we are constituted and classified. It makes no universal moral judgements and entails no utopian vision. In *The History of Sexuality*, therefore, Foucault starts by questioning Freud's 'repressive hypothesis' so that sexuality loses its 'essential' characteristics:

> The hypothesis of a power of repression seems to me quite inadequate if we are to explain this whole series of reinforcements and intensifications that our preliminary enquiry has discovered. [...] There has never existed one type of stable subjugation, given once and for all (1979, p. 72, p. 97).

Freud's work, and that of his followers, should not, however, be simply dismissed. Freud's insights have been particularly valuable within literary studies. Furthermore, Juliet Mitchell (1974) has convincingly argued that to reject Freud's work on the unconscious would be fatal for the feminist project. She praises Freud for his 'elimination of an absolute difference between abnormality and normality' (p. 10), and contends that on the basis of his insights gender identity is not fixed, as it is in theories of biological determinism. Unconscious meanings given to sexual experience are undoubtedly just as important as conscious ones. The forms of individual libidinous desire identified by Freud, and the neurotic expressions of its insatiability, have a crucial role to play in the formation and the sustaining of the gender differences that dominate our experiences of sex and deeply influence our social identity. Ultimately, however, as Weeks (1986, p. 73) writes, psychoanalysis does set up a prescriptive model of what sex 'should' be. Freud's famous statement that 'anatomy is destiny' has become almost legendary. The use of anatomical features, even if this is merely symbolical as Mitchell claims, is bound to lead to confusion. Ascribing total causal effect to the unconscious presents an ahistorical definition of sexuality that offers little hope of change.

Sexual power cannot, therefore, be solely ascribed to all men and no women. Such dualities are invalid categories, particularly in the contemporary globalised world, characterised by interconnectedness and collective responsibility. Against this background of multifaceted strands of oppression ideas of 'sexual liberation', such as those proposed by Wilhelm Reich (1951) or Herbert Marcuse (1962), appear hopelessly utopian and ahistorical. If there is no centralised locus of oppression then neither can there be, as a logical corollary, a single locus of resistance. As Weeks (1986, p. 25) notes, sexuality cannot be reduced to a 'life force we must release to save our civilisation'. However, a number of 'real' forms of subjugation and of injustice do exist, notably structured around class, race and gender. Sexuality as a construct is clearly fundamental to the supposed differences between men and women which maintain the power relations structuring their lives, particularly given the history of male domination over and female exclusion from the institutions which have produced sexual discourse. In terms of sexual power, woman, like the Foucauldian subject, is constantly caught between awareness of her victimisation and the desire to exert control. The feminist slogan 'the personal is political' would seem to conform exactly to Foucault's concentration on the microlevel of society. It is at this level too, that women reproduce the systems of domination in which they are entrapped.

Jana Sawicki's 'Foucauldian Feminism' (1991) thus extends Foucault's ideas to focus specifically on female bodies. The links between her two concepts are summarised thus:

> Foucault and feminists both focus upon sexuality as a key arena of political struggle. Both expand the domain of the "political" to include forms of social domination associated with the personal sphere. And both launch critiques against forms of biological determinism, and humanism. Finally, both are sceptical of the human sciences insofar as the latter have been implicated in modern forms of domination (p. 49).

She argues together with feminists such as Audrey Lorde for a 'politics of difference', a pluralist feminism which accepts and welcomes the fact that women are not all oppressed in the same way by patriarchy. This is, rather, dependent on issues of class, race, age, sexual preference, cultural and family background, religion, physical ability, and so on. Sawicki sees difference as a resource, rather than as a barrier to effective political action. Foucault too, she claims, has recognised the ambiguous power of difference in modern society. Carole Vance also argues for recognition of female sexual difference, in order that feminism does not fall into the traps of normative sexuality that it is desperate to escape.

The polymorphous and ambiguous shape of Foucauldian discourse implicitly suggests that it is the present itself that offers possibilities for social change, not a golden past or future utopia. Thus whilst some feminists concentrate on using the analysis of power given in Foucault's work to identify and understand the disciplinary technologies that map meaning onto women's bodies, others centre on 'cultures of resistance' (Sawicki, p. 14). One such culture is provided by those feminist writers who argue for acceptance of sexual variety, where concerns are mutual consideration, consent and pleasure rather than a pre-

27

scribed 'ideal'. As Vance (1992, p. xvi) notes: 'For women to experience auto-nomous desire and to act in ways that give them sexual pleasure in a society that would nurture and protect their delights is our culture's worst nightmare and feminism's best fantasy'. This multifaceted fantasy can best be expressed through art. In particular liberatory art by women, which has traditionally been, and still is, 'an important site for the articulation of oppression and of utopian hopes for a different future' (Weedon 1987, p. 144).

In this sense the concentration upon the links between Foucault's work and GDR writing by women is a feminist project. As Martin (1980, p. 60) argues: 'The points of convergence between feminist and poststructuralist thought make Foucault's characterisations of such developments useful in our attempts to elaborate the significance for us of [...] anti-patriarchal literature in the GDR'. These texts do not only have immediate informative value, they are not just substitute sociology. They are also important for their contribution to the ideas and debates of Western feminism. Both Irmtraud Morgner and Gabriele Stötzer-Kachold express their own form of feminist sexual fantasy, whilst remaining aware of the context in which these fantasies are produced. Their work is influenced by actual experiences, both in the specific sense of that related to the GDR, and in the wider sense of that pertaining to Western industrialised, patriarchal society. It thus engages with the theories discussed in this intro-duction, as well as with the literature which will be analysed in the next chapter.

Analysis of individual texts can, then, identify important patterns, both of repression and of resistance, whilst at the same pointing up diversity. For it is only when we begin to understand the multifaceted nature of sexual oppression that we can begin to challenge it. In this examination of East German literatures the sexual, as a cultural product, is thus seen as a point of convergence for both conscious and unconscious meanings, rather than as a unified source. Art is one area of discourse where these meanings are both constructed and reproduced. Representations, descriptions and depictions of sexuality are, therefore, open to multiple forms of comprehension. The issues raised by Freud and challenged by Foucault have influenced the consideration of concepts of sexual utopias, sexual liberation and sexual power. Feminist discourses of sexuality can provide new terms in which sexual debate may function, upsetting, if not undoing, matrixes of power. For despite being inessential, sexual differences remain remarkably permanent. Not only are they constantly reproduced in mainstream culture, but they are still crucial to the creation of self and identity. A feminist critique of sexual constructions is, therefore, a political endeavour.

1. 'Keine Tabus'. Sexuality in GDR Literatures, 1968-89

Erotic constructions in GDR art can be contextualised with reference to many wider trends which critics have noted as regards the development of GDR literatures in general. These include the increasing importance, from the late 1960s onwards, of themes traditionally regarded as private. One such theme was sexuality, which, in the early years of the GDR, had been a subject considered taboo. The dismantling of such taboos takes place across a wide range of discourses and is heterogeneous. It is officially recognised in 1971, with Honecker's famous 'no taboos' speech. The 1970s are also famed as the decade when writing by East German women flourished. These developments did not, of course, occur in isolation. Often the new personal, everyday literature was that written by women. Often taboos were challenged in works by female authors. It is these three, interlinked, contexts which are outlined in this chapter: the sexual as part of the 'private' in GDR art, the sexual as taboo and the significance of women writers within these discourses.

1.1   The Context for an Erotic Emancipation, 1968-1989
Notions of Privacy

The 'ästhetische Emanzipation' (Mittenzwei 1987, p. 1290) that characterises East German literature from the late 1960s onwards has been documented often and extensively.[11] Much of this documentation emphasises notions of privacy. Sonja Hilzinger (1985, p. 36), for example, contends that: 'die Sehnsucht nach Glück und *privater* Erfüllung tritt immer stärker in den Vordergrund' (My emphasis). Kurt Batt (1976a, p. 23) writes: 'der Blick fällt [...] auf die zum Teil sehr persönlichen Leiden und Hoffnungen der Menschen, auf das, was ehedem gern als das *Private* denunziert wurde' (My emphasis). The new genres of this

---

[11] See for example Emmerich 1989, Hartinger/Diersch 1976, Hans Kaufmann 1976, 1986, Reid 1990, Schlenstedt D. 1976, Tate 1984, and Weisbrod 1980. The reasons given for this development vary from social and political influences, to the needs of readers, to the increased independence of the author. Kaufmann, for example, contends that: 'Diese Entwicklung ist Widerspiegelung und wirkendes Moment der in der Gesellschaft vor sich gehenden Veränderungen' (1986, p. 72). None of these answers, in isolation, is sufficient to explain a complex and varied literary history. This study is concerned only with some of the results of the changes, rather than the origins.

more subjective literature dealt with fictionality and language, with issues of morality and of history, with the everyday or commonplace, and with the home rather than the factory. Relationships between men and women, in numerous variations, were analysed in increasing depth. The relationship with oneself also offered an abundance of literary material. Stylistically, strict socialist realism was abandoned and formerly outlawed aspects of modernism began to influence East as well as West German aesthetics. Seminal works in which these characteristics and these themes are determining include Christa Wolf's *Nachdenken über Christa T.*, Werner Heiduczek's *Abschied von den Engeln*, Günter De Bruyn's *Buridans Esel*, and Irmtraud Morgner's *Hochzeit in Konstantinopel*, all of which were published in 1968. Wolf's *Lesen und Schreiben*, from the same year, 'liest sich heute wie eine der Gründungs-urkunden der neueren Literatur in der DDR' (Schlenstedt D. 1988, p. 35). 1968 represents a reference point in the history of GDR literatures as a useful, if ultimately arbitrary, date with which to begin an examination of the private in GDR art.

The term 'private' is generally used to refer to subjects which Western society, in a strange dichotomy, situates as personal rather than political. It traditionally signifies that which is connected with the home environment rather than that open to public knowledge and public concern. By extension it evokes the 'female' sphere of social influence. The implication is that the private does not 'affect the community' (*OED*, p. 515). Werner Mittenzwei's description of the East German aesthetic emancipation questions such categorical divisions. 'Die Literatur', he writes, 'bekam etwas Leichtes, Spielerisches, anscheinend Privates, jene Eigenschaften, die vorher eher selten gewesen waren' (1987, p. 1290). The use of the word 'anscheinend' expresses a concern about the use of the concept of privacy where it is undefined, for distinctions between the private and the public are difficult to maintain once the boundaries of each realm are exposed as discursive and ideological constructs. As Mittenzwei suggests, art can play a role in this process of exposure, interacting between areas of discourse and crossing border lines.

The increased presence within GDR literatures of themes customarily held to be private thus did not make this fiction any less socially relevant. J.H. Reid (1984, p. 107) argues incorrectly that 'the striking feature of GDR literature today is how unpolitical it has become'. Literature became political in a different sense, a sense more in line with what the feminist movement in the West understood by politics. This broader understanding meant that the relationship between literature and society was both investigated and presented anew. It did not mean that this connection was ignored in favour of peculiarly individual and esoteric concerns. On the contrary, as David Bathrick (1991, p. 304) summarises: 'it was initially from within the literary sphere that questions of subjectivity and issues of everyday life often were made legitimate concerns for the public domain'.

Relationships between individuals are similarly socially and politically 'legitimate'; only 'anscheinend privat'. As Irene Dölling (1980, p. 66). argues: 'Geschlechterbeziehungen sind gesellschaftliche Verhältnisse'. A 'new' form of social contact can, then, influence artistic images of the erotic, just as artistic images can influence social contact. In the GDR sexologists thus imagined a 'neue Einstellung zur Liebe und Sexualität unter neuen gesellschaftlichen Verhältnissen' (My emphasis, Starke/Friedrich 1984, p. 26), whilst literary critics described: 'der neue Anspruch an Liebe und Ehe', which 'erweist sich als ein gesellschaftlicher' (My emphasis, Kaufmann, H. 1976, p. 41).

As the aesthetic 'emancipation' in GDR art had political and social relevance, so too did it signal a 'Verstärkung moralischer Fragestellungen' and a 'Moralintensität' (Berger 1977, p. 985. Gabler 1987, p. 727). The famed 'subjektive Faktor' was moral as well as artistic. According to Christel Berger many authors deployed moral issues in order to emphasise the responsibility of the individual, rather than that of the state. This aim becomes particularly clear where the private sphere is placed in the foreground of the work. One such author is Irmtraud Morgner, who sees her work as both a literary and a moral enterprise. Morgner calls herself a 'Moralist' and argues that:

> Man kann die Sitten nur ändern, indem man sie als seltsam und unangemessen ins Bewußtsein hebt, zum Beispiel mit Literatur, indem man Leser anregt zu einem schöpferischen Prozeß des Nachdenkens und der Verwunderung über sich selbst (in Huffzky 1975).

Writers such as Morgner became responsible partners rather than teachers; readers were confronted with figures whom they were expected to judge by their own moral norms. The sexual is a distinctly moral issue, one which provokes judgement. The development of this theme thus also fits into the paradigm identified by Berger.

Wolfgang Emmerich (1980, p. 110) then, describing the aesthetic developments of the 1970s, contends that:

> Das Marxsche Diktum von der "Aneignung der Natur durch den Menschen", [...] wird jetzt sehr umfassend begriffen: Es geht weniger um die Aneignung der äußeren Natur im materiellen Arbeitsprozeß als um die Aneignung der eigenen menschlichen Natur, was auch und vor allem Selbstverwirklichung in der eigenen (geschlechtlichen) Körperlichkeit, in erotischen Beziehungen bedeutet.

31

Nominally private themes, such as the sexual, continued to gain in importance throughout the decade. The events of 1976, including Biermann's expatriation and the repressive ninth Party Conference, did not affect this development. Indeed many argue that these events – set against a global background of fear of nuclear war, ecological disasters, the dominance of technology and concerns about the role of the humanist subject – contributed to a loss of political utopia and a concomitant rise in traditionally more personal matters. Emmerich (1989, p. 302) views the works of this era as 'privater', and 'letzlich kleiner in ihrem Anspruch'. The themes identified by Antonia Grunenberg (1990a, p. 161) for the prose works of both the 1970s and the 1980s include 'Ehe und Familie, Sexualität, Emanzipation, Individualität/Identität and 'Glück'.

Grunenberg's list is, however, made up of exactly those concerns which were first noted in the 1960s. They are concerns which represent, for some, the widening of definitions of politics, and for others, resignation and disillusionment. The difficulty concerning definition is clear in this confusion, as are the problems with judging literature by set historical dates. The importance of 1976 as an apparent breach in GDR literary history has been emphasised time and time again.[12] For many artists the period of free experimentation did indeed come to an end. Large numbers left (or were forced to leave) for the West and those who stayed were often no longer certain as to their role, or the role of their art.[13] Christa Wolf (1986, p. 422), for example, talks of 'eine Krise; eine Krise, die existenziell war'. Yet, as Weisbrod (1980, p. 201) states, the date does not represent a 'Wendepunkt', but rather, 'ein deutlicher Ausdruck der grundsätzlichen Widersprüchlichkeit und Ambivalenz der Kulturpolitik in der DDR'. These 'cultural' policies certainly influenced literary developments but they did not control them.

Aesthetic freedoms did not, therefore, disappear overnight, as the emphasis on certain key dates can suggest. For the 'alternative' and seemingly repressed GDR literatures of the late 1970s and 1980s, such autonomy was, paradoxically, extended, as linguistic experimentation was taken to extremes. Moreover, the notion of privacy was also extended, often to the very conditions of artistic production. Grunenberg (1990c, p. 25) writes of: 'eine private Publikations- und Zeitschriftenszene' whilst Emmerich (1994, p. 170) paints a picture of a communal lifestyle uninterrupted by outside influences, of artists hidden away in

[12] Grunenberg (1990b, p. 64) argues that the Biermann affair 'hatte die kulturpolitische Situation *schlagartig* verändert' (My emphasis).

[13] Including Jürgen Füchs, Sarah Kirsch, Karl-Heinz Jakobs, Jurek Becker, Erik Loest, Thomas Brasch, Günter Kunert, Rainer Kunze, Kurt Bartsch, Klaus Schlesinger and Hans Joachim Schädlich.

'ihr eigenes Reich alternativer Lebensformen und künstlerischer Produktivität'. The emphasis critics place upon the conditions of production of this art is clear from the term 'Die Prenzlauer Berg Szene', which has come to stand for an entire aesthetic movement. 'Happenings' and spontaneous performance or discussion offered a platform where young artists could develop their ideas. Texts first appeared in hand printed *Zeitschriften, Unikate* and *Lyrikmappen*, which were passed round 'underground'.[14] A 'Gegenöffentlichkeit' (Dahlke 1992, p. 228) was created, an apparent alternative to mainstream forms of communication.

Although often regarded as intrinsic to the nature of 'alternative' GDR literatures, 'privacy' had in fact – within this particular context – become a problematic concept from the mid-1980s onwards. 'Underground' art formed, then, part of what Bathrick (1991, p. 303) classes as 'a semiautonomous terrain of publicness'. Each publication was regarded by the authorities as illegal, regardless of the political position of the editors and contributors. In this sense alone, the work was not only private, but also public. Furthermore, as Western interest in this literature increased – fuelled by the publication of the anthology *Berührung ist nur eine Randerscheinung* in 1985 – the 'unofficial' became 'official', with its own publishing house[15] and Aufbau acceptance, all be it 'Außer der Reihe'. Nominal privacy had attracted public attention, attention which would of course change the nature of this literary movement.

Post-*Wende*, however, it was a supposed aura of opposition and privacy that led to the celebration of this art as the 'genuine' art of the GDR. Yet this celebration was cut short by later revelations concerning the *Stasi* collaboration of artists such as Sascha Anderson and Reiner Schedlinski, thus questioning and negating any such notions of privacy. As Emmerich (1994, p. 33) writes: 'die schöne Fiktion vollkommener lebensweltlicher Autonomie und Souveränität der alternativen Kunstszene der DDR war damit zerstört'. The highly charged *Literaturstreit* debates convincingly demonstrated that no art can be created, or received, in an ideolgical vacuum.

If, however, the privacy of GDR literatures in the late 1960s and 1970s had been regarded as political, social and moral, the privacy of later art was often

---

14 Eg: *schaden* (which became *Die Verwendung*), *Entwerter/Oder, UND, Mikado oder der Kaiser ist nackt, u.s.w., Liane, Zweite Person, chlochart, braegen, Ariadnefabrik, KONTEXT, Poe-sie-all-bum, Anschlag, Bizarre Städte, Ypsilon, Sondeur*. For places/dates of publication, and editors, see, eg. Arnold, 1990. The characteristic mix of graphic and written art in these 'folders' allowed a certain subversion of censorship regulations. Graphic artists were allowed to print their work in editions of up to 100 without official licence.

15 GALREV (Verlag backwards).

seen as inward looking and irrelevant. The earlier generation of writers, according to Emmerich (1989, p. 425), 'verstanden sich als Sozialisten; sie akzeptierten einen moralischen, sozialoperativen Auftrag der Literatur'. The younger authors, he claims, had a very different view of the role of art in society, their work 'will keine Botschaft mehr verkünden' (p. 431). Anneli Hartmann (1988, p. 12) too, argues that this literature replaced moral concerns with rejection of any fixed meaning. 'die Verweigerung der Politik', she maintains, 'kehrt sich in eine Politik der Verweigerung um'. In her opinion, it is only in the silences and gaps of the writing that the unsaid hope of a different future is articulated.

The authors of such texts, in Kolbe's famous words 'hineingeboren' into the GDR,[16] had been presented with a state which they saw as immutable and a language which appeared corrupt and distorted.[17] Both linguistically and thematically their art expresses and explores this situation. Offering no definite or totalising meanings, it remains resistant to single interpretations. Yet this does not mean that there is no 'political' message or moral hope. As Leeder (1991, p. 423) suggests, the texts embody 'a search for meaning, and, importantly, a response to the meaninglessness of a ritualized and formulaic ideological rhetoric, which suppresses the language of experience'. In her opinion, there is still a utopia expressed in the writing, namely: that 'to be found *within* the authentic experience of the individual' (p. 418). The subjective realm is emphasised in much of this poetry, often as a reaction against the lack of direction described by Kolbe. In the creation of a new language, critical of the 'verkrusteten Sprachgebungen' of the SED (Thulin 1990, p. 234), the body functions as an important source of poetics. Language becomes, for some writers, sensual rather than political, reflecting 'die Emanzipation der Sinne und eine sinnliche Emanzipation' (Thulin, p. 237). The sexual here offers semantic inspiration. It also offers thematic material, for this prose is not only linguistically new, but also eminently visual. In this sense too then, the writing is both 'private' and 'political'.

Notions of privacy have thus been consistently used to characterise very different GDR literatures. The erotic is traditionally regarded as a private issue which has both social and moral implications. It can, therefore, be analysed as a theme with relevance for each of these literatures. Such an analysis can further

---

16 Uwe Kolbe, *Hineingeboren. Gedichte 1975-79*. Cf. Leeder (1993, p. 51): 'The title [...] became the signal for the experience of an entire generation'.

17 Kolbe states in interview (Heukenkamp 1979, p. 46): 'Ich kann noch weitergehen und sagen, daß diese Generation völlig verunsichert ist, weder richtiges Heimischsein hier noch das Vorhandensein von Alternativen anderswo empfindet'.

demonstrate that ultimately, notions of privacy are themselves based upon false premises. The following section examines examples of constructions of sexuality in GDR literatures. It begins with those which, in the 1950s and 1960s, portrayed sexuality as taboo, and moves on to the wide range of erotic images and sexual topics representative of the 1970s and 1980s.

1.2 The Context for an Erotic Emancipation, 1968-1989 'Keine Tabus'?

In 1971 Erich Honecker famously announced a new era in GDR art, an era of 'no taboos':

> Wenn man von der festen Position des Sozialismus ausgeht, kann es meines Erachtens auf dem Gebiet von Kunst und Literatur keine Tabus geben. Das betrifft sowohl die Fragen der inhaltlichen Gestaltung als auch des Stils – kurz gesagt, die Fragen dessen, was man die künstlerische Meisterschaft nennt (1971, p. 287).

Literary historians have erected this speech as a monument to a rapid improvement in conditions of artistic production. The *Tauwetterperiode* had begun, a period which encouraged writers, publishers and critics to be more experimental. Challenging new works were published and debated. Ulrich Plenzdorf's *Die neuen Leiden des jungen W.*, for example, appeared in *Sinn und Form* in 1972 and unleashed a discussion as important as the text itself.[18] The earlier polemic, in the same journal, on the role of literary criticism in the GDR, had been equally controversial. Here Adolf Endler (1971, p. 1363-4) had accused Germanists of 'Ignoranz', 'eine abstrakt normative Betrachtungsweise', 'brutalen Dogmatismus' and even 'eine vollkommene Unfähigkeit zum Kunstgenuß'. Numerous replies took issue with these radical statements, contributing to a redefinition of the strict dogma of socialist realism. It was within this atmosphere of experimentation that themes such as the erotic were able to become established literary topics.

In the 1950s and early 1960s, on the other hand, the sexual had – for many authors and for many readers – been taboo. Emmerich (1980, p. 109) thus calls GDR writing of the early 1960s 'eine im wörtlichen Sinn körperlose Literatur' and Reid (1990, p. 111) writes: 'The early GDR novel was exceedingly

---

18 *Sinn und Form*, 2 (1972), 254-310. The debates continued throughout the 1973 editions and into 1974.

prudish'. He regards the erotic as potentially dangerous within an authoritarian society for, like death, it is an aspect of human life which cannot be controlled mathematically. It is a subject which arouses fear and thus censorship. In this way, as Foucault demonstrates, sexuality is ordered and disciplined. Important works of the 1960s, such as Hermann Kant's *Die Aula*, are noticeably restrained as far as erotic decription is concerned.[19] In Christa Wolf's love story *Der geteilte Himmel* the sexual is barely alluded to. Wolf details the stars and the moon rather than Rita and Manfred, whose 'natural' experiences are generalised and therefore played down:

> Wenn sie zurückkamen, waren es noch mehr Sterne geworden, noch mehr Lichter auf der Erde, und das nahm kein Ende, bis ihnen schwindlig wurde und sie sich aneinander festhielten und sich streichelten und lautlos beruhigten, wie es Liebesleute überall tun (p. 25).

As Ilse Braatz (1980, p. 40) notes, there is 'keinerlei Andeutung, daß es menschliche Körper gibt, stattdessen ist von Himmelskörpern die Rede'. Other possible symbolic representations of sex include a scene set in a car, where Rita urges her lover to drive ever faster, and after the climax, 'erschöpft und glücklich' (p. 63), Manfred smokes a cigarette. Christa T. is described in similarly non-erotic terms. She marries, has children, and even has an affair, but her sexuality is never mentioned. Even in Sarah Kirsch's documentary novel *Die Pantherfrau* sex is mostly absent, although the interviews do allude to relationships. In accordance with official policies work is presented as the most important factor in the lives of 'real' women from East Germany.

In the early years of the GDR artists were often seen merely as politicians in disguise. They were given, in the Five Year Plans and at the Bitterfeld Conferences, the task of re-educating the population. Their aesthetics were to be those of early socialist realism, which concentrated upon the building of socialism and the 'Kampf gegen jegliche Reste bürgerlichen Einflusses auf das Proletariat' (Zdanov 1936, p. 44). These 'remains' included 'Wankelmut und Leichtfertigkeit', 'Faulenzerei', 'Undiszipliniertheit und Individualismus' and 'habgieriges und gewissenloses Verhalten gegenüber dem gesellschaftlichen Eigentum' (ibid.). The themes encouraged by official aesthetic doctrine were thus traditionally social and political. Writers were to portray the outward lives of the worker and the farmer, their successes, their ideology. Sexuality did not fit into this framework, for it was regarded as purely personal and trivial. To

---

[19] Cf: Ilse Braatz (1980, p. 37): 'Sinnlich, auffällig, eigenartig, erotisch zwingend ist keine der flüchtigen Bekanntschaften'.

write about the erotic was to risk accusations not only of individualism and 'Leichtfertigkeit', but also of Western style pornography.

Pornography, conceived of as an essential element of formalism, was linked by cultural politicians to nihilism and anarchy.[20] The Soviet socialist realists had, in the 1930s, decreed that such portrayals of the erotic were evidence of the decay of bourgeois culture. Honecker, in the 1960s, similarly railed against the destructive influences of capitalist, and especially American, sex propaganda. 'Sexuelle Triebhaftigkeit' (1965, p. 1077) was not, in his eyes, a plausible explanation for human behaviour and should not be shown as such. Sex in the GDR was 'healthy' and 'normal', for: 'unsere DDR ist ein sauberer Staat. In ihr gibt es unverrückbare Maßstäbe der Ethik und Moral, für Anstand und gute Sitte' (p. 1076). The use of a terminology based upon notions of cleanliness and purity reveals associations with religious notions of sexuality.

These conservative attitudes persisted as sexual morality in the West, during the 'swinging sixties', became increasingly liberal. As late as 1975 the authors of the book *Einführung in den Sozialistischen Realismus* link Western 'Trivialliteratur' with sex and other 'vices'. Literature is, they claim, becoming unaesthetic, the sensual is being made vulgar and ugly. It is Western pop music, however, as a major 'Bestandteil imperialistischer Massenkultur' (Batt 1975, p. 46), that presents the most dangers:

> Neben der Verherrlichung der Gewalt durch den Schocker-Pop gehört Sex zu den Lieblingsthemen der Pop-Szenerie. Aber nicht Erotik ist gefördert, sondern Pornographie. Es herrscht da ein wahrer Kult des Penis und der Vagina, Brutalität, offener Sadismus, Sodomie, Bi- und Homosexualität.

The prejudices surrounding homosexuality, which would appear to be a form of brutal pornography, are particularly clear.

Literature written in the GDR cannot, of course, be understood solely with reference either to political discourse or to official aesthetic guidelines. Such a critique renders the individual aesthetic productions valueless. It also positions both the author and the reader as secondary to cultural politics. There was undoubtedly much written in the 1950s and 1960s that did not conform to Andrej Zdanov's revolutionary standards of 'Enthusiasmus und Heldentum'. There was much written that transcends the confines of Ulbricht's pedagogical art. Those artists returning from exile, for example, did not simply forget what they had written before the War. Successful texts, including those by Christa

---

20 Cf. Otto Grotewohl (1951, p. 208): 'Der Formalismus ist die unschöpferische Richtung in der Kunst. Er hat keine Zukunft, er ist ebenso zum Untergang verurteilt wie die kapitalistische Gesellschaft, die ihn geboren hat'.

Wolf, challenged the guidelines rather than conforming to them. Yet the harsh censorship regulations of the *Hauptverwaltung Verlage* did mean that authors had at least to be aware of official pronouncements.[21] Where their fiction came into direct contact with functionaries of *SED* it had to appear to conform to certain standards. It had to set love in the correct context.

1.2.1 Keine Tabus – Sexual Description and Characterisation

Honecker's speech officially redefined the boundaries of this 'correct' erotic context. One cannot, however, assume a direct correlation between texts which addressed taboo subjects and art. To do so would be to ignore issues of form and style. Neither can one assume that Honecker's speech represents the genesis of a homogenous linear and teleological literary history. As Reiner Nägele (1983, p. 193) reminds critics: 'man sollte freilich nicht die immer wieder zitierte Honecker-Rede [...] einfach in ursächlichen Zusammenhang mit der literarischen Produktion bringen'. The speech was as much an endorsement of aesthetic developments which began in the 1960s as the signal of a new direction. Different aesthetic strategies continued to exist in the GDR, as they exist in every culture. The famous works of 1968, for example, brought not only important, but also varied changes in GDR literary styles and themes. Only one of these changes was the questioning of taboos in the erotic.

Gilbert Badia (1976, p. 1170) thus believes that it is not Honecker's speech, but Günter De Bruyn's novel *Buridans Esel*, that marks 'das Ende der Tabus und die Anfänge einer entkrampften Literatur'. In this book the author memorably comments upon the 'übliche Lücke' (De Bruyn 1968, p. 110) left by many of his fellow writers in the field of the erotic. In De Bruyn's later novel *Preisverleihung* (1972) there is a similar reference to 'die übliche Lücke', when students in a literature seminar discuss reasons why there are so few portrayals of sex in modern GDR writing. One defiantly asks, 'Warum geben wir eigentlich nicht zu, daß unsere Sexual- und Ehemoral noch immer die protestantischer Kleinbürger ist?' (p. 39). Another complains: 'Unsere Literatur soll doch realistisch sein, aber über Liebe schreibt sie wie im Mittelalter [...] Alles in mystisches Dunkel getaucht' (p. 38). De Bruyn's choice of vocabulary parodies official pronouncements which link the mysterious with formalism and pornography. This state view, separating the private and the political, is also

---

21 Politicians wished their statements to provide 'eine zuverlässige Orientierung' for artists. (Hager 1972, p. 509).

represented: 'Solange die Amerikaner noch in Vietnam sind, haben unsere privaten Gefühle ganz unwichtig zu sein!' (p. 39)[22]

In *Buridans Esel* de Bruyn's statements are complemented by the author's own fictional attempts to break through the 'aussparende Absatz', the 'Verdunklung' and the 'Schleier des Schweigens (soweit Anstand, Geschmack und Ämter es erlauben)' (p. 110). His protagonist Erp's first sexual encounter with Fräulein Broder is described in terms of traditional male power, simple lust and routine: 'Er wollte sie nutzen' (p. 76). However, exactly half way through *Buridans Esel* de Bruyn creates a contrasting and enthusiastic poetic description of how: 'Zwei [wurden] eins, spürten einander, fügten sich ineinander, flossen ineinander, jauchzten, schrien miteinander, hatten endlich nicht mehr das Gefühl, nur Hälfte zu sein, wurden ein Ganzes' (p. 110). Suddenly Erp treats his lover as a person rather than an object. Hans Kaufmann (1976, p. 151) has described this union as 'die schönste Liebesszene in unserer Literatur'. It is also, in his opinion, a 'socialist' love scene, involving characters who exist in a specific society and a specific social situation. Their love, expressed through sex, has a function within the narrative, it is not gratuitous. Yet the somewhat exaggerated depiction is not fact, but one man's imagined prose, and it seems rather to simply confirm antiquated myths about sexuality. Two becoming one in harmonious bliss certainly fills the 'Lücke', but does little more. Although Fräulein Broder states that 'diese puren Bettfreuden gibt es in Wirklichkeit noch nicht' (p. 77), her own experiences seem to embody exactly that.

Honecker's speech cannot, therefore, be considered in isolation. Neither can De Bruyn's novels be placed outside general trends. Literature of the 1970s witnessed, as Reid (1990, p. 111) recognises, 'something approaching a sex wave'. An abundance of works appeared which dealt with the emotional, the psychological and the physical aspects of human relationships. The apparently most private of themes became valuable literary material for a wide range of artists. The erotic is used to describe and to characterise, to evoke pity, hatred, sympathy and humour. One cannot do proper justice to this diverse achievement in a single chapter. The examples used here are appropriate to the arguments and represent one possible strand of one possible literary history, not an absolute paradigm.

Günter De Bruyn filled the sexual gap with a joyous, if somewhat clichéd, description of erotic love. For Fräulein Broder, if not for Elisabeth, sex was enjoyable. For Elisabeth sex was mechanical, she was kissed: 'wie man Schuhe am Abtreter säubert, die Zähne putzt oder nach dem Frühstück zur Zigarette

---

22 Cf. *Buridans Esel*, where the couple experience 'das schlechte Gewissen (weil sie Vietnam und Indonesien und Spanien vergaßen)' (p. 111).

greift' (*Buridans Esel*, p. 89). It is her perspective which is increasingly emphasised in texts published in the 1970s. Whereas the women in Kirsch's *Die Pantherfrau* exclude the sexual from their descriptions, those interviewed by Maxie Wander (1977) talk about all aspects of their lives, including the physical. Many express disappointment and dissatisfaction. Katja P., for example, tells the author: 'Es war eigentlich so, daß ich jedesmal unbefriedigt blieb und leise heulte, während ich einschlief' (p. 172). As Sabine Kebir (1993, p. 145) notes, 'Aus Maxie Wanders Buch erfuhr man zum ersten Mal nicht nur als medizinische, sondern auch als kulturelle Tatsache, daß viele Frauen keinen Orgasmus erleben'.

The problems that sex often involved for women were expressed in many different forms of writing. This type of characterisation functioned to criticise both individual men and patriarchy as a system. Lack of female sexual pleasure could also be perceived as symbolic of the failure of society to progress in the direction envisaged by Engels in 1892. True monogamy, based on 'individuelle Geschlechtsliebe' (Engels, p. 188), was absent from these portrayals. Doris Berger (1988, p. 128) is correct in her argument that:

> Nachdem in früheren Texten oft nach einem verheißungsvollen Kuß ausgeblendet und das Paar seinem vermeintlichen Glück überlassen wurde, beschrieben Autorinnen nun Langeweile und Normierung in der Sexualität. Die von Männern gesetzten Sexnormen werden als unterdrückerisch – und letztlich für beide Seiten unbefriedigend – erkannt.

In this sense the erotic was in no way simply personal, but could be invested with meanings fundamental to both social and individual identities.

Brigitte Martin's (1977) protagonist Brigge, for example, carefully analyses the experience of sex, rather than cloaking it in clichés or mystery. She registers thoughts such as, 'Wir sind Ersatz füreinander, Ersatz für das Einmalige, Große, das wir nicht finden können' (p. 143), whilst going through the motions expected of her. Martin does not ignore the embarrassment of the situation, the common reality, she details all of Brigge's conflicting emotions:

> So ist es immer mit mir und der Liebe, denke ich grämlich, hebe die trägen Lider ein wenig auf und schaue auf den Vorgang über mir. Der Ablauf ist klar. Es war immer so, und es steigt diese Bitterkeit in mir auf, die im Hals würgt und die ich zu verbergen suche, Unmut, weil ich für Augenblicke die Angst vergessen, alles Ungeklärte von mir schieben, das Schwere erleichtern kann (p. 146).

Sex here is no more than a means of escape from the difficulties of life as a single mother. It is a process which can be learnt and repeated, not a moment of inspiration and love. Martin's analysis thus offers not just criticism, but also a new perspective on traditional ideas.

In one of Helga Königsdorf's best-known stories, 'Bolero' (1978), the narrator pushes her lover over the balcony, tired of their empty affair. Sex with this man was perfunctory and male dominated, a situation Königsdorf describes with openness and humour:

> Während ich also für seine Befriedigung schwer atmete und leise stöhnte, dachte ich daran, daß das blaue Sommerkleid zur Reinigung müsse. Ich legte seine Hand mit der Narbe zwischen meine Schenkel, doch er begriff nichts (p. 10).

The comedy offers resistance to a bleak situation. The reader laughs *at* the man, who is made to appear not only selfish, but also stupid. This is also the case in Monika Maron's novel *Flugasche* (1981) where Strutzer is similarly portrayed as egotistical and lazy. Here, however, there is little laughter, for Strutzer's wife is a nameless sexual object:

> Josefa sah, wie Strutzer sich auf die Frau wälzte, sich in ihr rieb, bis es ihm kam und er von der Frau abfiel. Strutzer hatte einen Schlafanzug an, die Frau ein angerauhtes Nachthemd, das Strutzer ihr gerade so weit hochgeschoben hatte, wie es nötig war (p. 117).

Criticism of specific men does not, however, always mean that the female role in patriarchy is one of passive victim. Until her final and spontaneous action, Königsdorf's narrator had accepted and even encouraged her lover's behaviour. She had cooked his favourite meals whilst he slept, taken the pill to please him, (although it made her sick) and had never interfered in his family life. Female characters such as this have internalised an ideology to such an extent that they accept it as normal. Prose which allows the reader to question this situation can offer resistance to such norms.

Christine Kautz's short text, which appeared in *Temperamente* in 1979, is less well known, but also characteristic of works which used the sexual to criticise male sexual behaviour. Kautz too employs sarcasm in conveying the 'schreckliche Monotonie' of her female subject's sex life:

> Mechanisch und lustlos ziehe ich mich aus und lege mich hin.... Programmierte, phantasielose Sexualität, Liebe nach Plan. Ich fühle mich wie ein Computer, der mit einem Glas Rotwein, ein paar Sätzen aus Köchelverzeichnis 525 und ein paar Worten [...] gefüttert wird und der daraufhin ein bißchen 'Labido' und ein paar Minuten 'Sexualmotorik' ausspuckt (p. 158).

All sense of the sexual as pleasurable is lost. As in the advanced technological society, everything runs according to plan, a plan designed by men. The most intimate experience becomes, through the use of words such as 'Computer' and 'Motorik', a comment on both patriarchy and industrial society's reliance on machines. This same comment is comically explored in Sarah Kirsch's sex change story *Blitz aus heiterem Himmel* (1974), where orgasm – 'den Quotienten O' – is worked out mathematically. Sex is regarded as an equation which provides scientifically calculable results: 'Katharina und Albert erzielten $n = 4$ bis 7 bei einer Streubreite O' von $\pm$ 0,005 um 1' (p. 12). The algebraic form of the erotic suggests, and again criticises, the prominence of the scientific in a society where the sexual is taboo.

Günter Görlich also delineates sex as a routine affair in his novel *Die Chance des Mannes* (1982). Here, however, in a letter written by the female protagonist Monika, the routine is seen as female failure, for that is how society sees it:

> Auch in der Liebe wurde allmählich alles auf Regelmäßigkeit gebracht. Am Wochenende der Beischlaf, eingeleitet durch ein unveränderliches Ritual. Es gelang mir nicht oder nur ganz selten im Urlaub, diese Gewohnheit zu durchbrechen. Das bedeutet doch Versagen für eine Frau (p. 174).

Other male authors use sexual habits in order to characterise men rather than women. Christoph Hein's tango player Dallow has various superficial sexual encounters, which reflect his general inability to come to terms with his society once he has left prison. Sex for Dallow, as indeed for Hein's 'Napoleonspieler', is an often sadomasochistic 'Spiel', a game in which women, the playing pieces, are described solely in terms of their physical attributes. Uwe Saeger's character Helmut Krüger is drawn in very similar terms. The numerous erotic adventures Krüger has in the openly sexual narrative *Warten auf Schnee* (1981) cannot give his life any meaning. He is condemned to 'wait'.

In Volker Braun's *Das ungezwungene Leben Kasts* (1979) Kast's love affairs are crucial for the development of his character. His report is labelled a 'Liebesbericht' (p. 178). Kast's ideas of sex are made clear in phrases such as the aggressive 'gleich würde ich sie besitzen' (p. 27) and the perfunctory:

> Wir reiben unsre Haut oder wenns hochkommt unsre Gedanken aneinander und kriegen ein paar schöne Gefühle dabei, und dann zieht sich jeder unter seine Vorhaut zurück (p. 64).

He is allowed to feel basic physical and lustful desire. Braun uses a picture by Kast – described by a Party member as 'schädlich und "philosophisch zuende gedacht" antirevolutionär' (p. 80) – as a cynical comment upon the sexual taboos which he challenges in his work. The picture shows a girl in an open blouse, which the Kafkaesque 'Sekretär K.' dismisses as 'die Dekadenz!' (p. 81). Braun's work too is decadent, but the decadence has a literary purpose.

The topics explored in Braun's *Hinze-Kunze-Roman* (1985) again include the sexual. Here the author ironically quotes Honecker in justification of this explicitly erotic text: 'von gewissen festen Positionen aus gibt es keine Tabus' (p. 8). 'Die Literatur', he comments, 'schreckt ja vor nichts mehr zurück' (p. 11). Kunze is represented particularly effectively through his perverse relationship to the opposite sex, which is treated as an illness. Braun thus plays with definitions of sexuality which are founded upon notions of health and disease. Varied examples of Kunze's 'abnormal' behaviour are also a strong comment on the patriarchal nature of many ruling GDR Party functionaries. A visit to the *Reeperbahn* is used to characterize both the West and the protagonist. Kunze's equation of his experiences with international politics adds humour to the situation. The description of the 'Völkerverständigung' (p. 91) between East Germany and Africa cynically adopts the discourse of diplomats, a discourse dependent upon money and violence.

Linguistically, Braun's experimentation with sexual vocabulary is particularly successful in this novel. He uses, for example, a cluster of different words for the male genitalia, thereby emphasising the androcentric bias of language. These include 'Geschlechtsteil' (p. 12), 'Die Zeugungsorgane' (p. 20), 'Schwanz' (p. 154) 'Sack', and 'das schwache Gestrüpp' (p. 187). Neologisms such as the verb 'vergewohltätigen' (p. 81) express how some men view rape and sex as one and the same. The introduction of sexual terminology into Kunze's political speech is heavily sarcastic. Marx's words are made to sound ridiculous rather than revolutionary:

> Wir müssen den Wettbewerb orgasimieren, von Haus zu Haus. Die Nachtschicht, um die Nachtschicht kommen wir nicht herum. [...] Gebt euch hin! Proletarier, vereinigt euch! [...] Es lebe der Frieden, es lebe der Orgasmus in der Welt! (pp. 120-21)

Braun exploits the possibilities of the sexual to break taboos, to characterise, to experiment with language and to add comic effect. In this respect his work can be compared with that of Sarah Kirsch, who also treats sex with humour and irony. Jessen, for example, in his critique of the story *Merkwürdiges Beispiel weiblicher Entschlossenheit* (1973) particularly notes Kirsch's use of language.

He cites the irreverent linking of 'das geheiligte Attribut "*gesellschaftlich*"' with a 'hart anstehende Sache'.[23]

Male figures such as Kunze, Dallow and Strutzer are essentially negative and unsympathetic. Their sexuality is both cause and effect of this negativity. Alternatives to these critical characterisations are, of course, also to be found, particularly in poetry. Many writers portray mutual affection as the basis for partnership. Stefan Döring's poem 'ergebnis' (1989, p. 88), for example, uses repetition – notably of 'er-' – and rhyming personal pronouns to create an image of equality and eternal love:

> ich ergebe mich
> und lasse dich lieben
> bis du tot umfällst
>
> und erwecke dich wieder zum lieben
>
> du ergibst dich
> und läßt mich lieben
> bis ich tot umfalle
>
> und erweckst mich wieder zum lieben

Sarah Kirsch's poetry too is generally acclaimed for its erotic content. Birgit Dahlke (1994, p. 53) writes of 'eine eigene Sprache weiblicher Erotik'. Hanne Castein (1987) and Adolf Endler (1975) also note the importance of Kirsch's eroticism, citing texts such as 'Don Juan kommt am Vormittag' and 'Muskelkater' from the anthology *Zaubersprüche* (1974). The titles alone subtly suggest a sexual content.

There are countless examples of such positively erotic and sensual poetry and prose in GDR literatures.[24] In Braun's *Unvollendete Geschichte* (1975) for example, the sexual act is described in reserved sentences such as: 'Karin küßte ihn auf die Brust, auf den Leib, und er legte sich auf sie und drang in sie ein' (p. 19). [25] The simple statement 'Es war zum ersten Mal schön' (p. 36) needs no

---

[23] The quotation Jessen refers to is: 'Frau Schmalfuß ließ durchblicken, daß sie gern mit dem Vogel über eine andere gesellschaftlich hart anstehende Sache geredet hätte, aber nicht hier bei dem Krach' (p. 12).

[24] See, for example Kurt Drawert (ed.) *Die Wärme die Kälte des Körpers des Andern. Liebesgedichte*.

[25] *Unvollendete Geschichte* was first published in the GDR in *Sinn und Form*, in 1975. It did not appear as a book until 1988.

further detail, in contrast to Kunze's activities. The body in this text represents a space that the state cannot reach:

> Für die Gedanken konnte man, der Körper ging keinen an. Der konnte nichts einsehen oder anders machen, der lebte wie es kam. [...] Für all die Theorien war er nicht zuhaus (p. 33).

Karin's pregnancy is thus 'das einzige bemerkenswerte Ereignis des Jahrhunderts' (p. 93); the 'personal' clearly has primacy over the outside world to which she is forced to conform.[26] The representation of love as an 'Insel in einer feindlichen Welt' is one which Karin Hirdina (1972, p. 6) rejects as typical only of capitalist love stories. She believes that in a socialist society love is no longer threatened by social circumstances. Fiction is not, however, simply an ideologically determined reflection of society, although it can, and often does, refer to it. Portrayals by Braun and others which represent the corporeal as refuge suggest, therefore, that socialism has not secured individual happiness.

Another East German critic, Hans Kaufmann, again dismisses poetry in which the sexual is shown as an idyll or a route of escape from social responsibility. Of work by Günter Kunert, for example, he complains: 'Der geschlechtliche Kontakt wird gefeiert als Oase in der Wüste, als Zu-Sich-Kommen in Abgeschiedenheit und Geschichtslosigkeit' (1976, p. 173). This meaning can indeed be read into certain of Kunert's poems. In 'Kleines Gedicht' (1972, p. 18) he links sexual drives with eternity:

> O kurze Frist der Liebe,
> Da man sich selbst vergißt
> und nur mit seinem Triebe
> die Zeitlichkeit durchmißt

The short moments of love appear separated from other aspects of life. The openly erotic language which characterises many of Kunert's poems can also give the impression that social aspects of the theme are unimportant. 'Das Fleisch' is 'nackte Wahrheit' ('Zuspruch, wortfrei' 1972, p. 11), the penis is 'das Glied der Glieder' ('Kleines Gedicht'). Such strong terminology can further suggest either an emancipatory, or a specifically male perspective. Morgner, for example, (in Voigtländer 1972, p. 205) describes Kunert as 'Ein Liebhaber von Pornographie im üblichen Sinn'. Such opposing interpretations,

---

26 This is not to say that the spheres of the family and of work are totally separate, Braun refers, for example, to how pressures at work affect marriage (p. 24), and to how Karin is unable to find work because she is four months pregnant (p. 96).

both of which seem valid, demonstrate the difficulty of attributing authorial intention to art.

The notion of the sexual as sanctuary is again expressed in one of the most openly erotic protocols in Wander's *Guten Morgen, du Schöne* (1977). In addition to her thoughts on German history and East German society, Rosi S. discusses her love affairs, various sexual practices and issues of contraception. Of sex in general she says:

> Im Sex drücke ich meine ganze Persönlichkeit aus, viel direkter als sonstwo, ja? Ich bin keine Sexmaschine, ich bin eine Frau. Und es geht wunderbar, sobald ein Mann das begriffen hat. (p. 63)

The body, then, is an important element of her narrative, particularly the female body. It represents nature, primitive drives and a form of freedom. Rosi's criticisms of socialism depict a society that is not free, having lost the ability to question. She thus creates a dichotomy between 'alles was natürlich ist' (p. 62) and 'unser sozialistischer Konformismus' (p. 69).

Metaphors of the body are significant in the work of many women writing in the 1980s. This trend has been anlysed by Dahlke, who considers texts by Annett Gröschner, Raja Lubinetzki, Barbara Köhler, Kerstin Hensel and Gabriele Stötzer-Kachold. The women use 'Körper-Worte' (Dahlke 1994, p. 179) and describe in detail experiences connected with female sexuality. For the men of the *Szene* there is, in general, a less concrete view of the body. As Dahlke (1994, p. 183) summarises:

> "Der Körper" spielt als Formel eine wichtige Rolle in vielen der inoffiziell publizierten Zeitschriften, jedoch in anderer Weise als in Stötzer-Kacholds, Hensels oder Gröschners Texten beschrieben. Er wird eher zum Losungswort eines künstlerischen Selbstverständnisses, das Sinneswahrnehmung und Experimente am eigenen Körper, [...] den umfassenden Entfremdungserfahrungen entgegensetzt.

The body becomes a cliché if it represents no more than natural sensuality. If it is further constructed as female this cliché is gendered and cemented. Dahlke criticises writers such as Michael Thulin for precisely this reason.

However, other male artists of the 1980s treat the body as a physical and sexual entity and not as a formula. Their work has been seen as innovative rather than androcentric. Bert Papenfuß Gorek uses both sensual and crude sexual imagery in his poetry, which, unlike his surroundings, is literally 'geschlechtlich' (1988, p. 123). In the poem 'mein credit' (1988, p. 158) he states:

strotzen meine gedichte vor votzen, wimmeln
von pimmeln, schwänzen & gespensten – kopf-
tripper!

Through the accumulation of rhymes, unexpected sexual terms such as *Votze* or *Pimmel* appear, and sound, lyrical. Dahlke (1994, p. 186) notes that 'Papenfuß-Goreks Texte strahlen eine Körperlichkeit aus' and Leeder (1993, p. 182) similarly contends: 'Papenfuß is out to break taboos with the explicit and casual sexuality in his texts'. Jan Faktor's Dada 'Manifeste der Trivialpoesie' (1989) are also openly erotic. His 'Beispiel Nr. 2' of such poetry is 'Ich will ficken', example number 8 'Beischlaf ohne Worte' (p. 87, p. 90). Poetry here is reduced to basic desires such as hunger and sex, the effect is 'subversiv und opp-ositionell' (p. 87).

In their attempts to portray Hirdina's harmonious socialist eroticism many writers are noticeably less experimental, merely repeating stereotypical similies of sexual experiences. Braun's Karin questions the construction of nature as pure, innocent and female: 'Überhaupt die JUNGFRÄULICHE Natur (die noch kein Mensch berührt hat) schien ihr fast kitschig' (*Unvollendete Geschichte*, p. 40). Others, however, instinctively link nature and sex, thus perpetuating an ideal of 'natural' sexuality beyond ideological constructions. Images of the earth are, for example, common in many erotic descriptions, often masking the realities of an uncomfortable situation. Manfred Jendryschik's short story 'Ein Sommer mit Wanda' (1976) depicts how 'wir die Erde verließen' (p. 42). Uwe Saeger (1988, p. 262) paints the relationship between Eva and Hans thus:

> Wir sind weit über der Welt und müssen nur achtgeben, daß wir sie nicht anbrennen an uns. [...] Es geschieht immer noch einmal, daß wir uns ablösen von der Erde und hi-nauftreiben; verwunderlich ist einzig, daß es uns gelingt, stets wieder an gleicher Stelle zu landen.

This fairy-tale scenario stands in sharp contrast to the events of the Prague Spring which form the historical background to the narrative of 'Unfachliche Notizen', and in such a context appears somewhat ridiculous. Eberhard Panitz's *Die sieben Affären der Dona Juanita* (1972) again lapses into bathos. Here the 'earth moves':

> Die Liebe einer Frau zu einem Mann könnte sich derart steigern, daß das Gefühl ent-stünde, die Erde bewege sich unter ihr, und das sei einmal im Leben möglich, meist nie, höchstens dreimal (p. 126).

Panitz's representation of a woman's love for a man not only dramatically limits female sexual pleasure, but also reinforces traditional sexual role models.

47

Such models are also particularly clear in Renate Apitz's novel *Hexenzeit* (1984). The sex which Mathilde has with Bert, for example, is typical:

> Sie halten sich in den Armen, ein erschöpfter Mann, nach einem guten, harterfochtenen Sieg, und eine Frau, ganz weich und noch ohne List. [...] Ihre Liebe ist wie ein Schrei in den beginnenden Morgen, in den glühenden Tag (p. 67, p. 72).

The similes of nature both here, and in later illustrations of the erotic, reinforce these clichés. Mathilde's breasts are 'Knospen', orgasm is 'vulkanisch und glücklich' (p. 109). This type of account is effectively parodied in Helga Schütz's novel *Julia oder Erziehung zum Chorgesang* (1980). Schütz's portrayal appears at first to conform to the established pattern. However, the grotesquely exaggerated use of natural ideas comes to an abrupt halt with the introduction of phrases such as 'dialektische Beipflicht' (pp. 239-40) into the description:

> Ich wachse aus seinem Mantel und fliege in die heiße Nacht, und abertausend blonde Schmetterlingsfühler stoßen gegen das flüssigkühle Mondlicht, das von den Kiefern herab über uns hinweg rieselt, seitlich von uns abrinnt, in die Erde hinein, und uns langsam mit hinunter nimmt. Wir sinken [...] Zwei Wochen später weiß ich von meiner Schwangerschaft.

The reality of this scenario is that Julia is pregnant.

Another seemingly ageless romantic myth is that of two effortlessly becoming one in love. In a manner reminiscent of De Bruyn's *Buridans Esel*, Jendryschik, in the short story 'Karla, ziemlich am Anfang' (1976), states: 'er küßte sie, bis sie es nicht mehr aushielt, [...] bis er in sie eindrang und aufhörte, er zu sein, und sie aufhörte, sie zu sein' (p. 82). Gerti Tetzner's Karen calls Peters, 'die andere Hälfte meines Körpers' (1974, p. 98). Their sexual relationship is also painted in terms of male possession, and is glorified through natural similies of colour:

> Und eines Nachts wurde ich wirklich seine Frau...Unter meinem Blick füllte sich das Fenster mit goldrotem Licht. Der braune Kleiderschrank wurde orange, der weiße Tisch gelb. [...] Und es ist, als begegneten wir uns seit der Geburt auf seinem Männer- und auf meinem Frauenpol wieder zum ersten Mal (ibid).

Thus Ricarda Schmidt (1992a, p. 153) discovers a 'Mills and Boon type of masculine attraction in the novel' together with various phallic images suggesting male sexual power. Dorothea Schmitz (1983) also criticises Tetzner's depictions of sex, claiming that they remain androcentric and bound by taboos. Analysing sexual constructions such as these, she argues:

Sexualität wird zum wichtigen Faktor im Befreiungsprozeß der Frauen. Aber immer noch überwiegt das indirekte Sprechen, immer noch wird häufig genug angedeutet, immer noch findet ein Rückzug auf tradierte Begriffe und Bilder statt, die mit den alten Vorstellungen von der Sexualität der Frau belastet sind (p. 146).

Examination of a wider and more varied range of sexual portrayals shows that GDR literatures did, notably in the 1970s and 1980s, challenge sexual taboos. Within this challenge other prejudices could, however, clearly be confirmed.

1.2.2 Keine Tabus – Sexual Themes

Sexuality is, as has been shown, a complex construct; and the introduction of previously taboo sexual subjects into GDR art can be read as both reinforcing and attacking sexual prejudice. However, if the erotic remains absent from literary description, prejudice – as the unspoken status quo – will also remain. Thus it is of notable importance that many new sexual themes can be traced in GDR literatures from the late 1960s. These include prostitution, pornography, sexual violence, homosexuality and references to the work of Freud. Some of these topics were undoubtedly unpopular with the censors until the late 1980s. Yet they are present within literature, as a preliminary analysis shows.

In *Guten Morgen du Schöne*, for example, Wander's narrators talk about their first sexual experience, about masturbation, about sex education, and about the role of the pill in their lives. This aspect of the book has often been commented upon by critics. The Hartingers (1984, p. 54) note that: 'existing taboos are bravely pushed aside' and Reid (1990, p. 111) writes: 'part of the popularity of Maxie Wander's interviews must have been due to the insights afforded into the sexual habits of some of those interviewed'. There existed, it would seem, a need for sexual issues to be raised, in cultural discourse as in other areas of society.

The apparent obscenity of Braun's *Hinze-Kunze-Roman* was one of the reasons for the four year delay in publishing; in this text love is a 'subversive[s] Thema' (p. 196). In his report for the censors Professor Werner Neubert (in Wiesner 1991, p. 153) rejected the manuscript, naming eleven different aspects that he regarded as problematic. These included:

> 8) Die Sex-Szene mit der Afrikanerin erscheint mir widerwärtig. Sie beleidigt meiner Auffassung nach auch nach "außen", d.h. international. [...]

> 10) Sinnlichkeit und Pornographie sind zwei *unterschiedliche Qualitäten* (ethisch und ästhetisch). Von Prüderie weit entfernt, bin ich einigermaßen bestürzt über diese Art der

Darstellung, die bereits den Elementar-Humanismus in Frage stellt. Volker Braun begibt sich in Gefahr schwerer Selbstbeschädigung.

Braun's references to pornography and prostitution are particularly rare in GDR literatures, as such reactions by the censors, echoing earlier remarks by Honecker, lead one to expect. Both activities were illegal in the GDR.

Kurt Bartsch (1980, p. 16) allows a pimp to comment upon this judicial situation. Through the act of such a criminal figure adopting the language of the statute books the passage is rendered highly ironic:

> Die Prostitution ist eine regelmäßige und geradezu unvermeidliche Begleiterscheinung der kapitalistischen Gesellschaftsordnung und konnte in ihr (trotz jahrhundertelanger Bekämpfung) nicht ausgerottet werden. Sie erwächst aus wirtschaftlicher Not und fehlender Gleichberechtigung der Frau [...] Diese Wurzeln sind ihr in der DDR und in allen sozialistischen Staaten entzogen.

Bartsch's text remained, however, unavailable in the GDR. Other themes broached therein which were unlikely to have found favour with the censors include prostitution, pimping, lesbian sex, casual sex, masturbation and sexually transmitted diseases. Prostitutes are mentioned in the extract from Werner Bräunig's *Rummelplatz* printed in *NDL* in 1965, but this text was later attacked by Honecker for its alleged obscenities and not published until 1981.[27] Helga Schütz, in *Julia oder Erziehung zum Chorgesang* (1980) refers to 'die Nuttenpreise in der DDR und in Polen' as well as to pornographic films and photographs. In both of these examples there are, however, no explicit sexual scenes as is the case in Braun's novel.

Uwe Saeger's *Das Überschreiten einer Grenze bei Nacht* (1989) portrays a policeman's son smuggling pornographic material across the Polish-German border. The author, through the figure of the father, is strongly critical of such 'fotografierte Schweinerei' (p. 117). Yet he suggests that similar material is copied and sold in the GDR on a very widespread basis:

> Die gehen weg wie warme Semmeln, pro Spiel krieg ich einen roten Lappen, und die hier, er klopft wieder auf die Karten in meiner Hand, die sind neu, Papa, die sind bei uns noch nicht rum (p. 118).

Sociological studies in the GDR painted a similar picture. Women's bodies were, according to critics such as Ina Merkel (1991), gradually re-sexualised. The icon of the female crane driver or the agricultural worker was replaced with

---

27 The text also includes a particularly strongly worded passage about VD and how to avoid it: 'Zuerst gehe ich immer mit dem Tabakfinger ran. Wenn sie da zuckt, ist die Fregatte leck' (p. 9). This was revised in the published version. See Reid 1990, p. 56.

those more appropriate to the new beauty contests. As Merkel (p. 72) argues, 'längst überwunden geglaubten Formen der Zurschaustellung des nackten Frauenkörpers [erlebten] eine wahre Renaissance – allerdings in den ästhetischen Formen der Vorzeit'. If there was a 'porno-wave' in the GDR of the late-1980s it was, of course, nothing in comparison to that which would hit the country post-*Wende*, as Western entrepreneurs exploited supposedly naive Eastern citizens.

Often traditional masculinity was criticised, as has been shown, through erotic images which emphasised aspects of boredom, routine and mechanisation. The fact that these relationships may also have been violent was portrayed less often, for to do so threatens not only social and moral conventions, but also supposed aesthetic decency. In Jendryschik's short story 'Karla, ziemlich am Anfang' (1976) male dominance is directly linked with aggression. Robert's 'Zärtlichkeiten, die keine mehr waren' (p. 61) turn into 'Gewalt', the word occurs five times in the narrative:

> Er konnte [...] ihren Mund aufbrechen, wirklich aufbrechen, anders konnte sie es nicht nennen [...] und in sie eindringen, als wärc das selbstverständlich [...] bis diese Gewalt kam, seine Gewalt (p. 68-69).

When he undresses Karla he hurts her, pressing her bra clasp into her back. The vocabulary chosen to describe their love making, such as 'über sie herfallen' (p. 73), also has connotations of violence. The way in which Robert holds Karla with his leg so that she cannot escape, an image that Rosemarie Zeplin uses in her short story *Schattenriß eines Liebhabers* (1980) further evinces his power.[28]

The narrative perspective of the sexual scenes in 'Karla, ziemlich am Anfang' is also used to express male sexual dominance. Ostensibly, the text gives the reader access to the thoughts and mind of a woman, yet sexually Karla is completely passive, she is never represented undressing or kissing Robert, she is merely the trapped object of his desires. The similarity of the two erotic scenes in the story suggests the automation of the procedure; a procedure which certainly does not conform to the 'Beziehung ohne Macht' and 'ohne Herrschaft' that Kaufmann (1976, p. 191) believes 'sozialistische Menschen als Liebende in der Beziehung zum Partner gewahr zu werden meinen'.

In the text 'Unterbrechung' (1978) by Helga Königsdorf it is, by contrast, the female character who is in control. She assumes the 'male' role in sex, expressed here by the verbs 'okkupieren' and 'Besitz ergreifen':

---

[28] Cf. Zeplin 1980, p. 43: 'Er schlief nur, wenn sein Leib den ihren mit soviel Fläche berührte, wie seine verwinkelten Glieder erreichen konnten'. This is used together with a whole range of symbolic gestures to express Pilgram's power over Annette.

Jetzt war sie es, die von ihm Besitz ergriff. Als hätten sie die Rollen getauscht, überließ er ihr seinen Körper. Manchmal, wenn sie ihn so okkupierte, steigerte sie sich in eine fast unerträgliche Wollust, in der sie mit unterdrücktem Schaudern ein Verlangen zu töten spürte (p. 12).

Yet the woman's violence is imaginary rather than actual. Whereas the results of male sexual desire affect their female partners, the results of Roswitha's sexual desires concern only her: 'Sie hatte sich einen Augenblick lang ausschließlich als Mann gefühlt und vergessen, daß sie davon ein Kind bekommen könnte' (p. 12). Königsdorf here, as elsewhere in her work, uses the erotic to question all sexual stereotypes, considering both social and biological aspects of the theme.

In Helga Schubert's story *Aus dem beruflichen Alltag* (1985) the roles are more usual. Here male violence takes the form of physical beatings. Lore's husband attacks her because she is in love with her boss. The terse description of the sentence 'Sehr geschlagen sieht sie aus' (p. 56) emphasises the fact that the man's actions are devoid of emotion, almost normal. The protagonist commits suicide. Her husband marries his lover six months later. Her boss, whose wife supposedly beats him, resumes his happy marriage. The men in the story are clearly the victors. Brigitte Reimann's eponymous heroine Franziska Linkerhand (1974), from the onset of menstruation, experiences her sexuality as 'böse und gemein' (p. 89), as an ordeal devoid of pleasure. Her husband's actions only serve to strengthen this impression:

Er war stark und gesund und ohne Phantasie, und nach drei Jahren hatte er noch nicht gemerkt, daß ich nichts empfand, aber ich dachte, es wär meine Schuld, ich schämte mich, als ob ich ihn betrüge, ich dachte, ich wär frigid, das andere kannte ich nur aus Romanen (p. 89).

As opposed to these other fictional portrayals, Reimann also describes how Franziska is beaten (p. 106). The character's earlier feelings of sexual guilt are thus transposed to an external, male figure. As with Lore, Franziska is hit in the face, her wounds are particularly visible and have to be confronted.

Male violence in *Franziska Linkerhand* is further linked to the anonymity of Neustadt, where a young girl is raped (p. 525). The cold buildings are made to produce cold emotions. Franziska's dreams of a more human form of architecture are, therefore, also dreams of a more human form of male-female relationship. In Sarah Kirsch's 'Die ungeheueren bergehohen Wellen auf See' (1973) a rape is again hinted at, but the perpetrators are men who speak a 'fremde Sprache' (p. 31), they are not socialists. It is to her *Vaterstaat* that the narrator must then turn for help, when she discovers that she is pregnant. Thus her daughter ultimately remains loyal to the port, the collective, rather than to her fiancé.

Kurt Bartsch's short story *Wadzeck*, which does show a rape by a socialist, appeared in 1980, but only in the FRG. At that time the author was living in West Berlin, having been expelled from the Writers' Union in 1979. Monika Maron's novel *Flugasche* suffered a similar fate, although the reason given for censorship was the modernist form, rather than the dream sequence in which the narrator is raped (pp. 211-12).[29] Although this rape is dreamt, it is particularly shocking, the one-legged man hits a pregnant woman, who bleeds from her eyes. After he has violently assaulted her he cynically demands 'War es gut?' (p. 212), only to find that the woman is dead. The dream expresses Josefa's anger, but also the loss of her sense of her own body, of her integrity and of any hope for the future. It thus reinforces the important change of narrative perspective from first to third person.

In the poem 'Male' (1980, p. 16) Uwe Kolbe describes daily forms of violence experienced by a subject who has grown up in 'peace time'. At the top of his list is rape:

Fünfmal
wurde mir von Vergewaltigungen
erzählt

The verb 'erzählen', standing alone, emphasises that this is not a topic which can be *read* about. Where depictions of rape occur in GDR prose works of the 1980s, it is often in connection with more general violence – particularly war-time violence. Renate Apitz openly portrays rape in *Hexenzeit* (1984) but only as revenge for the sufferings of a prisoner of war:

Er hielt mir den Mund zu, würgte mich, warf mich auf den Schreibtisch. Ich spürte einen Schmerz. Er ejakulierte schnell und genußvoll, riß mich vom Tisch und befahl: saubermachen. [...] Harry hatte sich an mir gerächt für Gefangenschaft und verlorene Jahre, für seine Schwester Margareta, für seinen vertrottelten Vater und seine bigotte Mutter, für seine sinnlose Heimkehr (p. 54).

The implications are that a 'normal' man would not have done the same thing and that the same thing could not happen in peace time. Harry, rather than Mathilde, appears as the victim. This rape is also relativised through the further

---

29 Maron wrote the novel in 1978. It was first published in the FRG in 1981, and in the GDR in 1990. Other reasons for the late publication could have included the themes of censorship within journalism, environmental pollution and the Jewish background of the narrator.

events of the novel. Mathilde suffers no after-effects from her experience and becomes a very happy mother. The sex which she experiences with other men is, by contrast, too harmonious in its clichés.

The theme of rape is again historicised in Christa Wolf's *Kassandra* (1983) where it becomes a metaphor.[30] Achill assaults the corpse of the Amazon leader Penthesilea, an event which is generalised by Wolf to represent any violence perpetrated by men against women:

> Wir fühlten es, wir Frauen alle. Was soll werden, wenn das um sich greift. Die Männer, schwach, zu Siegern hochgeputscht, brauchen, um sich überhaupt noch zu empfinden, uns als Opfer. Was soll da werden (p. 140).

In *Kindheitsmuster* (Wolf 1976) 'vergewaltigen' is a mysterious word which the child Nelly connects only with the Russian soldiers: 'Die Russen vergewaltigen alle deutschen Frauen: unbezweifelte Wahrheit' (p. 297). Again the stress is placed upon the historical aspect of the theme. Christoph Hein's sketch 'Die Vergewaltigung' (1989) also deals with the mass rapes carried out by Russian soldiers after the War. As in Wolf's novel, rape here is used as an example of the GDR's repression of their past. At a time when the Russian soldier had to be regarded solely as German saviour, such portrayals would have been taboo both in terms of socialist realism and of socialist politics. In the immediate post-war period East German *Trümmerfrauen* were to be encouraged to act as men, to build socialism along Soviet lines. They were not allowed to remember the suffering they suffered, as women, at the hands of Soviet soldiers. It is with this repression in mind that Hein (1989, p. 11) states: 'die Vergewaltigung der Großmutter ist nicht das Thema meiner Erzählung'. The theme is, he stresses, 'Verdrängungen'. The introduction of rape into GDR literatures thus coincides with the gradual rewriting of East Germany's history in the 1970s and 1980s.

Hein again depicts rape in *Der fremde Freund* (1982) and with particular effect in *Horns Ende* (1985). In the former novel he describes a character who is raped by her husband, but can do nothing about it. Here, the rape takes place in the present and the concentration is on specifically female rather than more general historical experience:

---

[30] Setting novels in the past was a strategy employed by artists in the GDR to avoid censorship. 'It may be possible', as Reid (1990, p. 175) notes, 'to infringe taboos by putting on the mask of history'.

Sie hat vier Kinder und einen Mann, der sie alle zwei Wochen vergewaltigt. Sie schlafen sonst regelmäßig und gut miteinander, wie sie sagt, aber ab und zu vergewaltigt er sie. Er brauche das, sagt sie (p. 13).[31]

The description, in the almost cold manner typical of Hein's female protagonist Claudia, is so shocking because it is inserted into the narrative as if it were just another fact of life in the GDR. Claudia's reaction, one of denial, emphasises the fact that Anne is alone with her problems. Claudia also rationalises other forms of sexual violence:

Nach der Frau schlägt man wie nach einem Hund, beiläufig, nebenher. Notwendige Erziehungsmaßnahmmen zum Nutzen des Geschlagenen. Die Umarmung kann dem Schlag unmittelbar folgen (p. 132).

Again, the effect is particularly powerful because of the matter-of-fact account. Hein's depictions of brutality are part of a wider atmosphere of abuse of sexual power which pervades his novel. As Reid (1990, p. 125) writes in his analysis: 'The exploitation of women by men is to be found on every other page; here, too, there is no evidence that actually existing socialism has created a new quality of human relationships'.

In *Horns Ende* Hein portrays the violent rape of a mentally disturbed girl, Marlene. Marlene's simple outline of the events in terms of marriage, and her references to her dead mother, make the scene even more horrific, as does Hein's choice of childish sexual terminology:

Mein Mann hat mich nicht geküßt und mich nicht gestreichelt. Er hat mich gepackt und auf die Erde geworfen, daß ich glaubte, ich werde ohnmächtig. Er hat meine Kleider zerrissen, weil er rasch zu meiner Muschi wollte. [...] Es tat weh, Mama, es tat weh (p. 202).

This novel, like 'Die Vergewaltigung', thematises the repression of the past in the GDR. Yet Marlene is not raped by Russian soldiers in war time, but by a drunken man in the park late at night. This image thus acquires much broader meaning, beyond the constraints of historical fact.

Despite these examples, the issue of rape remained problematic in GDR literatures, as the furious debate surrounding Annett Gröschner's story *Maria*

---

31 *Der fremde Freund* was published in the West (1983) as *Drachenblut.* Cf. also Wolf's *Nachdenken über Christa T.* (1968) where Christa T, in the sanitorium, meets a tram driver who is raped and beaten by her husband, but will do nothing about it (p. 130).

im Schnee (1987/88) shows.[32] Commenting on her text, Gröschner said 'Im Nachhinein fürchte ich nämlich, ich habe ein erfolgreich aufrecht gehaltenes Tabu übertreten' (1990, p. 56). The taboos she challenged concerned not just the fact of the rape itself, but also aesthetic and political conventions. The themes, the setting, and the style of Gröschner's narrative offended. Her sketch is detailed, precise and frighteningly naturalistic:

> Es kostete ihn nicht viel Kraft, meinen Kopf in den Schnee zu drücken und mir von hinten sein Glied in die Scheide zu stoßen. [...] mein Gesicht von Schnee, gegen das er seinen Schwanz preßte, der schlaff war und stank (1990, p. 49).

The fact that the rape portrayed here takes place in Moscow caused just as much controversy as the report of the attack itself.[33] The condescending reactions of the police are also stated exactly. The subject's experience of rape becomes, then, Bachmann's 'Es war Mord' (p. 48).[34] Through this deliberate intertextual allusion it appears that the author is attempting to place her text within a specific tradition of writing by women. She further writes of 'die Sprache der Männer', which is the language of violence, and 'das Schweigen der Frauen' (p. 49). Her protagonist can only overcome this silence by splitting herself into 'Ich' and 'Maria'. Such generalised categories also earned Gröschner reproach. Kerstin Hensel, for example, wrote: 'Die Geschichte selbst bleibt auf der "Schwanz-Ebene". [...] SO (sic) gestaltet ist der Fakt ein gerichtlicher, kein literarischer.'[35] She does, however, add: 'ein Zeichen der Zeit: die großen Tabu-Themen kommen auf den Tisch. Ein Fortschritt, zweifellos.' Klaus Laabs, on the other hand, insists: 'daß es auch im Sozialismus Vergewaltigungen gibt, ist kein Tabu mehr',[36] and concentrates on criticising the author for her mistakes in Russian grammar. These negative reactions betray the fact that the theme of rape is still taboo, as indeed do Gröschner's anecdotes from readings where women – encouraged by the text – began to talk about their own

---

[32] The critics' opinions on this text, and the text itself, were not allowed to appear in the journal *Temperamente. Blätter für junge Literatur*, as had been planned, and were published instead, 'unofficially', in *Bizarre Städte* and *Sondeur*.

[33] Gröschner herself says that she chose Moscow because her narrative is based on an actual event, 'Diese Geschichte zu schreiben, war eine der wenigen Möglichkeiten, diese Sache zu überleben'. In Birgit Dahlke '"Ich habe vielleicht immer das gemacht, wovon ich dachte, daß ich es machen muß. Ich habe versucht, meine eigene Spur zu finden". Gespräch mit Annett Gröschner' (1994, Vol. II, pp. 20-36, p. 26).

[34] Cf. *Malina* p. 356.

[35] 'Sechs Punkte über den Wert einer Geschichte', *Sondeur* 1990, p. 51.

[36] 'aufgemotzt - dahergeschwätzt - schlludrig - gedankenarm - verantwortungslos', *Sondeur* 1990, p. 52-53.

experiences of abuse. Furthermore, these stories show how literature in the GDR could fulfil the famed *Ersatzfunktion*.

Rape represents not just a historical memory but also abuse of sexual power. Depictions of this abuse can function as important criticism of it. Very different partnerships of true equality were explored in GDR art through the theme of homosexuality.[37] As Georgina Paul (1994, p. 230) notes, in comparison with texts written in the West, those from the GDR were 'concerned not so much with the (political) validation of lesbian experience as with the critical examination, via an alternative model of interpersonal relations, of the male-female relationship'. In the 1970s homosexuality was almost invisible in GDR society. This was inspite of a notably liberal legal situation. Homosexuality was not a criminal offence after 1968, when paragraph 175 of the *Strafgesetzbuch* was deleted. The age of consent was 18, until 1988, when it was reduced to 16, the same as that for heterosexual sex. Nevertheless, both lesbians and gay men suffered heavy discrimination and were constantly under *Stasi* surveillance. It was only in the mid-1980s that the situation for homosexuals living in the GDR became easier. The church offered a safe space to meet. Groups such as the *Sonntags Club* were given official sanction, as were research projects. Academic conferences concerned with homosexuality took place in Leipzig in 1985, Karl-Marx-Stadt in 1988 and Jena in 1990.

In the 1970s and 1980s, however, there were hints of homosexual relationships in art. As Ursula Sillge (1991, p. 14) states: 'bei einer Durchsicht der DDR-Literatur fällt auf, daß eine ganze Reihe von AutorInnen, vor allem Frauen, über Schwule geschrieben haben'. Female authors also chose to focus upon lesbian friendships, although this is less common. Christine Wolter's short story 'Ich habe wieder geheiratet' (1976), is about two women who have chosen to live together. They could not get married, for 'das erlauben die Umstände nicht' (p. 26). Doris Berger (1988, p. 130) argues that 'die Möglichkeit einer erotischen Annäherung zwischen den Frauen [klingt] spielerisch-ironisch an' but, despite these possibilities, the women are ultimately together because of their children and their unhappy former marriages. Their partnership is equal and harmonious, but not sexual. The story thus ends with Rosa leaving a party to spend the night with the narrator's ex-husband, reinstating the heterosexual norm. As Paul (1994, p. 231) contends, one cannot tell whether this reinstatement is due only to the pressures of literary censorship. For Sillge the text offers an inconsequent portrayal which renders lesbianism a part-time choice

---

[37] For a full list of texts which deal with the subject of homosexuality see Ursula Sillge 1991, pp. 180-3.

rather than a 'real' identity. This denial is, she claims, the dominant representation of lesbianism in GDR art, as it is in GDR society.

Maxie Wander's interviews also detail various alternatives to the traditional marriage officially encouraged in the GDR.[38] These include open marriages, communes and, again only hinted at, lesbian partnerships. An important counterweight to Lena K's marriage, for example, is her friendship with another woman: 'Bei ihr kann ich mich geben, wie ich bin, wir sind gleichberechtigte, liebende Partner' (p. 32). There are also hints of lesbianism in Barbara F's account. The evidence of homosexuality is, however, so discreet, 'that it merely serves to strengthen the impression that this was a subject almost beyond discussion in the GDR at the time' (Paul 1994, p. 232). Barbara, for example, begins by discussing Karin, but quickly changes the subject to Georg. Helga Königsdorf's second 'unsuitable' dream (1978) depicts a lesbian partnership, one which is, once again, characterised by female tenderness:

> Ich hatte noch nie eine Frau geküßt, und es war überraschend gut. [...] Danach fielen wir uns erneut um den Hals, kosten uns und genossen erregt die weibliche Weichheit (p. 67).

However, the union is enacted only in a dream and the narrator's lover is the fairy-tale Snow White. The episode is important and yet unreal, 'unverständlich wie zuvor' (p. 68).[39] Monika Maron, in the censored *Flugasche*, portrays a relationship which began in a female prison. Again, this a union more loving and tender than those with men (pp. 109-11). The fact that Josefa is not allowed to include this story in the newspaper she works for signals the taboos which Maron attempts to challenge.

The lesbian affair created by Waldtraut Lewin in the text 'Dich hat Amor gewiß' (1974) does not rely to the same extent on the dichotomy between harmonious homosexuality and problematic heterosexuality.[40] The narrator in this story, an opera librettist, is hopelessly in love with a young bisexual singer, on whose account she suffers greatly. Their relationship is illustrated primarily on an emotional and mental level. It is also physical, although the final paragraph of the narrative, which repeats an earlier sequence, leaves the reader

---

38 Cf: 'Die Familie ist die kleinste Zelle der Gesellschaft. Sie beruht auf der für das Leben geschlossene Ehe und auf den besonders engen Bindungen, die sich aus Gefühlsbeziehungen zwischen Mann und Frau und den Beziehungen gegenseitiger Liebe, Achtung und gegenseitigen Vertrauen zwischen allen Familienmitgliedern ergeben'. (Eberhardt, *Familiengesetzbuch*, p. 11). Cf. also Pieper (1986, p. 109), 'In the GDR's official policy, marriage is regarded as having no alternative'.

39 Königsdorf also portrays a lesbian relationship in *Gleich neben Afrika*, published in 1992.

40 In *Kuckucksrufe und Ohrfeigen. Erzählungen*, 1983, pp. 5-65.

unsure as to what is real and what is the narrator's fantasy. Nevertheless, the text offers, as Paul contends, the earliest depiction in GDR literature of an unequivocally lesbian role. Lesbianism here is central to the narrative rather than marginal or hidden. Lewin, notes Karen Jankowsky (1993, p. 108), 'explores a multiplicity of eroticisms which were not usually part of GDR literature'. This is perhaps why the author herself, and not just her texts, became popular in homosexual circles in the GDR. She was invited to give many talks at gay and lesbian groups, as Jankowsky documents. Here then, as with Gröschner's readings, is an example of how literature could function as a replacement for open debate.

In *Kassandra* (1983) Wolf adopts a bisexual heroine, in love with both Aineas and Myrine. This portrayal stands in contrast with that of Achill's homosexuality, which appears to function as a negative characteristic. For Uwe Saeger's Nöhr (1981) on the other hand, it is a homosexual friendship which provides the security and the comfort he so desperately seeks. Here then, there are clear parallels with the representations of lesbianism found in work by female authors. Whereas Nöhr's marriage is based on competition and feelings of inadequacy, the relationship with Peter Bols allows him to be himself:

> Peter Bols gehört mir allein, du darfst nicht an ihn rühren, und nichts, was mit ihm war, hat mit dir zu tun [...] wir haben uns festgehalten aneinander, Hella, nur einer am andern festgehalten haben wir uns, weil wir so lange schon keinen mehr hatten, an dem wir das konnten, und weil [...] weil ich sonst nicht überlebt hätte (p. 192).

This solidarity with a man can, however, only develop in the marginalised and somewhat artificial setting of a sanitorium. In the 'real' world the knowledge of this friendship must be repressed. Outwardly Nöhr himself reinforces his masculinity, both in his insistence that 'Ich war bei einer Frau' (p. 191) and by making jokes about gays. He thereby denies his feelings for Peter and simultaneously participates in the social mechanisms which make homosexuality taboo. His sexual insecurity is, as Reid (1990) has noted, one symbol of the crisis of identity which Saeger's narrative details.

Helga Königsdorf's novel *Ungelegener Befund* (1989) depicts a homosexual affair between Dieter Jhanz and his young lover Felix. The letters written to Felix are 'nicht zum Absenden bestimmt', this love affair too remains secret. In her documentary novel Christine Lambrecht (1986) talks with male homosexuals, and openly challenges such secrecy. Georg D., after three unsuccessful marriages, has discovered that he is gay. He describes his coming to terms with this, and his partnership with Rudolf. He also speaks about sexual practices, giving details which would simply not have appeared in literature a few years earlier. This is reflected, Georg says, in the lack of research and publications on this subject. It is reflected too in the reactions towards homosexuality of other men interviewed by Lambrecht. Hans B., for example, a gynaecologist, says: 'Die stoßen mich ab. Obwohl ich weiß, daß der arme Kerl mitunter gar nichts dafür kann' (p. 84). This interview is placed directly before that with Georg, thus emphasising both the links between the two, and the importance of the theme for the author. In Hans Löffler's short story 'Mein Leben mit S.' (1987) similar prejudices are evident. The narrator writes of a woman he is unable to comprehend, for 'Sie wußte nicht mehr, wie sie sich als Frau verhalten solle' (p. 68). He imagines an unhappy childhood, or possibly even rape, 'denn daß sie homosexuell sei, wollte ich nicht glauben' (p. 68).

The taboos surrounding homosexuality in the GDR are evidenced in those narratives which subjugate the theme through the use of dreams or unreal worlds. This technique is, of course, indebted to the writings of Freud. Thus erotic dreams not only queried sexual taboos, but also the taboos surrounding Freud's work. The subconscious drives at the root of Freudian theory represented a threat to orthodox communism, because they could not be controlled. This meant that official literary criticism ignored psychoanalysis, at least until the mid-1980s. As Marx and Wild (1984, p. 178) write:

> Aufgrund der ideologischen Verpönung der Psychoanalyse als "bürgerlicher Wissenschaft" kann im Fall der DDR-Germanistik nicht einmal von einer negativen Rezeption gesprochen werden, Psychoanalyse mit ihrem Angebot für das Verständnis von Literatur wird nicht zur Kenntnis genommen.

The first anthology of Freud's writings to be published in the GDR was edited by the author Franz Fühmann in 1982. This opened the way for further selections of Freud's work to appear, for example the short collection *Trauer und Melancholie* (1982). The editors of this edition are at pains to emphasise the social aspects of the author's theories:

> Im Gegensatz zu trivialen Vorwürfen, die immer wieder gegen ihn erhoben wurden und werden, war er keineswegs einer, der die Dämme durchstoßen hätte, um menschlichen Trieben, besonders der Sexualität, freien Lauf zu verschaffen (p. 5).

Noticeable is the fact that they need also, even in 1982, to defend Freud against charges of having liberated sexuality.

Franz Fühmann was also the author who, perhaps most memorably, introduced erotic dreams into GDR literatures. His 'Traum von Sigmund Freud' (1988) acknowledges in the title the influence of Freud on his work. In the dream the famous psychoanalyst bites the narrator in the shoulder and will not

let him go. He announces his intention to achieve 'ein gedankliches Durch-
dringen und gleichzeitig ein seelisches Sich-Feien' (p. 72). The narrator understands Freud's words, as others of his dreams also manifest. He recognises the
importance of the metaphorical bite: 'Er müsse mich so lange beißen, bis ich
keinen Schmerz mehr spüre und zugleich den Sinn des Beißens verstehe, dann
erst fänden wir beide ans Ziel' (p. 73).

The *ungehörigen Träume* (1978) imagined by Helga Königsdorf's narrator
are explicitly sexual. As Grunenberg (1990, p. 202) notes:

> Alle Träume handeln von Liebesbeziehungen. [...] Sowohl die traumhafte Vorstellungs-
> welt der Assoziationen, Gedanken und Sehnsüchte wie die Symbolsprache, in die diese
> gekleidet sind, kreisen um die Motive von Zärtlichkeit, körperlicher Lust, Gewalt und
> Angst.

Although Königsdorf names only Irmtraud Morgner as the influence upon her
fantasy, one can also adopt Freudian insights to analyse the imagery. Thus
specific objects, such as the religious apple, are accorded symbolic value, as is
the case in Freud's theories of dreams. Repeated references to 'Der Direktor'
suggest an external controlling force upon the subconscious, which would
appear to be analogous to the Superego.

The erotic emancipation of GDR literatures can, then, be traced in various
forms in a wide range of texts. Other new sexual subjects introduced throughout
the 1970s and 1980s include masturbation, menstruation, pregnancy, abortion
and orgasm. In *Sinon oder die gefällige Lüge* (1983) Saeger portrays a trans-
sexual, and the problems which he faces in gaining social acceptance.
Königsdorf's 'Bolero' (1978) thematises the contraceptive pill, and the negative
side effects associated with it. The question so typical of 1970s GDR literatures,
'War ich dann noch ich?' (p. 11), is here placed in a hormonal context. In the
same collection, the story 'Hochzeitstag in Pizunda' also deals with the pill.
Here it is used to show the double moral standards characteristic of patriarchal
attitudes towards sexual responsibility:

> Die Pille und das Recht, eine Schwangerschaft zu unterbrechen, haben der Frau endlich
> die Möglichkeit gegeben, ihren Körper selbst zu verwalten. [...] Die Pille und das Recht,
> eine Schwangerschaft zu unterbrechen, haben den Mann endgültig von der Verpflicht-
> ung befreit, sich über die Sache irgendwelche Gedanken zu machen (p. 137).

In works such as these, the harmonious bliss of De Bruyn's description is
nowhere to be found, the cold realities of sex have taken over. This does not
mean, however, that the texts are unaesthetic, merely documents designed to

facilitate discussion of taboo themes. Königsdorf's humour, for example, raises her work beyond the function of mere *Ersatz*.

Karl-Heinz Jakobs' *Die Interviewer* (1973) treats the subject of a relationship between a forty-three old man and a young girl of sixteen, who sees sex as her passage to adulthood. Unusually, it is the older man who is afraid of the prospect. General prejudice against such a partnership is also reported, judgements which are made to sound outdated and ridiculous:

> Er könnte ihr Vater sein. Ob wir das nicht melden müssen? Was wohl ihre Eltern dazu sagen. Er geht, als hätte er Plattfüße. Ihr sollte der Kopf geschoren werden, und ihn sollten sie an den Füßen aufhängen. Sie könnte seine Tochter sein. [...] Ausziehen beide und mit Ruten peitschen (pp. 195-6).

Jakobs also raises issues concerning childhood sexuality, extra-marital affairs and even group sex. The latter, through comparison with other 'staatsfeindliche' activities, is placed in a positive light;

> Sie tauschten dort Nacht für Nacht die Partner. Sie soffen nicht. Sie randalierten nicht. Sie prügelten sich nicht. Sie bildeten keine staatsfeindliche Gruppe. Sie waren immer guter Laune, freundlich und zuvorkommend zueinander und zu jedermann (pp. 229-30).

Again prejudice against such 'abnormal' sexual practices is portrayed – the group is reported to the police, the 'Kaderleitung', the trade union, the Party and the youth groups. In general the sexual forms part of the problematic mood of this book, in which the spheres of work and family are constantly intertwined.

Other writers emphasise the role that accommodation, or the lack of it, played in love. This is, in some senses, an especially East German aspect of the treatment of the erotic. Young couples were given priority when applying for housing, which often influenced the decision to marry. Beyond this social factor, questions of space have a much wider significance, symbolising other features of a relationship. In Hein's *Der Tangospieler* (1989) Elke has to move her child into the hall in order to be able to have sex with Dallow. His flat remains empty, as does his life. Hans and Eva, in Saeger's 'Unfachliche Notizen' (1988), are constantly struggling to find a place where they can sleep together undisturbed. This situation reflects the constant interweaving of their personal relationship with political events. In Saeger's *Warten auf Schnee* (1981) Astrid and Krüger are confined to his one-room apartment. His inability to cope with this is again representative of the lack of real direction in his life.

GDR literary history is thus patterned by change as regards constructions of sexuality. At the beginning of the 1980s, therefore, Ursula Püschel (1980, p.

163) finds no signs of any censorship as far as the erotic is concerned. On the contrary, she writes: 'daß Prüderie überwunden wurde, ist nicht lange her, und so treten die Darstellungen der Zweisamkeit, für die Raum erobert wurde, jetzt eher inflationistisch auf'. Reid similarly concludes that the prudishness he discovered in early GDR art is now the exception rather than the rule. No former East German publishing houses were aware of any 'konkrete Richt-linien, die bei erotischen Darstellungen zu beachten gewesen wären'.[41] Herr Nitzschke of the Greifenverlag denies any influence of 'Prüderie und Eng-stirnigkeit in bezug auf erotische Themen'. Herr Chowanetz from the Verlag Neues Leben similarly claims 'die Autoren konnten darüber frei schreiben'. The question by a West German journalist (Doerry 1994, p. 192), 'Warum spielt das Erotische in der DDR-Literatur keine nennenswerte Rolle?' thus shows a typical misunderstanding of the situation, based solely on stereotypes of the 1950s and 1960s and on extended clichés of East German gravity. Descriptions which departed from accepted, and so-called 'normal', erotic behaviour, did remain under-represented in GDR literatures, but they were certainly existent, as a cursory examination shows.

1.2.3 Keine Tabus – Film, Literary Criticism and Sexology

In this analysis of GDR literatures it has been suggested that writing, in some cases, provided a space in which sexual themes could be pursued. As regards the issues of, for example, prostitution, pornography, rape and homosexuality, the status of art in GDR society meant that certain discourses fulfilled an important role as substitute forum for discussion. Fictional realization of taboo issues could have the effect of questioning those taboos. Literary discourse does not, however, exist in isolation. Sexual taboos were not broken solely through the achievements of writers, but also in other cultural and social fields.

Plenzdorf's film *Die Legende von Paul und Paula* (1973) for example, found 'ein riesiges Echo' (Meyer 1985, p. 51), which:

---

41 Frau Matschie, Lektorin, Domina Verlag. She adds, however: 'Ich kann mir vorstellen, daß bei einer Annäherung an pornographische Darstellungen die allgemeine Zenzur, die die Hauptverwaltung Verlage und Buchhandel im Ministerium für Kultur ausübte, reagiert hätte. Sicherlich hat in dieser Hinsicht auch eine Art Selbstzensur bei Autoren und Verlagen existiert.'

erklärt sich nicht zuletzt aus der Tatsache, daß die in ihnen angesprochene Thematik – die Infragestellung tradierter Rollenbilder, die offene Darlegung des Sexuallebens, die Kritik an der Normierung des Privatlebens durch den Staat – bisher tabuisiert waren.[42]

The debate surrounding this openly erotic film in the journal *Filmspiegel* was intense.[43] Some of those who expressed an opinion found the sexuality Western and therefore automatically wrong. Others distinguished between successful erotic scenes, which made the film more 'real', and the gratuitous sexuality characteristic of capitalist films. If sex was 'schön' or 'natürlich' it was acceptable, anything obscene was not. Gisela Kubach (*Filmspiegel*, 7 (1973), p. 18), for example, writes 'unsere sozialistische Moral kann solche Liebesszenen durchaus verkraften, ja, es ist sogar in ihrem Sinne'. Bernhard Wolter too is in favour of more erotic films, provided that it is 'klar zu erkennen, welches Verhältnis die Beteiligten an diesen Szenen zur Intimität haben und welchem Zweck diese Intimität dient' (ibid. p. 18). The novel of *Paul und Paula* (1979) is also openly erotic. Paula is an especially sensual character, it is she who is the instigator in sex.[44]

Films made by DEFA in the 1980s became increasingly sexual, showing naked men and women, homosexuality, and even a love affair between an eighteen year old man and a fourteen year old girl.[45] 'Die andere Liebe', in which homosexual men and women talk about their lives, was produced by DEFA in 1988. Heinz Carow's *Coming Out*, which portrays the relationship between Philipp and Matthias, was released in November 1989. Both films concentrated upon male homosexuality. Such developments, similar to those in literature, aroused both approval and disapproval. Heinz Kersten (1981, p. 232) cites a letter asking: 'Warum muß in letzter Zeit in fast jedem DEFA-Film ein Nackedei auftauchen, und warum scheinen unsere Filme ohne Bettszenen nicht mehr auszukommen?' Sex is no longer associated solely with capitalism.

During the 1970s literary criticism too became more receptive towards issues concerning sexuality. Hans Kaufmann's important article 'Glück ohne Ruh'

---

42 The film was made in 1973 by DEFA and was directed by Heinz Carow.
43 A similar debate had taken place about the film *Reife Kirschen*, *Filmspiegel*, 26 (1972), p. 18, 3 (1973), p. 18 and 6 (1973), p. 18. Opinions expressed here echo Honecker's words from the 1960s: 'Wenn es so weiter geht, kommt es – wie in der Mode – immer mehr zum Nachäffen der westlichen Art. Es wird dann gar nicht mehr lange dauern, und unsere Schauspielerinnen müssen [...] auch nackt vor der Kamera agieren' (Ingeborg Pahlitzsch), 3 (1973).
44 This was published as *Legende vom Glück ohne Ende*.
45 *Verbotene Liebe*, 1989. See also a film made by Ina Merkel and others, *Die Nackten und die Roten* (Arimix, 1994) in which various DEFA films, where sexual taboos are broken, are discussed.

(1976, pp. 151-92) recognises the achievements of various authors, whilst itself breaking taboos. Sexuality, 'die Gestaltung erotischer Beziehungen im engeren Sinn' (p. 155), is now an important subject, and one which is set firmly within a political context. Kaufmann accords pure erotic literature, which he sees as somehow peculiarly Western and self-indulgent, very little value, although the Western examples of the genre that he examines are limited. According to Kaufmann this form of art may have broken some taboos, but it created or reinforced others:

> Die Funktion der kapitalistischen Konsumliteratur mit sexuellem Inhalt erschöpft sich nicht darin, dem Produzenten Profit, dem Konsumenten Zerstreuung zu bieten, sie hat vielmehr einen ausgesprochen apologetischen Charakter, sie bestätigt die herrschenden Verhältnisse (p. 163).

His criticisms of Miller, both of the man and of his work, are remarkably similar to those given by Kate Millett. Both accuse the author of portraying women solely as sex objects who 'wollen nichts als geschlechtlich konsumiert sein' (p. 161), and men as their potent consumers.

A new form of society requires, so Kaufmann continues, new images of sexuality, images of 'eine natürliche Sinnlichkeit, die nicht auf Macht und Unterwerfung beruhende Verhaltensklischees reproduziert' (p. 167). He thus praises 'unsere sozialistische Literatur', which offers 'bei der Darstellung intimer Vorgänge eine recht eindeutige Alternative zu den skizzierten spät-bürgerlichen Haltungen' (p. 165). Socialist authors have, he claims, success-fully integrated the erotic into a wider social framework. His analyses aim to show how these two spheres are intertwined. He therefore also raises the problem of sexual language, questioning the terminology we adopt for words such as the penis. Crude language, he concludes, can easily be used. What Kaufmann prefers is 'eine literarische und sprachliche Kultur, in der die natürliche Sinnlichkeit von Rohheit und Zynismus befreit ist' (p. 172). In his choice of the penis as example, as in his concentration on male artists, Kaufmann's analysis is notably that of a male critic. It also, borrowing from a clichéd vocabulary of 'natural' sexuality, reproduces bourgeois ideas of a biological essence outside modern discourse, whilst, paradoxically, stressing the inherent social aspects of the theme. Despite these contradictions, the article is notable for the serious academic interest it displays in the erotic. It reflects too the arguments presented in other fields of discourse within GDR society, where taboos were also being challenged. Kaufmann thus refers not only to art, but also to 'die Sexual-wissenschaft und -pädagogik' (p. 160).

The polyvocality of literary discourse means that it can offer an alternative to official mainstream ideology. As Foucault (1966, p. 44) shows when describing the development of language from the sixteenth century to the modern age, modern literature can form a 'counter-discourse', representing the space where 'language was to grow with no point of departure, no end, and no promise'. The use of metaphor and linguistic experimentation allows the reader to develop her own meanings within the texts. However, aesthetic literature is not always oppositional to public discussion, it is not always *Ersatz*. As regards the sexual, fictional writing from the GDR also added to, and concurred with, medical, psychological and sociological debate. Within these discursive spheres, the GDR claimed to have created 'die freieste und menschenwürdigste Sexualmoral [...], die es jemals gab' (Allendorf 1978, p. 119). This was a morality supposedly free from prejudice, from taboo, from dogma, from economic influences and from male domination. According to the sexologist Siegfried Schnabl (1969, p. 48), for example:

> Die marxistische Ethik bejaht die Liebe nicht nur als geistiges Band und tiefempfundenes Gefühl zwischen Mann und Frau, sondern auch als sinnlichgegenständliches Erleben ihrer innigen Zuneigung in der körperlichen Vereinigung.

This bodily union is of course 'sittlich wertvoll, gesellschaftlich verantwortlich,' and 'verbunden mit der Forderung nach moralischer Sauberkeit' (p. 48).

In another standard GDR work on sexual behaviour, *Liebe und Sexualität bis 30* (1984) Professor Kurt Starke pronounces that socialism has successfully rejected bourgeois morality in every area of society, including the sexual. The fact that by 1989 over 90% of women in the GDR worked outside the home – making up 50% of the workforce – contributed, he maintains, to a deconstruction of role models, both at work and at home, on the production line or in bed:

> Mit der Veränderung der gesellschaftlichen Stellung der Frau verändert sich auch deren konkretes Sexualverhalten. Wenn, wie in unserer Gesellschaft, die soziale Unterdrückung und Bevormundung der Frauen beseitigt ist und sie die Gleichberechtigung real erfahren, dann kommt es auch zu einer tiefgreifenden Umgestaltung ihrer Geschlechtsbeziehungen (p. 77).[46]

---

[46] In general I am paraphrasing here from an interview with Professor Starke, 19.1.1993. Maron ironises such views in her novel *Flugasche*, 'Die Männer reden in der letzten Zeit viel von der Freiheit unserer Körper und von der entdeckten Sexualität der Frau. [...] Wir aber sollten die Größe erkennen ihres Verdienstes und sollten nicht die Augen verschließen von der epochalen Wende, denn an uns ist begonnen worden die klitoridale Epoche. Dank unsern Männern' (1981, pp. 159-60).

Thus Professor Starke believed that earlier sexual taboos had been overcome and were now irrelevant.

Joachim Hohmann (1991) complements this picture in his sociological study. He lists innumerable books published, and surveys carried out, in the GDR from the 1950s onwards that deal with the subject of sexuality. The *Ehe- und Sexualberatungsstellen* (*ESBs*) set up in the 1960s aimed to make this knowledge available to the average member of the public. Sex education for students was also designed to banish the taboos that had no place in socialism. Hohmann (p. 40) categorically states that:

> Jugendliche in der DDR verhielten sich insgesamt reifer und lustbetonter als solche in Westdeutschland, wenn sie sexuelle Bindungen eingehen. Diese Feststellung überrascht nur den, der sich die DDR als von Sinnlichkeit und sexueller Kultur weitgehend leergeräumten Staat vorstellt. Die Tatsachen waren anders.

Young people in the GDR may, as surveys carried out suggest, have been more sexually open than those in the West.[47] The results of sex education are, however, extremely difficult to assess. Kristine Von Soden (1991), for example, argues, along very different lines, that the GDR merely reproduced teachings from the Weimar Republic. Ultimately surveys and sex manuals are as much of a discourse of fiction as more literary products.

Books such as those by Schnabl and Starke strongly emphasise that the sexual is influenced by political, economic, historical, cultural and ideological contexts. They stress too that in socialism sex is the result of love, love which is, ideally, found in a heterosexual marriage. Kaufmann's literary analysis supports these notions, interpreting the sexual, within socialist literature, as sensual, beautiful, innocent and 'natural'. He manages to ignore literary portrayals of homosexuality and of the more negative sides of the sexual – rape, pornography and prostitution. In this respect the literary developments outlined above can clearly be related to those in other fields of discourse, although the special function of literature within discourse cannot be ignored.

---

[47] Eg. Kurt Starke and Konrad Weller, *Differences in sexual conduct between East and West German Adolescents before unification* (Leipzig, 1990).

1.3 The Context for an Erotic Emancipation, 1968-1989 Women Writers and the Sexual

The 1970s is a decade known not only for the 'aesthetic emancipation' of GDR literatures, but also for the social, and literary, emancipation of women. By 1971 Honecker, in another unforgettable speech, was able to declare that:

> Es ist in der Tat eine der größten Errungenschaften des Sozialismus, die Gleichberechtigung der Frau in unserem Staat sowohl gesetzlich als auch im Leben weitgehend verwirklicht zu haben (in Allendorf 1978, p. 128).

There remained, of course, considerable limitations to the form of legal equality to which Honecker refers. Yet it did offer many women the chance to write.[48] Amongst other subjects, they chose to fictionalise the various problems connected with their so-called emancipation and about their own experiences of their state. Previously private areas of family life became a new site where politics could be contested, rather than idyllic spaces of retreat. History was not just revised, it was often revised from an angle which was constructed as female. Thus subjects such as rape were not merely historical, political and aesthetic but also feminist. The women writing about such themes formed a notable group, whose work was seen as one of the most important aspects of the cultural landscape in the GDR.

Dorothee Rosenberg, then, entitles her article on 'Schriftstellerinnen in der DDR' 'Neudefinierung des Öffentlichen und des Privaten' (1992). These new definitions meant, as has been shown, that the erotic became part of GDR literatures, whether as descriptions of sexual intercourse, or as thematic questions of, for example, homosexuality, abortion, contraception, sexual violence, and erotic dreams. Rosenberg's title would, however, appear to suggest that it was the female authors who were responsible for redefining aesthetic understandings in the GDR, that it was they who made the private

---

[48] Of course women wrote in the GDR before the 1970s, and wrote also about the contradictions of their own lives, as well as those of others. An exploration of this 'women's writing' is, however, outside the bounds of this study. The social factors influencing the developments in writing by women in the GDR are noted often, particularly by GDR critics. Hans Kaufmann (1976, p. 233, footnote 44), for example, argues that: 'Frauenemanzipation als Stoff und Tendenz sind Teilmoment und Symptom gewachsener und offensichtlich weiter wachsender Teilnahme von Frauen an der Emanzipation im umfassenden, Marx'schen Sinne des Begriffs.'

public. Sara Lennox (1976, p. 226) also feels that women writers were 'naturally' able to deal with specific themes better than men could:

> Es scheint, als ob gerade diese Widersprüche und Schwierigkeiten ihres Lebens zwischen öffentlicher und privater Sphäre zusammen mit dem traditionellen weiblichen Hang zum Intimen, zum Gefühl und zum Erotischen die Frauen in der DDR vor allen anderen dazu befähigt hat, auf die Fragen sowohl weiblicher als auch allgemein menschlicher Erfüllung im Sozialismus einzugehen.

These ideas are echoed by many critics.[49] In the *Pariser Gespräch* on GDR literature of the 1970s it is noted that the new challenging of sexual taboos is linked to both the increased numbers of women writing in the GDR and the subsequent interest in the theme of female and human emancipation. Michèle Tailleur (in Badia 1976, p. 1168) states 'solche Themen [werden] gerade von einer weiblichen Romangestalt angeschnitten. Das entspricht der [...] Übernahme dieser Themen in einer neuen literarischen Dimension [...] durch die Frauen'. Hans Kaufmann (1976, p. 41) too contends that it is 'an erster Stelle Frauen' who have recognised the potential of the themes of love and sexuality.

Many women writing in the GDR did fictionalise their private experiences, including the sexual. Yet it is by no means the case that all female authors broke sexual taboos, or that no male authors did so. Where women did use eroticism their descriptions not only offered new constructions of the sexual, but also reinforced clichés whereby women functioned as passive objects of male desire with no sexuality of their own. Often the basic temptress-Eve/virginal-Maria dichotomy was simply reproduced. Texts by some men on the other hand, notably De Bruyn, Braun and Hein, offer important and aesthetically valuable contributions to the sexual debate. Reid (1990) emphasises the role of Saeger's novels in this respect. Kaufmann (1976) analyses works by Kunert, Braun, Mickel, Kahlau, Jendryschik, Plenzdorf and Hacks, as well as the classic examples of GDR writing by women. He cautiously concludes with a generalisation:

> Die persönliche Betroffenheit, die naturgemäß beim Thema Geschlechterbeziehungen besonders stark zur Geltung kommt, bringt es mit sich, daß schreibende Männer andere Akzente setzen als schreibende Frauen (p. 179).

It is, however, a generalisation which remains bound by terms of nature. It would be more appropriate to emphasise difference rather than similarity, and the role of the reader rather than a gendered author figure.

---

[49] See eg. Emmerich 1989, p. 203. Auer 1990, p. 149.

Female figures and female sexuality are not necessarily superfluous if portrayed by a male artist, these images too can help to challenge fixed role models and stereotypes. What they cannot, however, achieve is to break through the historical wall of female silence – that is a task that only women can fulfil. As Annemarie Auer (1975, p. 256) polemically summarises, 'solange die Frauen sich in eigener Sache kaum zu Worte melden, geht es ruhig in der uralten Weise fort'. In any analysis of constructions of sexuality in GDR literatures two female writers have been particularly important in challenging the 'uralte Weise'. The role of Irmtraud Morgner, as a recognised member of the canon, has often been acknowledged. *Hochzeit in Konstantinopel* (1968) is, for example, as noteworthy in its use of the erotic as *Buridans Esel*. Her later works function as a microcosm of each of the innovations in erotic literature detailed above. The writing of the less well-known younger artist, Gabriele Stötzer-Kachold, is similarly seminal as far as the 1980s are concerned. For her there are, simply, 'keine Tabus'. The following chapters concentrate, therefore, upon sexuality in the work of these authors.

2. Sexuality in the work of Irmtraud Morgner – Part One

In her obituary for Irmtraud Morgner, who died in 1990, Alice Schwarzer (1990a, p. 66) describes the author as 'eine feministische Visionärin'. Born in Chemnitz in 1933, Morgner belongs to the same generation as the other 'female visionary' of the GDR, Christa Wolf, and like her, had a vital influence on both readers and other writers in her country and abroad. Her writing, which began in the 1950s, signals important developments in the history of GDR literatures, both thematically and stylistically. In particular, it signals developments within the erotic. Beyond this, Morgner's work evidences the increased importance of feminist aesthetic debate within the GDR, a debate which has particular meaning in the context of sexuality. Together with Sarah Kirsch and Maxie Wander, Wolf and Morgner traditionally formed, for most Western critics, the canon of East German women writers. Before Emmerich's demand for new paradigms can be answered productively, such canons must be reviewed and reassessed, new questions must be asked of texts which have acquired almost legendary status.

The fascination of Morgner's works lies in a vast spectrum of possibilities of approach and interpretation. As the author states: 'alle meiner Bücher sind tatsächlich viele Bücher' (in Eva Kaufmann 1984a, p. 1495). The approach here will concentrate upon the sexual, for amongst 'official' GDR writers it is Morgner who most convincingly and consequentially uses the theme of sexuality in her work. Her role in the 'erotic emancipation' of GDR literatures has been recognised by many critics. While this chapter will begin with the issue of taboos, to view Morgner's texts simply as examples of Honecker's 'Keine Tabus' policy would be a reductive exercise. Her work with the erotic is also part of the feminism for which the author has often been acclaimed. The second part of the chapter therefore considers how Morgner's novels were received by critics as feminist and as East German women's writing. This reception is situated within wider debates concerning female aesthetics, which took place in both East and West Germany from the early 1970s. This forms the context within which, in Chapter Three, Morgner's constructions of sexuality are analysed not in terms of taboo, but in terms of feminism.

'Wir liebten uns nach allen Regeln der Kunst, die nicht gelehrt wird' (*Ho,* p. 125)

Morgner's use of sexuality represents a breaking of taboos, for her art too was not 'taught' in the GDR. She began to change the rules long before Honecker's official sanction, introducing bold poetic variety within the erotic and ignoring advice. Beatriz is reminded by trade union officials that 'eine Schriftstellerin [dürfte sich] nicht verleiten lassen, nackte Männer zu beschreiben' (*B,* p. 126), yet her creator's 'schöne Literatur' describes both naked men and naked women. It openly, and aesthetically, depicts numerous sexual activities and sexual themes. Many recent critics have thus acclaimed this aspect of Morgner's writing. Kristine von Soden (1991, p. 106), as one among many, states that: 'Irmtraud Morgner war die erste Schriftstellerin der DDR, die die Sexualität offen zum Thema machte. Das gab es bis dahin nicht in der Literatur'. Like many others she emphasises the role of this originality in breaking down taboos. Fritz Rudolf Fries (1990) similarly writes:

> Während Erotik in der DDR vor allem auf Bestellung in Adlershof ins Bild rückte und unser makelloses Fernsehballett auch die alten Herren vom Politbüro "after hours" re-animierte, hatte Erotik in den Romanen der Erzählerin unsere Wirklichkeit längst sensibilisiert.

Earlier commentators, especially those from the GDR, had not been so enthusiastic. Morgner's first novels had closely adhered to the cultural and political demands of the 1950s. *Das Signal steht auf Fahrt* was published in 1959 and was marked by the currency of the Bitterfeld conferences. It was, Morgner (1973 *AE,* p. 21) later claims: 'nach einem Exposé angefertigt. [...] Bei seiner Herstellung habe ich freiwillig, unwillkürlich alle damals im Lande kursierenden Ratschläge berücksichtigt, die aufzunehmen ich fähig war'. *Ein Haus am Rande der Stadt* appeared in 1962 and is similarly written in a classic socialist realist style. The short text *Notturno*, from 1964, again conforms to expected aesthetic doctrine, but does, through the figure of Karla, anticipate the importance that the female protagonist will be given in Morgner's later work.[50] It also begins to evidence the author's interest in the sexual.

This piece was originally to have been included in the author's next major project, *Rumba auf einen Herbst.*[51] The novel was, however, only published

[50] This text was awarded the *Aufbau-Preis* in 1964.
[51] Bussmann (1992, p. 332) writes of this novel, 'an den Roman *Rumba* ging sie anders als an die Frühwerke; mit ihm machte sie den entscheidenden Schritt hin zu sich'. Cf. Morgner: '*Rumba auf einen Herbst* war das erste Buch, das ich schreiben mußte' (in Kaufmann 1984a, p. 1510).

posthumously in 1992, having disappeared in 1965 amidst the bureaucracy of GDR censorship, *Stasi* files and the notorious eleventh plenary session of the SED Central Committee.[52] References to the Cuban missile crisis, Stalinism, jazz music and generation conflicts, as well as the modernist form, were amongst the reasons for censorship, which also included the sexual elements of the four stories, notably the extra-marital affair between Lutz and Ev. As Kerstin Hensel (1993d, p. 107) emphasises when discussing Morgner's critique of marriage:

> Mit diesem massiven Angriff auf das Gesetz, auch auf den strapazierten Familienbegriff Engels "Die Familie als die kleinste Zelle des Staates" ist Irmtraud Morgner natürlich Gegenangriffen ausgesetzt gewesen, *ein* Grund, warum *Rumba* nicht erscheinen durfte.

The official censor's report on this chapter complains that 'es sind nichts mehr als Gefühlchen, die da beschrieben werden' (in Bussmann 1992, p. 334). Giving free rein to spontaneous sexual emotions did not fit into the official paradigm of Marxist Leninism. It is, then, no surprise that Morgner's work had to be censored in the Soviet Union.[53]

According to Eva Kaufmann (1984b, p. 1517), the experience of state intervention had a vital influence on Morgner's work, 'zum Beispiel auch darin, daß sie sich viel stärker komischen und phantastischen Gestaltungsmitteln zuwendet, daß sie einen Lakonismus entwickelt, der vieles indirekt auszusprechen erlaubt'.[54] However, as far as sexuality is concerned, Morgner's writing becomes increasingly direct. In the GDR this form of directness was, despite often lengthy delays in publication, accepted by the censors.[55] Morgner's next text, *Hochzeit in Konstantinopel*, represents her literary breakthrough. There is much about the story, first published in 1968, that challenged the official aesthetic codes of her earlier prose, including the use of the erotic. As Gabriele Scherer (1992, p. 52) notes, 'als neuartig empfunden

---

52 Agde (1991, p. 9) describes this event as 'der rigoroseste und folgenreichste Eingriff der SED-Führung in Kunstprozesse und Intellektuellendebatten'.

53 'In der Sowjetunion zum Beispiel ist kein einziges Buch von mir erschienen, ein paar Erzählungen wurden übersetzt, aber kein Buch. Grund: Pornographie' (in Schwarzer 1990b, p. 37).

54 Kaufmann also notes general developments in GDR aesthetics which influenced the author.

55 For later works there is, at present, no evidence to support Barbara Meyer's (1985, p. 70) general claim that: 'Es mag nicht erstaunen, daß Irmtraud Morgner mit ihrer freien Behandlung der Sexualität bei der offiziellen Literaturkritik auf Widerstand stieß'. Meyer herself does not justify this statement in any way. As further research is carried out into *Stasi* files and *HV Gutachten* such evidence may, of course, be discovered.

werden im wesentlichen die phantastischen Erzählelemente und die emanzipatorische Thematik, außerdem die klare Benennung der bis dahin in der DDR-Literatur tabuisierten Erotik'. These innovations were not immediately popular. Shortly after publication all remaining copies of the text were removed from the shelves, despite Morgner's change from first to third person narration.[56] Scherer compares the debates to which the work gave rise to those concerning Wolf's *Nachdenken über Christa T.*, published in the same year. In the GDR both writers were accused of concentrating on the apparently private sphere at the expense of the public.

The protagonist and narrator of *Hochzeit in Konstantinopel* is Bele H., who sees sex not just as private, but as an art form not yet taught in the GDR. Her own stories, which she tells her fiancé Paul, aim not only to save their relationship, but also to challenge this absence. Ironic comments upon sexual taboos are common:

> Paul entwickelte eine erotische Theorie über optimale Vertretung der menschlichen Gattung, die Beles innere Zensur verbot aufzuschreiben, sie lebte in einem anständigen Land (*Ho*, p. 24).

Such observations echo De Bruyn's words and also move beyond them. Bele's narrative is more radical in its use of the erotic than Erp's. Morgner's prose plays with expectations in order to circumvent, and challenge, sexual taboos. The texts *Gauklerlegende*, from 1970, and *Die wundersamen Reisen Gustav des Weltfahrers*, first published in 1972, are similarly sexually humorous and similarly fantastic.

Morgner's works of the late 1960s and early 1970s thus introduced new erotic elements into GDR literatures, in defiance of official pronouncements. As Scherer (1992, p. 81) writes: 'ein erotisches Leitmotiv findet sich seit *Hochzeit in Konstantinopel* in allen Romanen und klingt auch bereits in den Textfragmenten von *Rumba auf einen Herbst* an'. It was, however, with the novel *Leben und Abenteuer der Trobadora Beatriz nach Zeugnissen ihrer Spielfrau Laura* that the author established her reputation as 'eine der wenigen erotischen Schriftstellerinnen' (Schwarzer 1990b, p. 38). This epic montage combines themes, ideas and even extracts from *Rumba auf einen Herbst*,[57] *Hochzeit in Konstantinopel*, *Gauklerlegende* and *Die wundersamen Reisen Gustav des*

---

56 Cf. Bele's 'Nachbemerkung' (*Ho*, p. 191).
57 Doris Jahnsen (1992, p. 354) traces the hidden *Rumba* quotations in *Hochzeit in Konstantinopel*, *Gauklerlegende* and *Beatriz*. 'Dieses Verfahren', she states, 'ist nicht bloße Reaktion auf den zensierenden Eingriff, vielmehr auch konsequente Fortentwicklung der eigenenen Handschrift'.

Weltfahrers. Beatriz was planned as the first part of Morgner's *Salman trilogy*. The second part, *Amanda. Ein Hexenroman*, was published in 1983. Again the work has become a classic. Like its predecessor it successfully combines the mythological, the fantastic and present reality with intertextual borrowings from discourses of every area of society. The third part of this magnum opus was never finished. Planned sections are, however, available: *Der Schöne und das Tier* and 'Nekromantie im Marx-Engels-Auditorium'.[58] Both evidence the familiar interest in questions of social, and sexual, emancipation.

The difference, in terms of the erotic, between Morgner's early texts and the Salman trilogy is expressed by Nikolaus Markgraf (1975, p. 150) as one of 'attack':

> Zwar hatte schon die *Hochzeit in Konstantinopel* ihr Interesse für und Bekenntnis zu einer offenen Sinnlichkeit deutlich erkennen lassen; aber das erotische Selbstbewußtsein von Irmtraud Morgner befand sich da noch in kämpferischer Defensive. Nun ging sie zum Angriff über.

One side of this attack is formed by positive descriptions of female sexuality and of sexual female characters. French critics thus acclaim the 'beauty' of Morgner's 'normal' erotic depictions:

> Der Rückzug der Tabus zeigt sich unter anderem in der oft schönen Beschreibung erotischer Szenen, die nicht mehr vom Standpunkt des Mannes aus verfaßt sind, so wie bei Irmtraud Morgner [...] Die körperliche Bindung zwischen Mann und Frau wird in ihrem normalen Aspekt bestimmt (Badia 1976, p. 1167).

For Annemarie Auer (1976) the shocking effect of Morgner's eroticism lies in the female perspective that it presents. In her opinion obscenities in the lyrical were, by 1976, fully accepted, as long as they are based on the presumption that: 'das Weibswesen eine Art Naturareal sei, eine Landschaft oder auch Muschel und Rose oder krassestenfalls, einfach das gemeinte Stück Fleisch selbst' (1976, p. 130). In Morgner's case, however, 'erlaubt sich eine, aus dem Objektstand in den des Subjekts zu treten' (p. 119).

The other side of Morgner's sexual attack is to be found in her attempt to open GDR literatures to sexual themes which had very little to do with official concepts of love and the erotic. In this sense too, her work both precedes and predicts that of other East German authors. Thus she also accords artistic value to topics such as abortion, the pill, homosexuality, sexual abuse, prostitution, and pornography, as well as to the work of Freud. Whereas *Beatriz* emphasised

---

[58] Scherer (1992, p. 10) suggests that the novel was to be entitled *Die cherubischen Wandersfrauen*, Luchterhand proposes *Das heroische Testament* (*Der Schöne*, p. 41).

the first side of Morgner's sexual attack, in *Amanda* concern lies primarily with the second. In the 1980s other writers challenge prejudices concerning one issue. Morgner's novel, by comparison, covers every aspect of sexuality in order to expose oppression of women in this sphere. War, rather than sex, is to become the taboo.

Morgner's literary interest in illicit sexual themes is not, of course, manifested only in *Amanda*. In *Beatriz* she tackles, amongst other subjects, that of homosexuality. This is a sexual theme which, for many writers from the GDR, remained taboo even after 1971. Georgina Paul (1994) singles out Morgner as one of the authors who first challenged this situation. Valeska, for example, is bisexual, an identity which represents, as Agnès Cardinal (1991, p. 154) argues, 'the paradigm for a utopian sexuality deriving strength and pleasure from both genders'. In her *Orlando* story Valeska hints at the lesbian emotions between herself and Shenja that have had to be repressed: 'Die Seele trug man ungeniert, jedoch oberhalb der Gürtellinie. Anderes verschwiegen' (*B*, p. 432). These emotions can only be physically revealed when Valeska is a man, although – as Paul recognises – the female pronoun supports the earlier hints. In Valeska's 'hadischen Erzählungen' she writes, 'Manchmal möchte ich eine Pflanze sein, beispielsweise Löwenzahn, oder lesbisch' (*B*, p. 225). This is a desire she can only formulate in her imagination, prejudice against homosexuals being as strong in the East as it is in the West. As a soldier informs Beatriz, sexuality should be 'gesund' and 'sauber' (*B*, p. 99).

With these prejudices in mind, Valeska dispenses with her male physique during sex with Rudolf, 'um die landläufigen moralischen Vorstellungen nicht zu verletzen' (*B*, p. 443). In the same way as Christine Wolter, Morgner thus ends by apparently 'reinscribing the centrality of the heterosexual relationship' (Paul 1994, p. 232). However, this reinscription can also be read as offering a critical focus on a society which makes such a relationship central to its ideology. As Schmitz-Köster (1989, p. 76) writes, Valeska's actions are not 'Anpassung, sondern Kritik: Die heterosexuelle Norm wird als bloße Festlegung jenseits der Biologie gedeutet'. Despite her appearance, Valeska is a truly androgynous subject, her sexuality is no longer based on the binary opposition male/female and its correlations. Thus any sex that she has will, ultimately, be outside the hetero/homosexual framework. It is, perhaps, not surprising that this sex change narrative was not included in Edith Anderson's *Blitz aus heiterem Himmel* anthology as planned, but hidden in the much larger work *Beatriz*.

Prejudices surrounding homosexuality are again material for Morgner's art in *Amanda*. Such discrimination has, for example, convinced Laura that boys who grow up without a male identification partner can become gay:

> Daß Homosexualität eine Art Krankheit sein soll, glaubte Laura den Zeitschriften-artikeln nicht. Aber sie wollte ihrem Sohn selbstverständlich ersparen, als Außenseiter leben zu müssen. Die Sitten des Landes – nicht die Gesetze – diskriminierten männliche Homosexualität unerbittlich. Weibliche wurde erst gar nicht zur Kenntnis genommen (*A*, p. 278).

The lack of female identification partners for girls is not discussed in the magazines that Laura reads, her own models had been male – her father, Don Juan and Faust. 'Lesbe' is among the slander list of the duo arch-devil and arch-angel (*A*, p. 446). Lesbian marriage proposals are practically a crime, 'entsprechend den herrschenden Sittennormen' (*A*, p. 430). Dr. Dietrich calls the suspected author:

> Eine Provokateurin [...] eine Diversantin, die mit einem Prozeßtrick unbescholtene Bürger der DDR, das heißt letztlich den Staat DDR, kurz und gut den sozialistischen Staat, das sozialistische Lager und den Sozialismus überhaupt madig machen will mit lesbischen Annoncen (*A*, p. 431).

The sarcasm here is a bitter comment upon a state which creates an antagonism between sexuality and socialism.

Morgner too, in her attack against persecution, acts as a 'Provokateurin'. As regards the themes of prostitution and pornography she also provokes, ironically hinting that, despite the law, there are East German prostitutes, and that these women act as *Stasi* collaborators:

> Sozialistische Geschichten wären wirklich pikanter als andere: keine Heldin, die nicht berufstätig wäre, manche nahmen nicht mal Geld. Oder sie würden bezahlt von Helden nur für Geschichten erzählen, ach ihr armen, hilflosen, kleinen Geschöpfe am Bahnhof Friedrichstraße und so weiter (*A*, p. 270).

The stories that Tenner tells of his experiences in the West, however, paint a picture that is decidedly more grim (*A,* p. 273). Here women appear as plain meat, recalling Beatriz's own experiences as French prostitute. The poetess's reactions to the pornographic pictures adorning the walls of the caravans that she stays in in Paris are effectively portrayed through juxtaposition with her medieval thought patterns: 'Einstmals hatten nur adlige Herren gehuldigt, jetzt eiferten selbst nichtfranzösische Straßenbauarbeiter!' (*B*, p. 32). This comic alienation effect sets the contemporary in its historical context and thus belies any notion of progress. This Parisian stage of the once noblewoman's life is subsequently echoed in the setting of her third reawakening. Beatriz finds herself in a 'normal' station in a 'normal' West German city:

> wo Fleisch, genauer als dem natürlichen Auge natürlich wahrnehmbar, in perfekt erklügelten Stellungen bunt oder nackt oder angezogen ausgezogener als nackt von allen Wänden schrie. In allen Größen. Neben dem Gestänge, auf dem ich saß, zum Beispiel so hundert Quadratmeter Fotoreklame mit weiblichem Fleisch. [...] Menschenfleisch [stand] live zum Verkauf (*DS*, p. 11).

The constant repetition of 'Fleisch' reduces human beings to their original status as animals, civilisation has regressed.

Hard pornography can be regarded as an invitation to rape. After having fallen in love with the engineer who wakes her up, Beatriz too is raped:

> Sie wehrte sich mit aller Kraft. Da schlug ihr der Mann die Lippen blutig, überwältigte sie mit dem Gewicht seines fetten Leibes, beschimpfte sie unflätig und erleichterte dabei seinen Beutel (*B*, p. 19).

This account leaves a lasting impression, for it stands in such sharp contrast to both the poet's naive expectations and the text's opening image of a fairy-tale sleeping beauty. Fritz Raddatz's (1976) description of 'ein bißchen Vergewaltigung am Rande' undermines the importance of such a representation of the far-reaching effects of patriarchal systems. The concise description of the event, portrayed as if it were an everyday occurrence, expresses the prevalence of this sort of violence in the West, rather than any marginalisation. Rape, prostitution and pornography are not common themes in GDR literatures of the 1970s. In *Beatriz* Morgner's notably pertain to the capitalist West. Yet upon her arrival in East Berlin Beatriz is also greeted with a 'Schlag auf den Hintern' (*B*, p. 92). For her work in the 'VEB Zentralzirkus', 'muß der Maxirock natürlich auf beiden Seiten geschlitzt werden' (*B*, p. 101); as Melusine says, 'Ich habe mich angepaßt und ausgezogen' (*B*, p. 105). Although not on the same scale as the forms of sexual oppression depicted as Western, these examples – restrained enough to pass through censorship procedures – also comment upon dominant modes of sexuality. In this respect Morgner's novel is similar to much that was published in the GDR in the late 1970s and 1980s.

In *Amanda* the examples of sexual oppression are no longer restricted to a Western context. The Western porn films that Vilma describes alienate through their direct violence:

> Ich stolperte in einen kleinen, stickigen Raum, der von einer Vergewaltigungsszene erhellt wurde. Das Geschlecht der Frau und ihr angst- und schmerzverzerrtes Gesicht in Nahaufnahme. Schreckensschreie zu Barmusikbegleitung. Dann wurde gezeigt, wie das

Glied das Mannes sich in der Scheide der gefesselten Frau bewegte und wie seine Hand ihr Gesicht schlug. Der Mann bewegte und schlug sich schnell in Stimmung und Orgasmus. Die Frau stöhnte plötzlich auch vor Lust. Ich verließ allein in unangenehmer Aufregung das Kino (*A*, p. 383).

These films are also worshipped by men, but this time by men from the GDR. Vilma's comrades return to their hotel happily entertained, their double moral standards raising conflicts for their female companion.

The male GDR critic Jürgen Engler (1983, p. 143) interprets this scene as an 'Analyse der Empfindungen mancher Männer angesichts von Pornographie, die von ihnen ideologisch natürlich abgelehnt wird, wiewohl sie *natürlich* geheime Faszination verspüren'. Engler is here reminding his readers that this is the attitude they should have. A reminder, like Morgner's work, which was particularly necessary in the GDR of the late 1980s, where pornography was becoming more and more common, despite legal censorship. In 1986, for example, the Academy of the Arts had held a conference entitled 'Pornographie im Sozialismus'. Their concern, Morgner tells Schwarzer (1990b, p. 37), had been:

Daß unser Staat für harte Devisen Pornographie druckt, aber nur für den Export. Die Recken von der Akademie wünschten nur, daß wir davon auch im Inland haben sollten. [...] Ich fühlte mich wie in einem Biertischgespräch.

For her, pornography represents violence and abuse of power. It functions solely to cement the male/female binary division. Thus she argues elsewhere that: 'die Pornowelle [deutet] ja doch nur einen Notstand an und hat mit der Emanzipation von Prüderie nichts zu tun' (in Huffzky 1975). The portrayal of pornography in *Amanda* is one of the most detailed 'erotic' scenes of the novel, in contrast to the 'normal' and 'beautiful' representations of sex in *Beatriz*. The sexual is here used to very different effect, not only offering emancipation but also signalling danger for women.

Another sexual theme which remained underrepresented in GDR literatures was that of the contraceptive pill, a medical development at the root of many recent changes in attitudes towards female sexuality. This subject too symbolises both emancipation and danger. In Morgner's work the pill is first mentioned in *Hochzeit in Konstantinopel*. With incisive irony Bele cites a letter from the *Die Zeit*:

Es ist geradezu furchtbar, welche Unruhe mit der Pille in unsere Häuser kommt. Gerade jetzt, wo wir Männer nichts nötiger brauchen als Ruhe nach anstrengender Berufsarbeit! Ob die pharmazeutische Industrie das wohl bedacht hat? Schäferspiele und Verführungskünste sind ja für einen richtigen Mann sehr schön. Aber doch nicht in der Ehe! (*Ho*, p. 53)

Yet the pill and the technology that it represents are products of industrial society as a whole, not just the FRG. Thus Morgner not only attacks the West, but again subtly suggests that there are Eastern men with similar thoughts. The theme of the pill and its relevance for female sexuality are pursued in depth in *Amanda*, where it offers an interesting perspective on female creativity and on the wider issue of human control over nature, a particularly equivocal aspect of modern society. Morgner's work presents the pill as similarly double-edged, a sword which has not simply liberated women from the fear of unwanted pregnancy and period pains as in Laura's case. The negative side-effects of hormonal control are detailed at length by Vilma, who argues that constant simulated pregnancy can only enervate women and distort their relationship to the body and to art. Such a form of contraception also frees the man from responsibility, whilst increasing that of the woman. In many cases it is thus men, and not women, for whom the pill represents a form of liberation:

> Vor der Produktion der Pille und der Abschaffung des Paragraphen zweihundert-achtzehn hätten die Männer diesbezüglich relativ sorglos gelebt. Danach lebten sie absolut sorglos. Dank der Forschungsrichtung, die eingeschlagen worden wäre. Eine von Männern bestimmte Forschungsrichtung (*A*, p. 180).

Vilma's arguments are substantiated by textual evidence. When she persuades Laura to stop taking the pill her friend feels healthier and has more energy.

The discussion of this issue is often portrayed in an alienating and cold scientific language, a language which, in Brechtian mode, forces the reader to take art seriously. This academic theorising is, however, in a manner characteristic of Morgner's work, constantly entwined with corresponding fictional narration, such as Laura's own experiences, or Anita's story. The chapter in which Vilma and Laura discuss the pill is thus entitled 'Anita'. This young girl's cry for help provides a telling example of possible negative effects of sexual liberation, when this takes place in a patriarchal context:

> Auf der Disco wirst du gleich gefragt, ob du die Pille nimmst oder nicht, und wenn nein, tanzt erst gar keiner mit dir, und wenn gar raus ist, daß du dir sowieso nichts daraus machst, also wenn sich das herumgesprochen hat, bist du ruiniert (*A*, p. 302).

Sex has become fashionable, chastity is now the taboo, a sexual ethos with which Anita is unable to come to terms.

In its attempt to introduce issues of contraception into GDR literatures Morgner's work can be compared with texts by Helga Königsdorf. This is again the case where the reception of Freud's writings is concerned. In view of the early rejection of Freud's theories in the GDR it is noticeable how Morgner already refers to these ideas in 1968, again dismantling taboos. In *Hochzeit in Konstantinopel*, for example, she argues against his *Sublimierungstheorie*: 'Zumal Freud in dem Fall irrte, ohne Frau konnte Paul nicht arbeiten. Er war ein glänzender Liebhaber, je mehr er arbeitete, desto glänzender war er' (*Ho*, pp. 113-14). Morgner continues a dialectical engagement with the psychoanalyst throughout her work. She uses sexual dreams, Freudian symbolism and general Freudian concepts. In *Gustav*, for example, the traveller's dreams are full of erotic imagery, including 'das Traumschiff' (p. 130). The ship is, according to Freud, a symbol for the female genitals, among those objects that can enclose others within themselves.[59] Thus Königsdorf explicitly links her narrator's sexually fantastic dreams to the work of her contemporary. She writes: 'Ich vermute, es war Irmtraud M., die mir eine neue Phantasiewelle zufunkte' (1978, p. 61). In *Amanda* (p. 77, p. 409) Freud's words form one of the basic arguments of the narrative: '"Was man passiv erduldet, ist man bestrebt, aggressiv auszuleben", sagt Freud.' Patriarchy is, then, entrenched in the female psyche.

Valeska's 'Gute Botschaft', on the other hand, openly ridicules Freud's theories, concentrating on penis envy. Her new penis, the 'übler Scherz' (*B*, p. 428), hardly appears as a powerful object worthy of female desire:

> Valeska fiel in unmäßiges Gelächter. Angesichts des Gewächses, worauf Legionen von Mythen und Machttheorien gründeten. Beweisstück für Auserwähltsein, Schlüssel für priviligiertes Leben, Herrschaftszepter: etwas Fleisch mit runzliger, bestenfalls blutge-blähter Haut. Valeska fehlte die entsprechende Rollenerziehung für den ernsten, selbst-bewundernden Blick in die Mitte: das Vorurteil (*B*, pp. 428-29).

Freud's ideas seem merely to advance the male cause, his 'Wunschbild, daß Penisneid neben Passivität, Narzißmus und Masochismus die Natur der Frau charakterisieren, konnte Rudolf nicht unbequem sein' (*B*, p. 426). For Valeska, however, these opinions are not quite so comfortable. Neither are they so for Morgner, who treats them, and the men who support them, with vitriolic sarcasm. Directly addressing male readers, the author, speaking in her own name, reminds men that women cannot be reduced to the absence of a 'Mittel-stück' (*B*, p. 98). Morgner thus accepts the validity of certain of Freud's recog-

---

59 Cf: 'Das auch die Schiffe des Traumes Weiber bedeuten, machen uns die Etymologen glaubwürdig, die behaupten, Schiff sei ursprünglich der Name eines tönernen Gefäßes gewesen und sei dasselbe Wort wie 'Schaff'.' (Freud, 'Die Symbolik im Traum. Vorlesungen zur Einführung in die Psychoanalyse' (1916), in *Essays 2*, pp. 226-252, p. 242).

nitions whilst not, as some feminists have done, rejecting both the man and his work completely.

Alice Schwarzer (1990b, p. 35), in interview with Morgner just before her death, identifies two aspects of the author's work which she regards as especially provocative. The first she names as 'eine lebendige Erotik', the second 'Gelächter'. The two qualities are often associated in Morgner's texts, for she seees both as iconoclastic:

> Zufassen und Angriff machen, das ist eigentlich von alters her überliefert Domäne der Männer. Ein Thema wie Erotik, Sexualität einfach anzufassen und nicht über zehn Ecken, sondern direkt, das ist ein Privileg, das sich die Männer für sich zugesprochen haben. Es erfordert nämlich das Subjekt. Diese Art zuzufassen verletzt also Tabus, genauso wie das Lachen (ibid).

Eva Kaufmann (1984b, p. 1525) notes that Morgner's 'Tabudurchbrechungen' are not achieved with the 'Verbissenheit und Verkrampfung' common in such cases. She too praises the writer's use of humour.[60] Ingeborg Nordmann (1981, p. 445) correctly recognises that sexuality is one of the areas in which Morgner's 'satirische Schärfe und polemische Sicherheit' are most successful.

Valeska's desciptions of her penis do not, then, only challenge taboos, they also create humour. Both Freudian theory and the penis are satirised and made ridiculous. The author also directs her irony towards prejudiced sexual behaviour and attitudes, sexual morality in both West and East, the pill, divorce and numerous other erotic themes. The ability to laugh is particularly important for the women in *Amanda*, struggling to cope with their daily lives. As Beatriz states: 'Wird der Ernst so groß, daß die Schmerztränen versiegen, ist höchste Zeit, Tränen zu lachen' (*DS*, p. 39). This statement reflects Morgner's own views on the function of the comic, which is not only a form of challenge but also of resistance: 'eine Widerstandskraft gegen die Lähmung durch Angst' (Kaufmann 1984a, p. 1514). The author's treatment of sexuality, whether sarcastic, grotesque, scientific, documentary, poetic or sensual, is also resistance. Resistance against a morality which defines women as sexual objects, resistance which is, in every sense of the word, productive. Her breaking of taboos thus does not simply aim to shock or to provide substitute debate, but to change the discourse within which gendered meanings are attributed to the concept of sexuality. In this sense it can be described as feminist.

---

[60] Morgner was awarded the 'Literaturpreis für grotesken Humor' in 1989.

K. Ruthven (1984, p. 109) suggests that 'instead of asking what women's writing is, we should ask what it is thought to be, which means taking account of how it is received'. Critics have used Morgner's texts not only to show how they break taboos, but chiefly in order to illustrate her feminism, her critical marxism and both the original form and the humour of her writing.[61] Sexuality is a theme with particular relevance for feminism. It is, therefore, appropriate to concentrate here upon the reception of Morgner's work as feminist *Frauenliteratur*. There are countless examples of this approach, which aims to justify the writer's 'Ruf als "feministische" Autorin der DDR' (Jahnsen/Meier 1993, p. 209).

In this respect, as in others, critics focus mainly upon the 'Salman Trilogy'. Articles such as Michaela Grobbel's (1987), which consider only the three books written from 1968-1972, are rare. The only monograph to deal in any detail with the earliest texts is Gabriele Scherer's (1992), the most comprehensive account of Morgner's works to date. Marlis Gerhardt's (1990) collection of articles is particularly useful, as is Kristine von Soden's (1991). Eva Kaufmann's (1984) analysis is important and balanced, if, unfortunately, too short. Many general works on GDR literature do, of course, devote some attention to both the author and her work, again concentrating on *Beatriz* and *Amanda*. The context in which these novels are set is most often that of GDR writing by women. Typical here are works by Sonja Hilzinger (1985) and Dorothee Schmitz-Köster (1989).

Beatriz was recognised by all Western critics as one of the most important works both of GDR writing and of modern writing by women. Karen and Friedrich Achbergers' (1975, p. 121) comments are representative. They describe the work as: 'without a doubt the most important work of GDR literature to deal with women's emancipation'. The novel was memorably reviewed as 'so etwas wie eine Bibel aktueller Frauenemanzipation' (Markgraf 1975, p. 153) and as 'eine Art *Dr. Faustus* für Feministinnen' (Herminghouse 1979, p. 248). Morgner's text appeared in 1974, together with the other classic 'feminist' works of this year, Brigitte Reimann's *Franziska Linkerhand* and Gerti Tetzner's *Karen W*. Both in content and in style Morgner's is the most radical of these books. *Amanda* too, was generally received, at least in the West, as a feminist text. In this respect, as in others, it was often compared with Wolf's

---

61 Included in the work on form are a number of articles tracing the intertextual references Morgner adapts for her own work.

Kassandra, also published in 1983. Wolf too proposed a 'Handlungsweise, die sich nicht blind gegen Männer als solche richtet, sondern gegen die männlichen Männer, eine Widerstandsform also, die 'andere' Männer als Verbündete zuläßt' (Schmitz-Köster 1989, p. 132-33).[62] Both works depict a woman finding her own voice and offer a female rewriting of historical subjects. Both use mythology as part of this project. Further similarities include the role of nuclear war and ecological disaster, the portrayal of rape and the criticism aimed at both writers.

This general comparison of *Amanda* and *Kassandra* groups Wolf and Morgner together under the label of 'GDR women writers'. Such a process of canonisation, concentrating mainly on these two major authors, was characteristic of Western reception. It meant that the work of minor women writers and themes which were not common to the work of both Wolf and Morgner were obscured. In the creation of new canons differentiation between the work of individual writers is particularly necessary, in order to allow alternative comparisons to be made. An examination of the theme of sexuality can achieve such a differentiation. This is a theme which, in Morgner's work, is expressly connected to feminist concerns, yet is only rarely noted by commentators. Eva Kaufmann (1991), as one of the few critics to use the erotic as a defining aspect in GDR literary criticism, recognises that both Wolf and Morgner base their feminist utopias on the need for love. This love is, however, reflected very differently in their art. Wolf's concerns with love and with the body are cerebral and philosophical. In her work, as Birgit Dahlke (1994, p. 60) persuasively contends, the erotic 'spielt so gut wie keine Rolle'. Morgner's novels, on the other hand, possess, 'eine intensive erotische Dimension' and 'eine erotische Sprache'. Whereas Wolf's work appears more serious, Morgner's sexual texts tend to provoke, and reactions to her work were not always favourable. In the GDR in particular she was not as popular an author as Wolf was.

In her analysis of this subject too, however, Kaufmann concentrates upon *Beatriz*, as do Ilse Braatz (1980), Biddy Martin (1979, 1980), Barbara Meyer (1985) and Angelika Bammer (1990). Reference to the erotic has consistently failed to notice the development of the theme throughout the author's oeuvre. Scherer (1992) is one of the few writers to stress also the role that the erotic plays in earlier works. Karin Huffzky's oft-cited interview (1975) establishes the significance of the erotic for the author, but in no way links the biographical

---

[62] The authors would appear not to have known of each others' projects, Morgner ('Konkret-Interview. Frauenstaat', p. 55) states: 'Ich finde besonders gut, daß wir vollkommen unabhängig voneinander dahin gelangten'.

statements to the works of art.[63] Literary criticism rarely makes detailed use of Huffzky's evidence. Schmitz-Köster's review of Morgner's 'Auseinandersetzung mit Sexualität' (1989, p. 71) is, for example, extremely cursory. Of more use, then, is the discussion by both Angelika Bammer and Ute Sperling of Morgner's popularity with Western feminists. 'Ein vitaler Berührungspunkt mit den Anliegen der feministischen Bewegung' was, Sperling (1991, p. 48) claims, 'die Art, wie weibliche/männliche Sexualität und Erotik, [...] thematisiert wurde: Als Aufforderung an die Frauen, die Befriedigung ihrer erotischen Bedürfnisse selbst in die Hand zu nehmen'. Here one can immediately identify arguments reminiscent of 1970s Anglo-American feminist movements, for whom the personal was of primary political concern.

The presence of sexual constructions within writing by Morgner does not, however, automatically make it feminist. This is dependent both upon the historical and political context in which the concept is used and upon individual readers' understandings of the term. In *Amanda* (p. 376) Morgner successfully parodies the label given to her earlier novel: 'Ich habe keine Bibel des Feminismus geschrieben oder dergleichen'. In interviews from the 1970s she similarly rejects the reading of her work as feminist, stating (in Huffzky 1975) that she regards herself first and foremost as a communist interested in the plight of women:

> Das Wort 'Feministin' gefällt mir nicht, weil es einen modischen, unpolitischen Zug hat für mich, weil es die Vermutung provoziert, daß die Menschwerdung der Frau nur eine Frauensache sein könnte. Da wird aber ein Menschheitsproblem aufgeworfen. [...] *Trobadora Beatriz* ist von einer Kommunistin geschrieben.

Beatriz (p. 104, p. 385) thus presents the conviction that, 'eine Frau, die sich heute Charakter leisten will, kann nur Sozialistin sein'. By the mid-1980s, however, and in interview with a Western journalist ('Konkret-Interview', p. 55), Morgner had changed her opinions:

> Bei uns herrscht geradezu eine Berührungsangst vor dem Wort Feminismus. Das halte ich für unsinnig. [...] Es heißt für mich nicht Separatismus, es heißt nicht Männerfeindlichkeit. Es heißt für mich weiter nichts, als daß wir Frauen nicht erwarten können, daß wir Geschenke kriegen.

This is perhaps because socialism as it existed in the GDR had not led to female emancipation, and perhaps due to a better understanding of the diversity of Western feminism.

---

[63] Cf. also interviews by Ursula Krechel (1976) and Alice Schwarzer (1990).

The concept of *Frauenliteratur*, one closely linked to that of feminism, was also discarded as Western and discriminatory. In response to Gabriele Swiderski's (1983, p. 65) characterisation of *Beatriz* as 'ein wesentliches Werk der Frauenliteratur' Morgner asks fervently:

> Was heißt hier 'Frauenliteratur'? Literatur von weiblichen Autoren geschrieben? Literatur mit weiblichen Hauptpersonen? Literatur nur für weibliche Leser? [...] Kunst ist androgyn. [...] Die bereits in den allgemeinen Sprachgebrauch eingegangene Bezeichnung 'Frauenliteratur' ist unsinnig.

She thus questions the use of a term which suggests that writing by women is somehow intrinsically different from writing by men. In this respect, Morgner's views represent those of most other East German artists, both male and female. The term was generally connected not only with a separatist feminist movement, but also with *Trivial-* or *Unterhaltungsliteratur*.

Whilst Morgner, and other authors, remain sceptical of separatist feminism and of women's writing as a category, they do consider, through their work, what a 'female' aesthetic might be. The term 'weibliches Schreiben' is used to initiate reflections upon the act of writing and indeed upon the work of other female writers. Christa Wolf, for example, explores her role in relation to Karoline von Günderrode and Bettina von Arnim.[64] In the *Kassandra* project she explicitly, and famously, devotes much of her attention to this subject (*Voraussetzungen einer Erzählungen: Kassandra* , pp114-15). She allows her protagonist to speak with her own voice, to rediscover her voice, to learn, as a woman, to say 'I'. She does not only write about women (almost all of her protagonists are female) and their emancipation, she also claims to write consciously as a woman.

Throughout her work Wolf experiments with many forms; diaries, travelogues, letters, note books, poetry, essays and speeches. Hers are *Erzählungen* rather than novels or short stories. For Irmtraud Morgner too, traditional genres were unsuitable for women's writing. Her operative montages mix styles and forms, creating texts which function both as a whole and as separate elements. It is in these shorter pieces of her jigsaws that she sees a possible link to a female aesthetic, an aesthetic which reflects women's lives:

> Abgesehen von Temperament, entspricht kurze Prosa dem gesellschaftlich, nicht biologisch bedingten Lebensrhythmus einer gewöhnlichen Frau, die ständig von haushaltbedingten Abhaltungen zerstreut wird (*B*, p. 170).

[64] Eg. *Kein Ort. Nirgends*; 'Nun ja! Das nächste Leben geht aber heute an. Ein Brief über die Bettine', and 'Der Schatten eines Traumes. Karoline von Günderrode - ein Entwurf', in *Die Dimension des Autors II,* pp. 116-54, pp. 55-115.

Morgner believes that women have to live not only with interruptions, but also with fear, which can also affect their art. Again in *Beatriz* (p. 336) she allows Laura to express this idea: 'überhaupt wachsen Persönlichkeiten, die unter Angst leben, wenn überhaupt, ganz anders als andere. Denken anders, fühlen anders, produzieren anders mit Händen und Köpfen'. As committed Marxists, both writers cite historical rather than biological reasons for the existence of this separate female aesthetic. Morgner's fear is caused by patriarchy rather than any essential female passivity. Her use of the word 'Persönlichkeiten' emphasises that this is not a strictly gendered issue.

Morgner's statements, together with those of Christa Wolf, were taken by Western critics as evidence that feminist aesthetic theory had reached the GDR. Many critics chose to emphasise, and thereby generalise, both the work of these two major canonised artists and criteria of gender. Sara Lennox (1981), for example, claims that Wolf's prose offers the most radical feminist critique to be found in modern German literature. Patricia Herminghouse (1985, p. 348) cites *Nachdenken über Christa T.* as representative of 'einen Durchbruch in der Geschichte der deutschen Frauenliteratur'. In Morgner's case, as Ute Sperling (1991, p. 60) comments:

> wurden ihre Romane von der feministischen Literaturkritik uneingeschränkt als Beitrag zu einer Art feministischer Ästhetiktheorie rezipiert, ohne das damals eine detaillierte Auseinandersetzung mit der Morgner-These von der Androgynität der Kunst stattgefunden hätte.

Alison Lewis (1989, p. 245) thus portrays Morgner's use of fantasy as feminist and subversive, as 'a form of emancipatory politics and consciously oppositional cultural practice'. Both Brigitte Ebersbach (1983) and Klara Obermüller (1980) argue that the author uses conventional feminine characteristics such as spontaneity, emotionality, illogicality and irrationality to create an artistic style. Sonja Hilzinger (1985) compares the form of *Beatriz* to the traditionally female craft of weaving. For Marlis Gerhardt (1990, p. 95), on the other hand, the novel represents 'Usurpation der großen männlichen Form', rather than the 'Kleinmeisterei' usually associated with the female aesthetic.

Using comments by the author in order to 'prove' authorial intention is, however, questionable. Such quotations do not close the texts to alternative readings. The fact that Wolf, Morgner and others write about and discuss a female aesthetic does not necessarily mean that their writing embodies this aesthetic, as Sibylle Cramer's (1979) criticisms of Wolf's *Kassandra* story show. She accuses Wolf of creating in Kassandra the very type of hero figure that she associates with 'male' art and in her monologue a traditionally 'male' linear narrative. Similarly, the form of Morgner's work does not have to be seen either as 'female' or as 'male'. It is, rather, an experiment, and as such 'nicht kanonisierbar' (Damm 1975, p. 146). Her aesthetic is primarily subjective and functions as a model for a society which accepts variety – 'female', 'male' and 'androgynous' qualities, thereby mirroring the themes of the works. Morgner combines the sensuous with the academic and the imaginary with the documentary. Her use of operative montage can, then, be placed within the traditions of modernism, rather than of any specifically female genre, thus avoiding possible clichés of style.

The Western reception of Morgner's writing outlined here can be seen as representative for that of much of the prose written by women in the GDR from the 1970s onwards. J.H. Reid (1990, p. 103), for example, finds 'a new quality [...] in women's writing. One in which strong elements of a specifically feminist consciousness are being expressed'. Biddy Martin (1980) writes of a body of feminist literature which appeared in the 1970s in the GDR, Schwarzer (1976, p. 58) of 'Emanzipationsliteratur'. Extracting the term from the specific discourse of its Western 1970s context, *Frauenliteratur* too was applied to these East German works, often without any discussion as to what the critic understood by this concept.

Schmitz-Köster uses the terms *Frauenliteratur* and *weibliches Schreiben* in her titles. She does, however, define what she understands by the former term and admits that it is one which is controversial in the GDR. Her justification for expanding quotations by Wolf, Morgner and Maron to cover a whole variety of literatures rests on the cult of the author, who has become, as Foucault (1969) writes, a guarantor of supposed authenticity and truth. Wolfgang Emmerich (1989, p. 199), on the other hand, justifies his use of Western discourse with reference to a universal system of patriarchy: 'daß nun eine Frauenliteratur nicht nur in den kapitalistischen Ländern, sondern auch in der DDR entstehen mußte, liegt daran, daß sich das Patriarchat auch in den "realen Sozialismus" hinübergerettet hat'. His claim here ignores differences between Eastern and Western forms of patriarchy and indeed between Eastern and Western forms of writing by women. Lutz Wolf (1976, p. 251) is more circumspect in introducing his collection of short stories entitled *Frauen in der DDR*, 'dabei sollte nicht der Eindruck entstehen als gäbe es in der DDR eine besondere *Frauen-Literatur*'.

The need to classify this Eastern literature with Western terminology arose partly because of its popularity amongst Western readers. Western 'feminist' art was often regarded as more negative in its content and less aesthetically challenging. East German women's accounts offered new reflections upon the themes with which Western feminists were concerned, whilst still providing for a utopian future. Despite the absence of an openly feminist context, these narratives developed 'indirect and metaphorical, subtle and fantastic forms of critiques of patriarchy' (Weigel 1984, p. 7). Here was an example of what David Bathrick (1991, p. 299) terms 'one's own historical investment as an enabler of categories'. The GDR, and thus literatures from the GDR, were read as 'the potentially utopian *other*' (Herminghouse 1993, p. 94) of Western critics' own political disillusionments. Gabi Ahlings and Ingeborg Nordmann (1979) emphasise the additional role that simple curiosity played in this phenomenon. The authors' works were seen to mirror a different political and social context and were thus invested with informational value. The prose achieved the status of sociological or historical sources, a status which often led to aesthetic criteria being regarded as secondary to content. Ute Brandes (1992, p. 13) concisely summarises the various aspects of Western reception thus:

> Die Texte von DDR-Schriftstellerinnen werden somit zum einen analysiert als Dokumente politischer Haltungen, die in der Kultur des Herkunftlandes verankert sind und von denen sich eine Autorin jeweils abgrenzt oder nicht; zum anderen als grenzüberschreitender Ausdruck von weiblichen Lebenszusammenhängen und feministischen Befreiungsutopien. Entstanden unter anderen gesellschaftlichen Voraussetzungen, wird diese Literatur zudem im Kontext der realen Lebensbedingungen von Frauen in der DDR reflektiert.

The simple adoption of the term *Frauenliteratur* does not do sufficient justice to these complex structures.

East German critics welcomed the numbers of women writing in their country as a social phenomenon that reflected the emancipated roles offered to women by socialism. The discussions initiated by this writing were, however, reacted to with caution, critics stressed the ideal of problems being solved together with men in a communist state. This was an understandable reaction, to pay too much attention to the female sex would seem to suggest not only that they were not quite as emancipated as official publications would have liked one to believe, but also that gender was becoming more important than class as a historical factor. In the GDR feminism was a concept laden with negative connotations. It was regarded as a bourgeois word invented by Western women in the 1960s. Often it was equated with militant separatism. Officially, there was no need for such a movement, as Bärbel Klässner (1990, pp. 46-7) writes:

> Und da Feminismus die Lüge von der angeblich erreichten Gleichberechtigung der Frau im Sozialismus hätte in Frage stellen können und zudem unsere führenden Politiker fast alle Männer waren, wurde er mehr und mehr noch als alle anderen linken und gesell-

schaftskritischen Bewegungen im Westen kurzerhand abqualifiziert und für indiskutabel erklärt.[65]

As far as Morgner's work was concerned, GDR reviewers of *Beatriz* thus concentrated mostly upon questions of the fantastic and of the montage style, emphasising that 'die Autorin sieht das, worüber sie schreibt, sozialistisch' (Neubert 1974, p. 105). *Amanda*, together with Wolf's *Kassandra*, was heavily criticised for its apparently feminist content. Both texts linked the threat of nuclear war, so dominant in the early 1980s, with male hegemony. In *Sinn und Form* Wilhelm Girnus (1983, p. 439) famously accused Wolf of toeing the Western feminist line and of simplifying history, of giving the impression that: 'Die Geschichte sei nicht in ihrem tiefsten Grunde der Kampf zwischen Ausbeutern und Ausgebeuteten, sondern zwischen Männern und Frauen, ja noch grotesker: zwischen "männlichem" und "weiblichem" Denken'. Morgner was similarly censored:

> Aus der nachgewiesenen doppelten Unterdrückung der Frau in der antagonistischen Klassengesellschaft sollte man nicht kurzschlüssig folgern, daß sich allein und bei allen Männern Methoden der Unterdrückung zu geschlechtsspezifischen Eigenschaften formten (Berger 1983).

Such a comment clearly distorts the author's highly differentiated and panoramic picture of society.

These accusations represent an attempt to foreclose the critical debate on female aesthetics which was beginning to take place in the GDR. A similar foreclosure, during the 1970s, was effected in the reluctance of GDR critics to even use the terms *Frauenliteratur* and *weibliches Schreiben*. This was partly due to a lack of suitable definitions of the labels, and also to the influence of ideology and politics. Ilse Nagelschmidt (1991, p. 26), for example, describes post-*Wende*, 'Wie kompliziert war es [...] sich zu dem Begriff der Frauen-literatur zu bekennen, wie schwierig, einmal zu hinterfragen, ob und warum Frauen anders als Männer schreiben'. Many commentators thus eliminated the issue of authorship from this term. Eberhard Panitz (1978, p. 72) claimed that male authors could also write *Frauenliteratur*, that: 'die Frage der Befreiung der Frau ziemlich weltweit eine Antwort in der Literatur gefunden [hat], die

---

65 Cf. Inge Lange (1979, pp. 232-57, p. 252): 'Übrigens hat die Tatsache, daß es bei uns keinen Feminismus gibt, ihre schlichte Ursache darin, daß sich in der revolutionären deutscher Arbeiterbewegung von Anfang an bis zur Gegenwart die kameradschaftliche Zusammenarbeit von Frauen und Männern – auch in bezug auf die Gleichberechtigung der Frau – immer bewährte.'

90

eher politisch und sozial als geschlechts- und tiefenpsychologisch zu charakterisieren wäre'.

This response is characteristic. Karin Hirdina's article 'Die Schwierigkeit, ich zu sagen' (1981), which considers some of the issues of subjectivity with which Western feminists were concerned, asked the question 'bräuchten wir etwa einen sozialistischen Feminismus?' (p. 4). She finds much to criticise in the work of authors, both male and female, who deal with women and their lives. Many, in her opinion, simply reproduce traditional clichés. As exceptions she singles out Christa Wolf and Günter De Bruyn, one female and one male author. Again, the sex of the author seems unimportant. Hirdina thus concludes that: 'die welthistorische Aufgabe Emanzipation ist nur in Bezug auf Frauen *und* Männer zu lösen'. She mentions neither *Frauenliteratur* nor *weibliches Schreiben*. Hans Kaufmann's essay on relationships as portrayed in GDR literatures has a special chapter devoted to literature by women, the rest deals purely with writing by men. He contrasts the famous works of the early 1970s with those he has considered previously in his article and finds that there are generalisations that can be made. He immediately denies, however, that he is creating a 'Männer- und eine Frauen-Literatur', for:

> es gibt gute Gründe zum Mißtrauen, wenn soziale Erscheinungen auf anthropologische oder biologische Begriffe, z.B. auf die Generations- oder Geschlechterfrage, zurückgeführt werden. [...] Es sind sozialistische Werke, die sich an jeden wenden, der sie lesen mag (1976, p. 187).

Characteristically, gender appears to be of secondary importance.

In the late 1970s and 1980s the importance of the women authors both as a group and individually was increasingly recognised and favourably noted. A careful reassessment of the theoretical situation began too, but only by some, of whom the majority were women. The terms *Frauenliteratur* and *weibliches Schreiben*, rather than the usual circumlocutions, appeared in journals in both East and West Germany. Whereas the writer Ruth Werner (1979, p. 118) says, 'leider gibt es noch so etwas bei uns wie "Frauenliteratur" und da klingt eine Art Abwertung mit', her interviewer, Elizabeth Simons (1979, p. 133), cautiously defends the term as signifying 'jene Leistung unserer Literatur, die auch internationale Anerkennung für viele nachdenkenswerte Aussagen über Lebensfragen der Frau im Sozialismus eingebracht hat'. Eva Kaufmann (1982) reporting on an Italian conference on 'die Frauenfrage in der DDR', is insistent upon the need for East German investigations of an East German phenomenon. Throughout the decade such demands were responded to and important research into the work of female artists was begun.

Ursula Heukenkamp, in 1985, analyses images of women in famous literary texts by men before moving on to modern women authors, exactly those members of the female canon established by Western critics: Wolf, Morgner, Tetzner, Reimann, Wander and Königsdorf. She states that: 'das Bekenntnis zur weiblichen Art, die Welt anzuschauen und zu erfahren, wird in der zweiten Hälfte der 70er Jahre zu einer Leitlinie der Frauenliteratur' (1985, p. 40-41). She does not define what she understands by a 'weibliche Art'. She does, however, clarify the genre: 'das Thema der Frauenliteratur ist die Frau in der Gesellschaft. Ohne den Sozialismus wäre diese Literatur nicht denkbar' (p. 38). Far from being a Western import, the concept is now fundamentally socialist, linked here to the emancipated social situation of women in the GDR. Ilse Nagelschmidt's detailed study (1989) also sets up a 'sozialistische Frauen-literatur' (p. 450), which she defines as intrinsically different to women's writing produced in the West; although she does allow for links between the two. The latter she sees as a rejection of patriarchal society, the former a discussion of problems for woman in a society with which the author is basically in agreement.

Nagelschmidt (1989, p. 454) specifies three main questions which she maintains are the concern of socialist women's writing:

1. Erwachsen den Frauen mit den neuen Ansprüchen und Möglichkeiten auch neue Konflikte?
2. Was bedeutet Frau-Sein im Sozialismus?
3. Wie kann man als Frau unter den gegebenen gesellschaftlichen Bedingungen seine Selbstverwirklichung erreichen?

She further compares the writing of the 1970s, which she sees as more descriptive or naturalistic, with the increased variety of the 1980s. This literature is portrayed as an integral part of GDR art as a whole, there is 'keine Abgrenzung von der von Männern geschriebene Literatur' (p. 460), activities she attributes to Western women's writing. Later, however, she contradicts herself when she isolates a 'Traditionslinie weiblichen Schreibens' that is important for 'sowohl den Autor*innen* westlicher Länder als auch den Schrift-steller*innen* der DDR' (My emphasis, p. 466). She does not define any one genre as being especially suitable for this writing; 'Sozialistische Frauen-literatur' uses 'alle ästhetischen Formen' (p. 467).

Wolfgang Gabler (1987, p. 739) presents an alternative argument as to how *Frauenliteratur* could be defined. In the prose of many women writing in the 1970s he finds a negative portrayal of the male. Here, he states 'könnte tatsächlich ein Ausgangspunkt für die Bestimmung sogenannter 'Frauenliteratur' sein, wenn die literarischen Werke auf ein Solidarisierungsgefühl von Leserinnen in Distanz zu "den" Männern organisieren wollen'. This is a definition which comes increasingly close to those used in the West to label feminist works. Gabriele Lindner entitles her article, published in 1988, 'Weibliches Schreiben. Annäherung an ein Problem'. She laments the fact that the work of Wolf and Morgner is accorded more importance in the West than in the East and thus discusses the issues that it raises. For her it is possible that women and men write differently, for 'zu den Unterschieden in den Lebens-bedingungen und der Lebensweise innerhalb unserer Gesellschaft gehören auch die zwischen den Geschlechtern' (1988, p. 59). Literature, she states, cannot be seen in a vacuum, writers are influenced by the context in which they produce their art, and GDR women live in a state that has given them a form of equality that has created a specific 'female' situation, a situation that can have some relevance for Westerners. Like critics writing in the West, she stresses what has been achieved by the GDR in legal and statistical terms, emphasising the interplay of social and literary developments. The influence of art produced by men is, however, also regarded as important.

As part of the increased debates surrounding issues of female aesthetics, critics also reviewed writing by women from other countries and other traditions. As early as 1982 Edith Anderson, the editor of the seminal anthology *Blitz aus heiterem Himmel*, had written about 'feministische Utopien' in American feminist texts and analysed their relevance for East German concerns. In 1985 Brigitte Burmeister studied some of the writings by French feminists, an important sign that Western literary theory was now, at least in academic circles, being discussed seriously in the GDR. Concentration on these texts allowed Burmeister to consider ideas of female aesthetics which emphasised the role of the bodily in writing. Her bibliography, like Wolf's in the *Kassandra* lectures, consists of works by Bovenschen, Stephan, Gerhardt, Weigel and other West German feminists.

The examples given, encompassing a wide variety of viewpoints, show that gender is certainly a valid criterion by which to study GDR literatures, or indeed literature in general. Beyond that they also prove the need to carefully define terminology which has, by now, become a generalised label rather than a helpful classification. To treat Morgner's work as *Frauenliteratur* is mis-leading. As Weigel (1984, p. 53, p. 55) argues, 'there is hardly a more contro-versial concept in contemporary German literature [...] women's literature implies more than literature by women. It embraces an entire movement including both production and reception'. The term belongs to a specific era in West German writing and literary reception. Weigel (1987, p. 48) describes it as a 'diskursives Ereignis', an 'event' linked to the politics of the women's movement, to the popularity of subjective and autobiographical writing in the 1970s and to the success of Verena Stefan's 'feminist bible' *Häutungen*.[66] The 'Symbol für den Durchbruch der Frauenliteratur' (Weigel 1987, p. 102), this novel encouraged a flood of texts recording women's personal oppression and the process of their emancipation, including Svende Merian's *Der Tod des Märchenprinzen* and Brigitte Schwaiger's *Wie kommt das Salz ins Meer*. These works offered female readers the opportunity to identify with protagonists whose lives reflected their own. They were seen as texts which possessed a therapeutic function, both for author and audience. Stefan herself ('Anmerkungen' 1977, p. 127) stresses this social and psychological side: 'Dieses hier hat im persönlichen, im politischen und im literarischen bereich diskussionen ausgelöst, die noch andauern. das ist das wichtigste daran'.

The marketing of the concept of *Frauenliteratur* by publishers has obscured its original sense. The media have been responsible for the negative connotations which the label now suggests. *Frauenliteratur* has become synonomous with *Trivialliteratur*, it is regarded as naive rather than aesthetically valuable. Anything written by a woman, and sometimes by a man, can be classed as *Frauenliteratur*. The reader is left unsure as to the book's actual content, although s/he may assume, according to Weigel (1984, p. 82), some form of 'autobiographical confession', which 'is essentially harmless'. This characterisation falls woefully short in respect of Morgner's work. Although elements of her biography are refracted through the lens of various characters, female and male, no one narrator stands for Irmtraud Morgner. Indeed, this is a position parodied rather than accorded primary importance. In *Amanda* 'die Morgner' (p. 316) even accuses herself of 'innere Zensur' (p. 18). There is little room for confession in novels of a challenging, didactic nature. The reader must actively engage with the text, rather than sit back and listen to a litany of events.

If the term *Frauenliteratur* is, in many senses, inappropriate to Morgner's prose, that of feminism is more applicable. Her work does, as Cardinal (1991, p. 149) argues, 'reach far beyond the narrow confines of political and social demands for female equality'. However, the author specifically constructs forms of female experience. She tells *herstories*, she allows women to speak, to create their own images, role models, history and stories. Of course female protagonists are not, in themselves, material enough for feminist novels. It is the fact that Morgner addresses, through their narratives, issues of power, specifi-

---

66 Cf. Weigel (1987, p. 56): 'Die Publikation von Verena Stefans Buch "Häutungen" kann als Zeichen dafür gelten, daß die "Frauenliteratur" als eigenständige literarische Bewegung aus dieser Geschichte entsteht'.

cally of male power over women, that makes her writing feminist. As with Morgner's other feminist motifs, sexuality is a theme which is in no way simply of interest to the documentary historian, 'wenn einmal die Mentalitäts-geschichte der DDR geschrieben werden soll' (Clason 1990, p. 1129). More generally relevant, it is of major importance in a reappraisal of the canons of East German literatures. Analysed in the following chapter, then, are those feminist aspects of Morgner's constructions of sexuality which endow her work with a significance beyond a 'Keine Tabus' GDR context.

3. Sexuality in the work of Irmtraud Morgner – Part Two

'Aber es wird sicher noch eine Weile dauern, bis das weibliche Geschlecht gelernt hat,
die Produktivkraft Sexualität souverän zu nutzen' (*B*, p. 336; *A*, p. 181)

Irmtraud Morgner regards the sexual as foundational for her work. 'Was für mich Erotik ist', she states, 'das kann man in meinen Büchern lesen' (in Schwarzer 1990b, p. 36). Her writing is driven by the need for love, a love to which she responds intuitively rather than at a purely abstract, intellectual level. Her response is sexual, for, she tells Karin Huffzky (1975):

Sexualität ist eine kostbare Unruhe, die erotische Beziehungen ermöglicht [...] Ohne sie gibt es keinen Enthusiasmus, kein Feuer des Geistes, keinen Esprit. Kein Denker, kein Politiker, kein Wissenschaftler, kein Dichter, kein Komponist arbeitet nur mit dem Kopf. Er arbeitet als Ganzheit. [...] Das gilt für Frauen ebenso wie für Männer.

Linked to the real and to the imaginary, sexuality is seen as a 'Produktivkraft', both in life and in art. This 'Produktivkraft' is a force which offers the foundations of a new morality, a morality in which women are free from sexual oppression and in control of their bodies. Thus Morgner's aim is not to provide erotic titillation, but to embed the sexual in a panoramic context of cultural and political discourse – medical, historical, legal, literary, technical, scientific, fictional and factual – in order to cerebrally stimulate the reader.

'Es wird sicher noch eine ganze Weile dauern...'

In the early 1970s GDR literatures were still generally restrained with regard to the erotic. Morgner's liberated sexual art represents one of the few exceptions. In *Beatriz* (p. 39, p. 274) the author repeats that:

Neulich sagte die Gattin eines Dichters, von Frauen wären keine Liebesgedichte zu lesen. Die Gattin hat recht, nur wenige Damen möchten ihren Ruf dem Geruch der Abnormität preisgeben.

The statement emphasises that there is a long way to go before such poetry becomes an acceptable form of female artistic expression. It will also be 'eine ganze Weile' before women are fully in control of their bodies, this is again something that must be learnt. The sexual is, therefore, linked to Morgner's utopian visions of a human future, 'die dritte Ordnung. Die weder patriar-chalisch noch matriarchalisch sein soll, sondern menschlich' (*B*, p. 20).[67]

The novel *Beatriz* thus offers numerous utopian sexual visions. Characters such as Bele, Beatriz and Valeska, and their various experiments, portray, as Ingeborg Nordmann (1981, p. 446) writes: 'einen neuen Modus intersubjektiver Erfahrungen, der unter den Bedingungen der bisherigen Geschichte noch nicht entwickelt werden konnte und als reale Antizipation des noch nicht Erreichten zu begreifen ist'. Laura's relationship with Benno, which begins as a magical dream, is one such utopia. Both Nordmann and Biddy Martin (1980) criticise the fact that this relationship of the future is depicted in terms of a traditional marriage, which, they claim, relativises its utopian potential. They ignore the possibility that a utopian marriage has little to do with its institutionalised counterpart relied upon in patriarchal systems. Benno's dream is 'für so was Ähnliches wie Ehe' (*B*, p. 273), it is not for traditional marriage. The utopia is, however, relativised in Morgner's later novel with Benno's mundane death in a car accident, which is caused through alcohol and the inability to cope with his wife's success.

In *Amanda* the utopian aspects of the erotic sphere are again given primary importance. Differentiated from the sexual act, the erotic represents real love, 'Erotik zur Welt' (*A*, p. 494), a form of love that is necessary if the world is to survive. Thus sexuality is employed by Morgner in its widest sense, a sense encapsulated in the word 'Produktivkraft'. It is directly linked to the major themes of the novel – the imminent danger of nuclear war and of ecological disaster, and the role of literature within this situation. The patriarchal, destructive romantic ideal, in which one man can offer everything to one woman, must be replaced in order to release active powers of love for both sexes. Angelika Bammer (1990, p. 204) writes, therefore, of: 'Morgners Versuch, das erstarrte Marxismuskonzept durch Erotik und Phantasie aufzu-brechen'. Jürgen Engler (1983, p. 143) similarly states, 'Irmtraud Morgner [...] ficht für die, um es metaphorisch zu sagen, Erotisierung des ganzen Daseins', an aim which Anneliese Stawström (1991, p. 12) uses in order to compare *Amanda* with *Beatriz*:

> Während im Trobadora-Roman die Bedeutung der Liebe zwischen den Geschlechtern besonders betont wird, tritt in *Amanda* die Liebe zur Natur und zur Erde angesichts der zunehmenden Bedrohung unseres Planeten stärker in den Vordergrund.

[67] This is a vision characteristic of mainstream writing by East German women. As Birgit Dahlke (1994, p. 47) notes: 'der Anspruch auf Emanzipation der Frau [wurde] stets in der Suche nach einer neuen Gesellschaftsordnung eingebettet, welche die "Emanzipation des Menschen" zu gewährleisten hätte'.

The love which is idealised in *Amanda* is constructed as androgynous. In order to achieve this androgony the text proposes that historically developed female qualities be brought into society in order to combat the hierarchical, aggressive thought that has led to the present dangerous world situation. It is only when 'die andere Hälfte der Menschheit, die Frauen, bestimmte, bisher nur für private Zwecke entwickelte Fähigkeiten und Tugenden in die große Politik einbringen' that 'atomare und ökologische Katastrophen abgewendet werden [können]' (*A*, p. 306). This new female potential is represented in *Amanda* by Pandora, seen by Morgner (and by Goethe) as a 'Humanitätssymbol' (p. 78, p. 209), and described by Herbert Marcuse (1962, p. 146) as 'the female principle' in the male world of Prometheus, symbolising 'sexuality and pleasure'. The ideal utopia will be achieved when Pandora returns, bringing true communism. A fourth human race will then be born, 'imstande, seine Interessen- und Meinungsverschiedenheiten unblutig zu bewältigen und Sitten zu entwickeln, die Kompromisse höher schätzen als Siege und den Krieg tabuisieren' (*A*, p. 129). In this respect too, sexuality, the female and communism are married in an image of hope for the future.

Utopian visions are, in the 1980s, increasingly rare in GDR literatures. Morgner's too is, by 1983, tempered by a strong sense of disillusionment, as Benno's death evinces. The concrete hope of *Beatriz* has become a faint, but critical, yearning. In some respects this reflects the social, cultural and historical changes which took place between 1974 and 1983.[68] Socialism did not move forward in the direction anticipated in the early 1970s, women would have to wait 'noch eine Weile'. Laura's former optimistic conversation with Beatriz, in which she talks of the productive force of sexuality, is, then, requoted in its entirety in the second part of her trilogy. The chapter, which deals with the pill and abortion, is cleverly entitled 'Geschluckte Wahrheiten' (*A*, p. 181, *B* p. 336), a title that suggests the author being forced to swallow her own words and implies that since Beatriz's death the envisaged change in sexual morality has not materialised. There is little enthusiasm for the future; 'die Erinnerung stimmte Laura melancholisch. Denn der naive Fortschrittsglaube, der diese Äußerung trug, war ihr verlorengegangen' (*A*, p. 181).

This repetition emphasises the significance of the theme of sexuality for the author, particularly when it occurs again in *Der Schöne und das Tier*. Here the loss of optimism is displayed even more strongly: 'Wer sagt, die Liebe ist eine

---

68 Cf. Morgner (in Swiderski 1983, p. 66): 'Der Beatriz-Roman ist unter der starken Hoffnung der Entspannungspolitik geschrieben [...] *Amanda. Ein Hexenroman* ist überschattet. Der Weltzustand hat sich verschlechtert, die Kriegsgefahr ist unfaßbar beängstigend geworden'.

Produktivkraft, ist krank. Denn sie ist natürlich eine Krankheit. Die verrückt macht. Vor Freude verrückt und vor Sehnsucht sowieso' (*DS*, p. 32). Sexual neuroses now appear to be more important than sexual productivity. Yet this form of illness is still preferable to a life of fear, the fear which is so dominant in *Amanda*. Beatriz continues: 'Nachmachen, Leute! Vor Angst krank oder verrückt werden kann heute jeder Rotzlöffel' (p. 32). Love for one other individual, traditional sexuality, has, in this third part of the trilogy, replaced the all-encompassing 'Erotik zur Welt' preached in the earlier text. Individual forms of utopia are advocated as the prerequisite to the 'grand narrative' outlined in *Amanda*:

> Die ganze Menschheit lieben oder glücklich machen, Millionen umschlingen wollen, ist leicht, weil nicht nachprüfbar. Aber einen einzigen Menschen glücklich machen... Nur wer das kann, ist legitimiert und mitunter sogar befähigt, Völkern Ratschläge zu erteilen oder mehr (*DS*, pp. 34-35).

The utopian elements of the theme have not, however, been entirely abandoned. Morgner, in all of her prose, retains a belief in a better future, despite increasing uncertainty about how this future will develop.

Western feminists have been accused of creating a vision of liberated female sexuality which offered a curiously essential 'Paß zur Autonomie' (Sichtermann 1989, p. 59). Such a vision represented, according to Barbara Sichtermann (pp. 70-71), 'eine vereinseitigende Radikalisierung der weiblichen Rolle [...] ein leerlaufender Narzißmus, der uns nicht weit trägt, ein Phantom'. The adoption of Marcuse's theories in the 1960s encouraged such generalising erotic utopias. Foucault's writings, amongst others, have shown how complex a construction sexuality is. As Jana Sawicki (1991, p. 11) contends: 'Foucault would have been critical of feminist approaches that appealed to an essential and liberatory feminine desire repressed within patriarchal society'. The assumption that this construction can be freed from discursive contexts to offer a new future is an illusion. The recognition that women are oppressed in this field is, on the other hand, vital, as is resistance to that oppression.

Morgner's utopian visions do not open her work to similar censure. Sawicki continues: 'a Foucauldian could consistently defend the idea of a sexual liber-ationist politics as long as it was neither totalistic, essentialist or ahistorical' (p. 13). Morgner clearly delineates sexuality as a discursive issue appertaining to the historical, the cultural and the ideological, rather than as a biological entity. Her work is not totalistic, essentialist or ahistorical. Sexual power is not portrayed as a whole, emanating purely from one central source, but as 'micro-structural', as constituted 'at the level of psychosexual relations' (Martin 1980,

p. 61). In this respect the texts go beyond traditional Marxism, offering no totalising solutions. Utopian images are constantly balanced with strong and effective criticism of patriarchy as it exists in the present. The author maintains a constant tension between hope and despair, between affirmation and critique. This tension is one of the means by which her prose is opened to various possibilities of interpretation. The argument put forward by Nordmann and Martin (1980, p. 61) that Morgner's Marxism ultimately closes her work and 'constrains the emancipatory possibilities that it opens up' relies upon authorial intention. Individual readers without detailed knowledge of Marxist theories are enabled to read the text differently, as the enthusisatic reception of Morgner's 'feminism' in the West shows.

Erotic imagery in Morgner's work does not merely provide visions of the future, for the erotic is, in the present, 'die letzte Domäne der Männer' (B, p. 112). The sex that Beatriz, for example, experiences is often that of a male dominated world – at worst violent, at best unimaginative and routine. As Nordmann (1981, p. 440) writes, 'Die Trobadora durchläuft so ziemlich alle Stationen der sexuellen Ausbeutung'. The group sex she has is not liberating but boring. The sex that she is subjected to by one of her admiring workmen is described thus:

> Nachts lag Beatriz der Kalfaktor auf dem Bauch. [...] Der Mann stieg von rechts auf, bewegte sich kaum eine Minute wie eine Nähmaschine, ließ sich links herabfallen und begann zu schnarchen (B, p. 37).

In this scene, reminiscent of many in GDR literatures, there is no sense of tenderness, let alone love. The mechanical encounter lasts only one sentence and is reiterated through subversive and critical irony. Beatriz also has to endure sexual violence in the forms of both rape and prostitution. Treated as a sexual object, she is forced to marry one of her Parisian clients. In Italy the situation appears even worse. In this narrow context the GDR does seem to be the promised land. Morgner's concrete descriptions evidence the need for socialism, and in the West at least, for feminist projects. It is thus no coincidence that Beatriz awakes when she does, for the left-wing revolutions of 1968 gave rise to the new women's movement and new strength to the French communist party. Yet Beatriz's experiences of sexual objectification are repeated, on a smaller scale, in the GDR. Here too then, there still remains much to change, with or without feminism.

Both Morgner's visions of the future and her criticisms of patriarchal sexuality are intricately linked with notions of morality. One of her major concerns is to show the effects of 'Sitten' in determining women's lives in the present. Bele, for example, bemoans a 'selten erlebte Harmonie zwischen Moral und Lust' (*Ho*, p. 11). Female desire does not appear 'useful' in a technological world and is thus not 'moral'. In *Hochzeit in Konstantinopel* sexual problems linked to this morality are directly attacked. Frau Kunsch says:

> Männern gestünde man offiziell ein Geschlechtsleben zu, Frauen nicht. Sie dürften zwar im richtigen Moment eins haben: das freute die Männer; eine Frau mit nicht unterdrückter Sexualität gelte jedoch bereits als nymphoman, die meisten Frauen arbeiteten das Problem weg (p. 136).

Yet these words go unheard, followed only by an absurd comment (by a man) about the export of Beatles wigs. The issue of female sexuality is thus lost in general conversation, reflecting society's censorship of an issue that is rarely taken seriously. This sentence is not, however, lost in Morgner's work, for it is repeated twice in *Beatriz* (p. 39, p. 274), and again in *Der Schöne und das Tier* (p. 17) – the problem remains unsolved.

Amanda, then, voices concerns similar to those of Frau Kunsch: 'Ein Zufluchtsort der doppelten Moral muß auch dem Sozialismus mehr als schaden' (*A*, p. 446). The examples given by Morgner of the double sexual standards so characteristic of patriarchy are countless. One of the most effective is Laura's 'zu wahre Geschichte' and its pendant. Her 'unerhörte Umgangsformen' (*B*, p. 111) are the 'gewöhnliche' that women have to face, the 'durchschnittliche' (p. 314) for men. The parable makes it clear that taking the sexual initiative is still a male prerogative. Another example is given by Valeska:

> Die Sitte neutralisierte eine von Abbau gezeichnete Frau, während ein Mann mit grauen Schläfen als interessant gewertet wurde. Und für eine junge Frau zumutbar. Im umgekehrten Fall sprach man von "Mumienschändung" und "Großmutter besteigen" (*B*, p. 441).

Konrad can thus have sexual affairs and watch endless television, Vilma has to swallow her words and wait. As Hilda discovers: 'einem weiblichen Leiter dürfen nie und nirgends auch nur Anflüge von Affären zu Mitarbeitern oder dergleichen unterlaufen' (*A*, p. 145). Barbara's 'Heiratsschwindeln' is a crime, similar male behaviour is the norm.

This then is the present which Morgner's characters face. To question such prejudices, to discover a new sexual morality, they must learn to use 'die Produktivkraft Sexualität'. If feminist analysis is to inspire rather than to remain bound by dogma, both critique of patriarchy and utopian fantasies are necessary and vital. As Sawicki (1991, p. 102) states:

Attempts to free ourselves from certain forms of experience and self-understanding inherited under conditions of domination and subordination are not enough. We must also continue to struggle for rights, justice and liberties within the constraints of modernity. We must also continue to envision alternative future possibilities.

Morgner's fiction both struggles and envisions, providing, as Martin (1979, p. 436) summarises: 'an historical perspective on the importance and the potential for change in traditional moral attitudes and sexuality'.

'bis das weibliche Geschlecht gelernt hat...'

In Morgner's visions it is her female characters who are granted responsibility for 'die Produktivkraft Sexualität'. Physical and open, they are figures who learn to express their own sexuality with independence, humour and impatience. 'Der Eintritt der Frauen in die Historie' (Walther 1973, p. 49), the necessity for women to discover their own identity, including their own sexuality, is one of Morgner's major themes. As Beatriz proclaims: 'Ich bin aus der Historie ausgetreten, weil ich in die Historie eintreten wollte. Mir Natur aneignen. Zuerst meine eigene: die Menschwerdung in Angriff nehmen' (*B*, p. 113).[69] Shenja similarly urges Valeska to reconstruct what appears natural, to become human rather than female. This 'Menschwerdung' necessitates true emancipation in all spheres of life. As Eva Kaufmann (1984b, p. 1525) recognises, the most important of these spheres is the erotic:

> Mehrfach wird im Roman betont, daß der Eintritt der Frau in die Geschichte bedeutet, sich zuerst die eigene Natur aneignen. Dieser Begriff umgreift die praktische und die geistige Existenz der Frauen im weitesten Sinne, meint hier *vor allem die Erotik*, jene Sphäre weiblichen Lebens, in der Verkrüppelungen besonders tief reichen und durch juristische und soziale Errungenschaften nicht automatisch behoben werden. [...] Der Zusammenhang zwischen der immer wieder beschworenen "Vermenschlichung des Menschen" und einem befreiten erotischen Selbstbewußtsein der Frau liegt auf der Hand. (My emphasis).

Ev, Karla and Persephone, for example, are not simply the socialist *Superfrauen* typical of writing from the early 1960s. As idealised male projections, such mythical figures were more likely to provoke disbelief, cynicism, guilt or depression than encourage imitation and identification. As Patricia Herminghouse (1985, p. 343) argues: 'die Frau wird Objekt, nicht Subjekt der literarischen Darstellung, ohne jegliche Analyse ihrer wirklichen Bedürfnisse oder der

[69] Cf. *Gustav*, p. 157.

Strategien für ihre Emanzipation'. Morgner's protagonists, on the other hand, are subjects rather than objects. They are women with both bodies and bodily desires. Persephone functions as the first in a long line of memorable female narrators, characters who actively assert their subjectivity. As Ursula Heuken-kamp (1993, p. 144) writes:

> Ein solches Selbstgefühl und Einverständnis mit dem eigenen Geschlecht weist keine spätere Frauenfigur bei Irmtraud Morgner auf. [...] Persephone hat das erste und das letzte Wort im Roman und ist zudem die einzige, die sich selbst erzählt, die Frau also, die "ich" sagt.

This form of characterisation recurs in all of the author's subsequent texts.

Persephone is followed by the memorable Bele H., a figure who reappears in various guises as protagonist, minor character, narrator, author and editor. Like her grandfather Gustav she possesses the 'Schöpferkraft der Machtlosen' (*G*, p. 16) and like him she constructs her own history. According to Michaela Grobbel (1987, p. 5) then, 'Bele stellt auch die schöpferische Figur dar, die die "Produktivkraft Sexualität" in sich trägt'. Her vivid imagination is constantly devising new images of love. A 'geschäftigte Liebhaberin und Geliebte' (Franke 1969), she appreciates both Paul's intelligence and the fact that he is a good lover. Sex is an important part of both her honeymoon and her stories. In this respect too, there are links with Morgner's literary model. As Gabriele Scherer (1992, p. 62) notes: 'es ist nicht zuletzt der erotische Reiz, der von der orientalischen Märchensammlung ausgeht, mit dem Bele ihre Hochzeitsreise in Verbinding bringen möchte'. In *Die wundersamen Reisen Gustav des Welt-fahrers* the physical is again of importance for Bele. The subject is introduced in a humorous manner: 'Mein Liebhaber und späterer Ehemann begleitete mich. Da ich in einem Studentenheim wohnte und er in Untermiete, bevorzugten wir Nachtwachen' (p. 9). The humour emphasises that Bele is allowed to enjoy her sexuality despite university regulations. It also points forward to the role that the sexual plays in the main narrative.

Bele's positive relationship to her body is mirrored in Morgner's other major female characters, Beatriz, Laura, Amanda and Valeska: 'sie kennen ihre Bedürfnisse genau und können sie befriedigen, indem sie sich zum Beispiel aktiv und werbend Männern gegenüber verhalten' (Schmitz 1983, p. 139). Whereas the literary woman conventionally appears in a role subservient to, and reliant upon, the male hero, Morgners heroines stand alone. Beatriz, a 'Grenz-überschreiterin' (*DH*, p. 17), and 'eine große Liebende' (Kaufmann E. 1984b, p. 1525), acts in defiance of sexual taboos. The poet is as physical and passionate as her predecessor Bele. Once she has reached the GDR she has the sort of sexual adventures that are usually the prerogative of men. The ideals which she embodies pose a threat to androcentric order, and to monogamy as an absolute value at the heart of this order.

Like the female socialist Alexandra Kollontai, Beatriz rejects the notion of love as a necessary basis for sex, an axiom which has traditionally been used in romantic fiction to establish Engel's 'Monogamie [...] gegründet auf die Herrschaft des Mannes, mit dem ausdrücklichen Zweck der Erzeugung von Kindern mit unbestrittener Vaterschaft' (1892, p. 176). Beatriz's liberated sexuality represents the 'subversively feminine', she 'brings the fantastic, the extravagant, the impossible and the erotic to bear on the apparently "natural" order, its discursive underpinnings and its literary representation' (Martin 1980, p. 61). Her sexual autonomy threatens the split between the worlds of work and the home on which patriarchal constructions of gender rely, blurring distinctions between production and reproduction.

The figure of Beatrice has been stylised in art as Dante's beautiful muse. Morgner's Beatriz subverts this stylisation by taking men as her poetic inspiration. The first of these men was Raimbaut d'Aurenga, 'umgearbeitet, um ihn bedichtenswert zu machen' (*B*, p. 23). In her second life affairs with both Lutz and Alain stimulate her art. Reborn for the third time, Beatriz writes for a young male prostitute, whom she depicts primarily through his physical features. The siren finds herself unable to resist: 'Wir liebten uns im Keller eine Nacht oder eine Woche. [...] Keine Schmerzen oder Brutalitäten [...] Nur allerlei Kämpfe, Kampflüste, Lustkämpfe' (*DS*, p. 28, p. 30). Beatriz admits, and acts upon, her desire without scruples. Her first union with her young lover is a literal image of 'vögeln', sex in flight:

> Ich flog im Smog über die Stadt sieben Runden. Der Mann wälzte im Flugwind den Kopf wie im Kissen. Ich konnte beide Ohren, in Lockennestern versteckt, abwechselnd besehen und bebeißen (*DS*, p. 27).

This leads, however, to the loss of Beatriz's bird-like covering, and like Eve she awakens from her sexual experiences naked. The discovery of her nakedness is also, in this case, the rediscovery of her voice.

Beatriz's main relationship is one of friendship and of solidarity rather than of sex. It is that with Laura, Morgner's most pragmatic figure. Laura realises how futile Beatriz's attempts to control her own sexuality are, and it is she who explains to her friend that the erotic is the last male domain. Laura is portrayed as a woman who has had many relationships, she talks openly about her abortion and about her pregnancy. Other than with Benno, she is, however, given little opportunity to indulge her sexual fantasies, detailed clearly in her

'Liebeslegende' (*B*, pp. 125-32). In *Amanda* Laura has even less opportunity to enjoy her sexuality. In accordance with the general loss of optimism which characterises the second part of Morgner's trilogy, her life has become sadly unerotic. It is her friendships with other women which are now more important. After the early death of Benno Laura does not experience erotic love again, other than that of a mother for her son. As Lia Secci (1988, p. 431) writes: 'Laura opfert Wesselin einen der bei Irmtraud Morgner erstrebenswertesten Ansprüche, die freie weibliche Sexualität'. She subjects herself to night shifts mainly in order to find a father for Wesselin and not for her own pleasure. The sex that she has with Konrad, whilst drunk, is described only ambiguously, through juxtaposition with a nearby sculpture: 'Das Paar aus Stein ist nackt. Das andere hatte mit den Unbilden der Kleidung und der Witterung zu kämpfen' (*A*, p. 276-77). It is measured according to passing tube trains and afterwards the couple part. Laura's sexual relationships with Sven are nothing more than 'garantiert harmlosen Freundschaftsdienst für Anita' (*A*, p. 335) Her love of her job, however, 'konnte durchaus in euphorische Zustände versetzen, die denen der Liebe vergleichbar waren' (*A*, p. 517), and she mostly has to make do with this substitute.

'Laura', writes Beatriz, 'durfte nie vergessen, sich nicht fallenlassen' (*A*, p. 126). Like Valeska's friend Lena, she simply has no time for anything other than the necessary day-to-day living.[70] Even her experiments in alchemy are designed primarily with suicide, rather than pleasure, in mind. As Morgner states in interview (*DH*, p. 69), sex is reliant on practical factors of time and lifestyle, not just physical lust:

> Neulich las man bei uns einen Artikel. Männer jammerten, es gäbe zu wenig Zärtlichkeit, zu wenig Zuwendung, und die zärtlichen Vorspiele wären zu kurz. Darüber vergessen die Leute: Eines der Vorspiele sind die achtzig Prozent der Hausarbeit.

Although she has no housework to do, in *Amanda* Beatriz too is not only metaphorically but also literally confined. In this life her only companions are Arke, other animals and Nature. The sexual adventures of her first rebirth have been replaced by loneliness and isolation. Her tongue, symbolic not only of speech but also of the erotic, has been stolen from her, this siren is unable to tempt either sailors or other men.

---

[70] 'Lena hetzte durch die Tage, sechs Uhr aufstehen, Kind in den Kindergarten bringen, heizen, aufräumen, dichten, einkaufen, Kind holen und etwas bespielen, Wäsche waschen, kochen, Kind baden und ins Bett bringen, Wohnung saubermachen, womöglich ein Buch lesen oder fernsehen, solche Hetzerei ist der Liebesfähigkeit abträglich' (*B*, p. 439-40).

Ursula Heukenkamp (1984) suggests that the characters in *Amanda* have little sensual pleasure because their actions are driven purely by fear of war and ecological disaster. She sees Morgner's use of mythological motifs as a narrative reflection of this lack of the directly erotic:

> Die Synopse der Mythologien im Roman [dokumentiert] nicht nur die Ablösung des Matriarchats, [...] sondern eben auch die Unterdrückung der Sinnlichkeit [...] Daß die mythologische, zweite Welt so wenig an sensualistische Weltbilder anschließt, ist vielleicht eine Schwäche des Buches. Sie spiegelt aber auch Notwendigkeiten (p. 568).

The 'private' sexual sphere is thus intricately linked with the major 'political' themes of the novel. The absence of positive sexual description in *Amanda* functions as just as revealing and meaningful as the comparative wealth of such material in *Beatriz*. What Gabriele Pleßke (1986, p. 228) describes as the 'Ent-Sinnlichung Lauras' has, therefore, a distinctly critical function.

The one notably sensual character in *Amanda* is Laura's other half Amanda, whose 'entfesselte Sinnlichkeit' (Pleßke 1986, p. 228) stands in sharp contrast to Laura's constant feelings of exhaustion and desperation. Amanda's rebellion includes the erotic. Even for her though, there are patriarchal demands which have to be fulfilled, sexuality is never shown in a vacuum. Amanda's physicality is used to provide pleasure for the brothel customers, including Tenner. As Pleßke (p. 228) states, 'während die Sinnlichkeit Lauras medikamentös gebändigt wurde, ist die Amandas teuflisch institutionalisiert'.[71] The difference between the two women is manifested most clearly in their mouths:

> Auffälligster Unterschied der beiden Erscheinungen: ihre Münder. Vergleichsweise erschien Lauras großer Mund herb, ja verkniffen. Der andere konnte in allen Gefühls- und Spekuliertonarten aufspielen (*A*, p. 221).

Amanda's mouth is large, full and extremely expressive. The rest of her face is subordinate to this one feature, which becomes Amanda, it is 'der Mund des Besuchs' (*A*, p. 131) which acts. The owner's harmonika playing also centres around this part of her body. The devil's comment, 'für Fellatio nicht übel' (*A*, p. 331), emphasises the sexual connotations. Laura's mouth, on the other hand, is described as a 'schlichte Einrichtung zum Essen, Sprechen, Küssen' (*A*, p. 131), although she does much more eating and talking than kissing. For her, food becomes a sexual substitute.

The mouth is a highly complex symbol, especially for women. As Ros Coward (1984, p. 122) argues, it represents 'a site of drama, a drama between the desire to pursue active needs and the prohibitions levelled against women's

---

[71] The 'medicine' referred to here is the contraceptive pill.

behaviour'. The mouth is traditionally the locus of the erotic, as countless images of kissing testify. The lips also offer immediate associations with the female genitalia. The mouth is, however, much more than this, it is also the immediate source of speech, speech that is necessary in order to assert one's subjectivity. Beyond this it is connected with food and with eating, activities which are also vital for women's images of themselves.

Food in general is often linked to the sexual in Morgner's work. In *Gauklerlegende*, for example, Wanda and her minstrel eat a sumptuous five course meal during their imaginative courtship. He then explains to her the stimulatory qualities of certain delicacies. This foreplay has the desired effect: 'Da zeigte ihm Wanda ihr Zimmer. Nachdem er es im Augenschein genommen hatte, tauchte er seine Zunge in Ohren, Mund, Nabel und Schoß, sie beschliefen einander in sieben Stellungen' (p. 69). Conspicuous here is the fact that this is primarily oral sex, beginning with the tongue. The language, which controls the humour of the situation, is deliberately exaggerated, from the graphic 'tauchen' to the emphasis on erogenous zones. For Wanda's 'real' partner Hubert, on the other hand, food is secondary to work.[72] Whilst Wanda 'verschlänge ihn mit den Augen' (p. 59), he quickly eats only rolls and cakes during the conference papers. The difference between the two male figures is thus evidenced through their attitudes towards food.

Gustav's stories are accompanied by steaming bowls of soup served up by his wife, food which once again functions as an aphrodisiac. Klara herself does not sample her cooking, her pleasure is in watching the two men eat. Before the tales begin they lick their spoons, undo their trousers and greedily devour the soup, arousing their (sexual) appetites. The verbs used, such as 'vergnügen' and 'verzehren', have sexual connotations. The spheres of food and sex are, after each story, noticeably juxtaposed:

> Den Abend verbrachte er auf, neben und unter seiner Frau. Nachts träumte er. Als er erwachte, wußte er nicht, was er geträumt hatte, fluchte und verlangte Speck und Käse. Seine Frau brachte ihm Salami, Speck und Käse und sah ihm zu beim Essen (*G*, p. 54).

The wife's role is, again, to provide the food rather than to enjoy it. After sex Gustav also eats 'Käse und Pumpernickel' (p. 34), 'Lachsherring' (p. 69), 'einen Apfelkuchen, den ihm seine Frau gebacken hatte' (p. 91) and 'Sauermilch mit Pumpernickel' (p. 113). The range of mismatched foods serves not only to characterise the hedonistic protagonist, but also to provide humour within the narrative.

---

[72] In this respect Hubert can be compared with Paul (*Ho*) who also eats sensible and boring carbohydrates and works while he eats.

Gustav's sixth journey takes the reader to a land where women are served naked for dinner, literally to be *had* on a plate:

> Nach dem Essen trugen uns die Kellner eine auf einem silbernen Tablett stehende Dame auf. Der Geschäftsführer erklärte uns, daß das Ausziehen einer Dame zum Mittagsgedeck eines jeden anständigen frigiderischen Restaurants gehörte (*G*, p. 119).

The alliterative irony, contained in the juxtaposition of 'Ausziehen' and 'anständig', clearly implies criticism of a society so cold that it makes women commodities. Indeed this form of prostitution is taken to frighteningly edible extremes:

> Für elf Eismark durfte man der servierten Dame die Haut abziehen und die Hände auf Leber, Galle, Milz und andere Innereien legen. Für fünfzehn Eismark durfte man die Milz behalten (ibid).

In this instance it is society, rather than individual men, which is characterised and condemned by its stance towards the sexual – literal frigidity is the norm.

Beatriz is also food server and flesh served, roles which again underline stereotypical female positions in relation to victuals. She cooks for the Parisian workers and provides her husband with both 'kulinarische Delikatessen und erotische Dienstleistungen' (*B*, p. 56). Commenting upon her own function, the pornographic pictures she discovers depict women 'Porendrall und mit Wassertropfen behangen wie ein bißlüstern servierter Apfel' (*DS*, p. 11). Valeska, on the other hand, reverses the expected roles. A food scientist rather than a physicist, she is both sexual subject and consuming subject. Her first story takes love bites to extremes: 'Im Verlaufe von Liebesspielen hatte es Valeska nämlich des öfteren gelüstet, von Clemens Fleisch zu kosten' (*B*, p. 222). This nutritional activity is also given an ironic biblical dimension, whilst Valeska chews around the collar bone Clemens cries: 'Wer mein Fleisch ißt und mein Blut trinkt, der hat das ewige Leben' (ibid). The irony does not, however, merely furnish laughter and a counterpoint to the long scientific descriptions given in Valeska's 'Hadische Erzählungen'. It further suggests that Valeska's desire for a harmonious relationship with men is one with religious overtones. Her stories, with their utopian ideals, are gospels.

Like Valeska, Morgner's witches are allowed to indulge themselves. These female characters too are representative of rebellion and female strength. Hidden in the Hugenottendom outside society's ideological constraints, food represents for them a source of pleasure rather than of responsibility: 'Lauter Kalorienschwergerichte aßen sie: ungarische Salami, Eisbein, Schlagsahne, Konfekt. Fühlten sie denn keine persönliche Verantwortung für ihre Figur?' (*A*,

p. 253) The mismatch of foods is suggestive of the meals enjoyed by Gustav during his appetizing flights of fancy. Here, however, it is women who are allowed to revel, to the extent that Laura asks: 'Fühlten sie denn keine persönliche Verantwortung für ihre Figur, keine gesellschaftliche Verantwortung für die Gesunderhaltung ihrer Arbeitskraft?' (*A*, p. 253). It is a question which mocks not only East German notions of social responsibility, but also Western notions of dieting. The women's feasting is accompanied by 'scharfe sexuelle und politische Witze' (p. 253), again discourses usually the prerogative of men.

Morgner's associations of food with sexuality offer yet another link to feminist concerns. Her excessive, and comic, portrayal of women as subordinate in relation to food shows how they are also regarded as subordinate in sex. As Lorraine Gamman and Merja Makinen (1994, p. 159) pithily state: 'traditionally, our culture constructed masculinity as he who fucks, femininity as she who cooks'. With the Western emphasis on dieting and the ideal slim feminine figure, has come the notion that to eat is to sin, to indulge. It is a platitude that sex too was traditionally considered sinful, unless for the purpose of reproduction. Dieting has become a way of life with strong religious overtones. Both sex and food, then, mean problems for women. Both are encoded through their links to issues of power and subordination, of denial and of guilt, of pleasure and of desire, which is constantly defined and stimulated. Feminists have attempted to prove the ideological prejudice at the root of these judgements, on which, for example, many adverts rely. Both food and sex represent business. Coward (1984, p. 99) writes of 'food pornography'. Others have shown how the discourse of love often uses food terminology. Jeremy Macclancy (1992) notes the linguistic parallels where one activity is constructed in terms of the other. The associations, in a variety of discursive fields, are countless. Food is the great metaphor for sex. Morgner's art exploits this metaphor to the full, challenging and questioning the links between the two spheres. Her work with the erotic thus moves beyond mere characterisation, the personal is, once again, discursive, ideological and public.

Morgner's female characters function, therefore, as narrative subjects and as sexual subjects. This aspect of her work is, firstly, part of its feminism. If women are to resist oppression then they must act for themselves to change the discourse which creates the meanings given to concepts of femininity. Secondly it relates to the utopia envisaged by the author, both in the narrow sense of women having control of their bodies, and in the wider sense of the 'female' potential being harnessed in order to further peace. Morgner's female characters are practicians of love. Yet they also suffer sexually and in this respect their characterisation is part of the texts' criticism of patriarchy. As fictional representations they do not simply reflect reality, but rather they literally embody the past, the present and a new morality.

Morgner does not only use the erotic as a means of characterisation where women are concerned. Her male figures too are constructed with regard to sexual codes. They are, for example, described in physical detail, often by women.[73] Laura eloquently evokes her lover's body, the man becomes her sexual image:

> Armoberseiten und Rücken bis zur Gürtellinie sommersprossig, augenfällige Muskel-bildung auf Schultern und Rippen, dann undeutlich, von der Halsgrube abwärts schütter behaart. Schmalhüftig, tiefe eingeebnete Taille, kurze Beine mit vorragenden Knien, mittelgroßes hübsches Gemächt (B, pp. 128-29).

Beatriz's speech for Guntram Pomerenke, based on the one given for her a year earlier, humourously paints the male artist too as an object; nothing more than his body (B, p. 98, p. 396). Such drawings again position women as subjects of sexual desire. From *Rumba auf einen Herbst* onwards the author thus answers her own question:

> Was werden [die Damen] als Menschen sagen über die Männer, nicht als Bilder, die sich die Männer von ihnen gemacht haben? Was wird geschehen, wenn sie äußern, was sie fühlen, nicht was zu fühlen wir von ihnen erwarten? (B, p. 39, p. 274. *DS*, p. 17).

Similarly detailed descriptions of women are less common in Morgner's work, a further critical reversal of traditional aesthetic and literary expectations. The physical portrayal of Beatriz, for example, is highly ironic, she is designed to appeal to male readers, 'dem heutigen Schönheitsideal vollkommen ent-sprechend' (B, p. 98).

Many texts published in the GDR from the 1970s onwards both personify and criticise men through delineation of their attitudes towards sex. This trend is particularly notable in Morgner's work. For Paul love is a rational occupation, connected to physics rather than to the fantastic: 'nur die Leistung gilt' (*Ho*, p. 146). After sex he spends the rest of the night with his books and not with Bele. Hubert too is more concerned with his scientific conference and complicated mathematical definitions than with Wanda. His pragmatic sexual views are evinced through numerous comparisons with those of the minstrel. Even revolutionaries such as Alain are sexually egotistical, an experience which

---

73 Cf. Morgner (*DH*, p. 85): 'Ich kann einen Mann nur von aussen beschreiben. Was er macht und wie er sich verhält. Aber von innen, da hätte ich Hemmung, weil es so hervorragende Analysen gibt von Männern über Männer'.

relates to those of many feminists involved in the student movements. For this man Beatriz is nothing more than sexual object. Alain is French, but his views are more widespread and more conventional. Lutz, for example, judges women according to only one category, 'schlafen oder nicht schlafen' (*B*, p. 155).

Karla's unhappy marriage to Lutz is thus characterised partly through the descriptions of sex in *Rumba auf einen Herbst*. Lutz is the only participant to enjoy the experience when his wife conceives their third child. The emotions detailed are, however, Karla's:

> Ein paar Griffe, ein Kuß auf die linke Brust, immer auf dieselbe Stelle, los. Druck des schweren Leibes, harte, rhythmische Schläge, langsam zuerst, dann immer schneller werdend, Schweiß, sinnlose Worte, der Schrei. Wie immer. Nur die Unterbrechung fehlte. [...] Er dachte nur an sich (*R*, p. 209).

Such images of machinery and methodical routine were repeated in many later works. Here the bleak atmosphere of this scene is emphasised through juxtaposition with the romantic landscapes of with Lutz's affair with Ev. The unsympathetic erotic characterisation of Lutz can be contrasted with the more complex picture of Uwe. Uwe's problematic relationships with women are related to his psychological need for a figure of authority. While he feels subservient he is unable to fulfil the demands made upon him by traditional codes of masculinity. He cannot become a 'father' himself. His socially determined frigidity is emphasised through comparison with the erotic openness and control of his wives and girlfriend. Both Laura and Valeska are 'bewundernswerte Geschöpfe von denen er wußte, daß sie ihn auf die Dauer impotent machten' (*B*, p. 75). Beatriz too, with whom Uwe immediately falls in love, is an 'überlegene Frau' (*B*, p. 75). Unlike Lutz, Uwe has no sexual power, as a man he too he is oppressed by patriarchal role models.

Men are thus portrayed as scientists uninterested in the sexual, capitalist oppressors, impotent and disturbed, or sensitive and only available in dreams. These portrayals can, of course, be interpreted as nothing more than clichés. The rational, unerotic man and the irrational yet creative and sensual woman – these were seen by some critics as stereotypes that belonged more to Western feminism than to Eastern communism. Paul and Hubert are reminiscent of Wolf's Manfred, a figure that appears time and time again in GDR writing by women. Lutz, Uwe and Benno are, according to Petra Reuffer (1988, p. 338), simply 'drei verschiedene Männertypen [...] insbesondere in ihrem Verhältnis zu Frauen'. Christa Wolf faced similar accusations over her short story *Selbstversuch*. She was severely criticised for her use of such reductionalism, whereby the female is made to represent humanitarianism. Critics claimed that true socialist literature should transcend this Western tradition.[74] However, as Morgner writes in *Amanda* (p. 357): 'In Klischees sind Aussagen über Zustände eingeschlossen. Über gesellschaftliche Zustände, die auch charakterbildend sind'. The erotic ideals to which women and men were expected to conform in GDR society were still those of a bourgeois world, a world criticised by the author. Stereotypes of masculinity can thus offer a re-vision of feminine equivalents, particularly where alternative models are juxtaposed, as is the case with Lutz and Uwe. If Morgner's male figures are, in some cases, types, the same cannot be said of her women. None is merely representative, all are individuals. Thus the literary domination of men is also challenged at this level.

Morgner does not only use the sexual in order to describe people. This method of characterisation is extended to places, events and even aesthetics. Bele's narration, for example, is depicted as the diary of a woman through apparently trivial asides related to female sexuality. Thus the reader is informed that: 'Bele wartete bereits zwei Tage auf die Regel' (*Ho*, p. 114). The naturalistic description of birth given in *Hochzeit in Konstantinopel* again positions the writing subject as female. This is not a wonderful gift of nature, but rather a painful experience: 'Ich dachte, nie wieder. [...] Gott wäre ein Mann, eine Frau hätte sich für das Geschäft was Besseres einfallen lassen' (pp. 78-79). In the hospital female sexuality is regarded as nothing more than mechanical baby production, an impression which is heightened by the repetition of Bele's cold reception both in the ward and by the midwife. Implicit in such a representation is the need for change.

The atmosphere of the hospital is reproduced in the Amazonian dystopia of Gustav's fourth journey, where sexual intercourse is replaced by scientifically controlled sperm banks and separation of the sexes. The ice world of the sixth journey is similarly depicted by its stance towards the sexual. Gustav's final journey into space represents a future where children are picked off trees rather than conceived in love. Life is 'befreit von Leidenschaften, Komplexen und Neurosen. Die Morallehre hatte ihren attraktivsten Gegenstand verloren, der Lesehunger die zuverlässige Stimulanz' (*G*, p. 147). Sex, with all its connotations, has disappeared. This is, again, a world which Gustav flees, escaping one-sided perfection. These visions make clear that modern Western society is increasingly reliant on a form of cold industrialisation which takes little account of human relationships. It is against these intemperately rational developments that Morgner's sensual and fantastic imagery offers a warning.

---

[74] See for example Sigrid Damm and Jürgen Engler (1975).

113

In *Amanda* Morgner's bewitched world of the borderland between East and West is another place that relies on sexual oppression. This esoteric domain is portrayed as a modern brothel, equipped with all the necessary modern appliances for the production of desire.[75] The witches' heads, which they have to veil when they are at 'work', are their 'Schamteil' (*A*, p. 525), otherwise nakedness is the obligatory uniform. They are merely their bodies, their role is to provide relaxation for men. The Hörselberg is given the name 'Lusttempel', whereas the Blocksberg where the male witches live is known as the 'Vernunft-tempel' (*A*, p. 235); the labels playing with the clichés of masculinity and femininity that Morgner is accused by her critics of reproducing. The brothel is also known as the 'Venushöhle' (*A*, p. 520), again a paronomasia, for the vagina can, idiomatically, be termed the *Venushügel* or the *Schamberg*. Amanda states that the brothel witches serve the 'Erhaltung des heilen Moralbilds der DDR' (*A*, p. 445), and that:

> Schloß Blocksberg mit Dependance Hörselberg besorgt nämlich, daß patriarchalische Gewohnheiten nicht aussterben. Ein Sozialismus aber, der die Männervorherrschaft nicht abschafft, kann keinen Kommunismus aufbauen (*A*, p. 447).

Her comments upon such strong images of prostitution thus suggest the anachronistic patriarchy of both capitalism and communism.

By linking witchcraft and sexuality in this 'Hexenroman' Morgner further recalls traditional images of the witch as a heretic who attended sex orgies, danced naked and had intercourse with the Devil. As Lucy Mair (1969), writes, stereotypical witches have insatiable or perverted sexual lusts, are thought to commit incest and are regarded as nymphomaniacs. Confessions extracted from women about to be burnt to death during the witch hunts contain hysterical accounts of orgies. Academics and theologians produced great tracts on the size and shape of the Devil's penis, his sperm and his sexual prowess, tracts which read like early pornography.[76] Men's experiences were not discussed, male writers focussed on women. Morgner too focusses on women, and even allows the Devil to propose to Laura, but her appropriation of this tradition is purely

---

[75] Sex aids in this brothel include: 'Sitzmöbel und Tische, nach nackten Männer- und Frauenkörpern naturalistisch modelliert, supernaturalistisch, besonders in den Details, die die primären und die sekundären Geschlechtsorgane abbildeten. Auch allerlei Sex-maschinen, komplette Sadismus- und Masochismus-Ausstattungen mit Hifi-Schrei-verstärkungen sowie original japanische Beischlafgerätschatullen und dergleichen' (*A*, p. 337).

[76] Cf. R.H. Robbins (1959, p. 466ff).

satirical. It represents another link to feminist projects, whereby the the image of the witch has been reclaimed and transformed into an icon of power.

Morgner's sexual characterisation thus achieves much more than a mere exchange of role models. Women do not simply take on traditionally masculine sexual characteristics and men do not become passive, caring and giving. It is in the playing with, and questioning of, such gendered qualities, that the success of Morgner's work lies. As Sigrid Damm (1975, p. 143) writes, the use of the erotic is successful:

> wo sie aggressiv und heitersarkastisch Rollenbewußtsein bloßlegt, überlebte Verhaltens-normen angreift, in einer Art polemischer Bestandsaufnahme bei uns existierende Widersprüche zwischen der Revolutionierung gesellschaftlicher Verhältnisse und der Revolutionierung der Sitten und Gewohnheiten aufdecken läßt.

The contradictions Morgner exposes are not merely those of the GDR. They belong, in addition, to patriarchal discourse. Resistance to this discourse is feminist as well as Marxist.

'die Produktivkraft Sexualität...'

The juxtapostion of the words 'Produktivkraft' and 'Sexualität' is a linguistic achievement for which Irmtraud Morgner is famous. Iconoclastic, the term is central to her attempt to create active female subjects and accord women sexual sovereignty. The phrase suggests, however, much more than a sexual utopia. For readers schooled in Communist theories one immediate connection is with the writings of Karl Marx, where the concept of 'Produktivkraft' occurs endless times. The development of this force is necessary if Communism is to succeed:

> Die sozialen Verhältnisse sind eng verknüpft mit den Produktivkräften. Mit der Erwer-bung neuer Produktivkräfte verändern die Menschen ihre Produktionsweise, und mit der Veränderung der Produktionsweise, der Art, ihren Lebensunterhalt zu gewinnen, verändern sie alle ihre gesellschaftlichen Verhältnisse ('Das Elend der Philosophie', p. 130).

'Produktivkraft' here is a notion linked to the economic rather than to the sexual. It is regarded as a material 'Arbeitskraft' of male production rather than of female *re*production. 'Die größte Produktivkraft' is, in Marx's opinion, 'die revolutionäre Klasse selbst' (ibid, p. 181), yet he would appear to concentrate upon the male revolutionaries rather than the female.

In the context of 'der *Mensch*', Marx also accorded meaning to 'natural' forces or 'Lebenskräfte': 'als Naturwesen und als lebendiges Naturwesen ist er teils mit *natürlichen Kräften*, mit *Lebenskräften* ausgerüstet, [...] diese Kräfte existieren in ihm als Anliegen und Fähigkeiten, als Triebe' (1844, p. 578). These human drives appear to correspond to the traditional understanding of the sexual. This correspondence is even clearer where Marx places these natural forces in the context of the relationship between man and woman. He repeats, as does Morgner, that:

> Das Verhältnis des Mannes zum Weib ist das *natürlichste* Verhältnis des Menschen zum Menschen. In ihm zeigt sich also, inwieweit das *natürliche* Verhalten des Menschen *menschlich* oder inwieweit das *menschliche* Wesen ihm zur *Natur* geworden ist (Marx, p. 535, *B*, p. 64).

These, then, are further concepts and ideas upon which Morgner amplifies. Sexuality, like economic forces, must be understood and worked with, by women as well as by men. However, whereas Marx presents his 'Triebe' as an idealised inner essence, Morgner constructs her sexual drives within specific social and discursive constraints. Her male-female relationships, as opposed to those of Marx, are determined by notions of gender and not just of 'nature'.

The GDR's *Kleines Politisches Wörterbuch* emphasises material goods in its definition of 'Produktivkräfte'.[77] In an East German context the phrase 'Produktivkraft' further evokes both the 'Produktivkraft Wissenschaft und Technik' and the 'Produktivkraft Proletariat'. These terms were extremely prevalent in official East German discourse, expressing the value given to industry and science by modern industrial states, and the role of the workers in communism. Uwe, for example, is writing an article entitled 'Produktivkraft Wissenschaft'. In the institute where he attends conferences, physics is a new religion, scientists the new 'Heilige' (*R*, p. 249). Physics is also 'eine männliche Wissenschaft' (ibid). From *Rumba auf einen Herbst* onwards Morgner questions this one-sided bias, stressing the need for a productive union of science and art. The redressing of this unbalance is an aim embodied in the critical juxtaposition of the familiar 'Produktivkraft' with the unfamiliar 'Sexualität'. In *Rumba auf einen Herbst* therefore, as Hensel (1993d, p. 105) writes: 'wurde die Industriewelt nicht als unbeherrschbar und bedrohend empfunden, sondern auf seltsame Weise erotisiert'. Similarly, in *Hochzeit in Konstantinopel*, the spheres of the erotic and industry are constantly intertwined.

---

[77] 'Die Gesamtheit der subjektiven und gegenständlichen Faktoren des Produktionsprozesses sowie deren Zusammenwirkung bei der Produktion materieller Güter' (1973, p. 676).

Gabi Ahlings and Ingeborg Nordmann (1979, p. 94) have argued that Morgner's adoption of this discourse is restrictive rather than provocative:

Die den herrschenden Begriff technisch-ökonomischen "Produktivkräfte" kritisierende Konstruktion "Produktivkraft Sexualität" ist affirmativ an jenen zurückgebunden. Zu sehr verläßt sich die Morgner auf das Verständnis davon, was als produktiv gelten kann; es geht ihr offensichtlich nur um die Gleichberechtigung eines bisher unterdrückten Bereichs.

Such statements fail to recognise the full range of meanings implicit in Morgner's phrase. Her 'Produktivkraft' suggests, as Ahlings and Nordmann recognise, that the sexual too is an economic and social theme, an impression supported by the treatment of prostitution and pornography in her writing. These are sexual spheres in which money controls the female body. Yet it further suggests that sexuality is not just determined by economics, but also that the sexual can be regarded as the primary determining force in society, and thus more important than the economic. This too becomes a 'Produktivkraft', in the senses described by Marx and more. As Martin (1979, p. 434) contends:

Beatriz, and Morgner through her, calls for a more progressive view of productivity, one which integrates imagination and shared decision-making powers with increased technological advances and increased production. An essential aspect of Morgner's concept of productivity and subjectivity is her concentration on sexuality and the importance of liberating eroticism.

Morgner's appropriation of the language of traditional Marxist discourse is thus primarily subversive rather than affirmative.

Morgner's 'Produktivkraft Sexualität' also adds a specifically feminist dimension to the original terminology, as can be seen by comparison with other feminist writers. Ulrike Prokop (1976, p. 71), for example, gives signifiers of production wide signifieds. She argues that: 'die "Produktivkräfte" der Frau enthalten eine kulturelle (soziale und psychische) Komponente: Arten und Weisen der Wahrnehmung, der Phantasie, der Spontanität, der *Imagination*'. As examples she cites housework, cooking, clothing, decoration and relationships. These, like sexuality, are forms of production traditionally undervalued in society because they have been regarded as female spheres. Morgner aims also to accord the supposedly 'feminine', subjective qualities of 'Erdenliebe, Sinn für Harmonie und Hegen, Kompromißfähigkeit, Frieden' (*A*, p. 67), the importance which Marx gives the economic. The personal is, once again, made an inherently political issue. As in Western feminist theory, false definitions and distinctions, the foundations of patriarchy, are deconstructed. It is in these links to Western feminism that one of the reasons for the popularity of

Morgner's writing in the West can be found. As Angelika Bammer (1990, p. 204) states:

Denn wenn Sehnsucht und Erotik Produktivkräfte sind, wie Morgner in Trobadora Beatriz behauptet, dann können sie natürlich auch Sprengkräfte sein. Damit berührt Morgner einen der Kernpunkte feministischer Praxis und Theorie. Die "Subjektwerdung der Frau" nämlich – und dies ist letzten Endes die verbindende, Differenzen übergreifende und konkrete Utopie aller gegenwärtigen Feminismen – bedeutet Befreiung sowohl im materiellen wie im libidinösen Bereich des Bewußtseins und Begehrens.

Linked to the political, the legal situation is also of particular importance in defining female sexuality. The term 'Produktivkraft Sexualität' occurs in the context of Laura's celebration of the East German abortion law of 1972. Morgner quotes extensively from the speech given by the minister for health on the day the law was passed (B, pp. 329-335). The emphasis she places upon this is set against the background of Laura's resort to the knitting needle in the early 1950s, and a woman's necessary reliance on her partner and on her doctor. One of Beatriz's utopian visions is 'die Abtreibungsverbotparagraphen abzuschaffen' (B, p. 166), for before 1972 a woman was not able to make her own decisions concerning reproduction. On the day the law is passed Laura exclaims 'Erst jetzt gehört uns, was uns wirklich gehört' (B, p. 336). This exclamation echoes the slogan 'Mein Bauch gehört mir', used by West German feminists during the debates surrrounding the notorious Paragraph 218. Here again then Morgner reflects feminist concerns beyond specifically GDR confines.

The right to abortion on demand is productive in that it offers women a form of sexual autonomy and control, a way of resisting the supposedly natural linking of female sexuality with reproduction. When necessary, it can represent liberation from the confines of motherhood. The premises on which East German law was based thus support the aims behind Morgner's semantic experimentation. In this respect this chapter, ironically entitled 'Darin schließlich geheiratet wird', represents a turning point in the text. Laura is now free to marry her ideal man Benno, without the law she was trapped into marrying Uwe. Control of the physical nature of female sexuality is thus foundational for Morgner's utopian partnership. As she states in interview (Huffzky 1975), the 'ausgesprochen frauenfreundliche Gesetzgebung' of the GDR 'ragt die Zukunft in unseren Alltag'.

A further legal measure taken in the GDR to reinforce the message of the abortion law and secure basic freedom of choice for women was the free availability of contraceptives. Control of female sexuality is also offered by the hormonal pill. In Amanda this issue too is elided with Morgner's productive forces, but here the elision is negative. After Laura's repetition of her former enthusiastic speech Vilma, in the swallowed truths of the chapter's title, claims:

> Die Pille hat uns von einer physischen Unfreiheit in die andere gestürzt. [...] Die Angst sind wir los, aber die *Produktivkraft Sexualität* gleich mit. Denn die Pille dämpft. Und wir verlieren auf diese Weise nicht nur die Lust auf den Spaß, was schon ungeheuer viel ist, wir verlieren auch die Triebfeder der Unruhe, die aller schöpferischen Arbeit physischer und psychischer Urgrund ist (*A*, p. 181, My emphasis).

The repetition of the phrase 'Produktivkraft Sexualität' in this new context emphasises the author's earlier 'naive Fortschrittsgläubigkeit' (*A*, p. 182). As Barbara Meyer (1983, p. 757) writes, 'anstelle eines bedingungslosen Glaubens an die "Produktivkraft Sexualität" ist die Erkenntnis von der sexuellen Befreiung als neuer Form weiblicher Unterdrückung getreten'.

The pill does not offer emancipation but represents, as Vilma argues, exploitation. The moral, and feminist, dimension of the situation is made apparent through the word 'Ausbeutung' (*A*, p. 182), a word with important connotations within the GDR context. Morgner thus presents the pill as an ambivalent blessing and, in so doing, answers in detail the charges made against her by Ahlings and Nordmann (1979, p. 94), who assert, with reference to *Beatriz*, that: 'die Überlegung, daß die Perspektive, zwischen Pille und Abtreibung wählen zu können, sich ja immer noch auf vorgegebene Muster männlichen Sexualverhaltens bezieht, wird nicht thematisiert'. The linking of debates surrounding contraception and abortion with the reference to the 'Produktivkraft Sexualität' does not just mean that 'die Freisetzung der Produktivkraft Sexualität mit der Aufhebung des Abtreibungsparagraphen gleichgesetzt wird' (Ahlings and Nordmann 1979, p. 93). Legal measures are only a small part of the issue.

The results of the 1972 abortion law are, for example, not seen in a solely positive light. Abortion is again a motif in *Amanda*, where both Sven's sister and Hilde are still reliant on doctors who can choose not to comply with the law. Other legal and economic steps taken to allow women to combine a successful career with motherhood are portrayed as less conducive to a fulfilling sex life, as Morgner's depiction of Laura shows. Legal and economic acts, successful or not, are only a necessary first step towards change, towards Morgner's new sexual morality. A new consciousness cannot be imposed by the state as laws or social measures can, 'das geht allmählich, [...] muß wachsen, ist ein schöpferischer Prozeß der ganzen Gesellschaft' (Morgner in Krechel 1976, p. 24). The role of creative art in this process is particularly important.

Ingeborg Nordmann (1981, p. 447) claims that: 'Die Aufforderung Lauras an die Frauen, ihre Sexualität souverän als Produktivkraft zu gebrauchen, [wird] im Roman an eine fiktive Voraussetzung gebunden: den utopischen Mann'. She omits, however, the possibility of sexuality being a productive force in more senses than simple heterosexual intercourse. One of the most important facets of Morgner's statement is the idea of the erotic as artistically productive, as foundational for all forms of creativity. The links between sexuality and the literary are expressed in various interviews with the author. Both are regarded as agencies which can be fruitfully used to create relationships. The courage needed to write is itself a 'Produktivkraft' (*AE* 1973, p. 19) , for women have consistently been told they could not write without this energy:

> Ein bekannter Philosoph [Schopenhauer] hat einmal gesagt, von Frauen wären keine produktiven Leistungen zu erwarten, weil sie nichts zu sublimieren hätten. Diese Theorie unterstellt, daß Frauen keine Sexualität haben. [...] Der Philosoph beschreibt als Naturzustand, was sittliches Gebot war. Die anständige Frau hatte keine Sexualität zu haben (Morgner in Huffzky 1975).

Recognition of one's sexuality is here portayed as the necessary prerequisite to artistic achievement. Within Morgner's writing the links between art and the sexual are reflected in the varied love stories and poems which structure her intertextual mosaics. These texts represent 'die ungeschriebene Geschichte, die nicht von Männern gemacht wurde' (*B*, p. 181). Knowledge of one's past is vital if women are to create a future in which they can participate. However, history, constructed by the powerful, is traditionally male. A female version of *her*story has yet to be written. Beatriz and her female companions construct this narrative, which will lead to Morgner's utopian androgony.

Bele's 'lockere Beischlafgeschichten' (Auer 1976, p. 118) are mostly told in bed and often in a particularly erotic vein. 'Schattenspiel', for example, evokes the narrator's relationship with the poet Franz and his house. The opening scenes of loss, search and welcome discovery, are strangely sensual, accompanied by sonnetts of 'Eos, Scheißhäusern und anderen unerhörten Gegenständen' (*Ho*, p. 20). Franz offers the narrator his shadow to protect her from loneliness, a gift which she refuses, 'denn ich liebe die Männer, die alle meine Werke sind' (ibid). This foreplay of images, together with the reference to the flower of the Romantics, adds passion to an otherwise strangely cold offer of sex:

Dann stand er auf, pflückte eine von den blauen Blumen, die auf seinem Kopf wuchsen, reichte sie mir, wobei er die rechte Hand auf die linke Brust legte und sich tief verneigte, und fragte, ob ich ihm gestatten würde, mich zu vögeln. Ich gestattete (*Ho*, p. 21).

The description is short, precise and open, ending with female consent. The myth that sexuality must involve love is exploded once again.

In 'Für die Katz' the narrator, as a cat, eats her owner Richard. Like the other men conjured up by Bele, Richard possesses many of Paul's characteristics. This 'fressen' (*Ho*, p. 85) is, however, accompanied by stroking, purring, ruffling of hair and ear-biting, and it allows Bele the active eroticism that her relationship with the real Paul is lacking. In the story 'Gericht' Bele and Wenzel literally eat one another, a meal which makes the walls of the restaurant come alive with pictures of naked women, angels and various animals. 'Das Hotel' relates a night that Bele spends with Jan, 'Faungesicht' an episode with Ben. All of these stories are symbolic of Bele's own relationship with Paul and in some senses they are a surrogate for what they do not share. The men Bele describes are, literally, 'meine Werke', she becomes their creator.

Beatriz is determined to give women a sexual voice in all areas of society, including the cultural. Like her creator she 'muß sich': 'ausgerechnet mit dieser letzten, gesetzlich kaum faßbaren Domäne, die die Männer begreiflicherweise hartnäckig verteidigen, beruflich anlegen', she 'kann nicht was anderes' (*B*, p. 112). Bele's stories are ambiguous and limited in comparison with the 'Verse von leibhaftiger liebe' and 'sinnenhafter weiblicher Poesie' (Kaufmann E. 1984b, p. 1525) produced by her successor. The *Minnesängerin* Beatriz de Dia was a paradoxical female love poet in a male world where *Minne* was ritualised and made into a courtly emotion. Beatriz's immediate expression of her feelings meant that she 'fiel [...] reichlich aus dem Rahmen' (*B*, p. 28). Her love poems to Raimbaut d'Orange were considered so scandalous that her husband burnt them. Only five of these poems survive, two of which are included in *Beatriz:*

"Sehr möcht ich eines abends ihn
in meinen nackten Armen schaun
und meine Brust ihm anvertraun,
die seinem Haupt als Kissen dien.
  Das würde mehr an Lust mir geben,
als Floris Blancaflora gab.
Sein sind mein Haar, Hauch, Herzensschlag,
  sein meine Augen und mein Leben" (*B*, p. 24)[78]

[78] See also p. 96.

Both texts are openly sexual, as is expressed here in the use of vocabulary such as 'nackt' and 'Lust'. The woman, in defiance of expectations, willingly offers herself to the man, both physically and emotionally.

The reborn poet's first poem to Alain, 'Seegang' (*B*, p. 59), is again highly erotic. It suggests Freud's ideas of the ship as an image of the female body and his linking of water to both birth and the penis. The religious symbolism of water is also evident:

> Ich sagte:
> "Bist du es,
> so heiß mich zu dir kommen
> auf dem Wasser"

The female 'Ich' is dramatically present in the poem, demanding that her partner ask her to 'come'. The increasingly sexual poems that form the fifth and sixth chapters of the second book are directly related to *Minnesang*, inspired by Beatriz's 'niederen Liebe zum falschen Alain' and her 'hohen Liebe zum richtigen Alain' (*B*, pp. 62-63). 'Dach' is simply a poetic description of a male orgasm.[79] The 'skandalöse Verse und Ärmel für Lutz' (*B*, p. 140) are again connected with Middle High poetry, through the idea of the gift of the sleeve. The text that Laura discovers is female erotica:

> Diesem Geschlecht
> kein hübschres sah ich
> mach sie
> ihre Tränen: Vorsekrete der Lust.
> Mein Mund erwartet das Brennen
>   des Samens
> Taufschrei
> auch küß ich die verrätrischen Hände (*B*, p. 141).

Even the poems that Beatriz 'writes' with the Verschmiede are mainly love poems, although they are the most expensive genre. 'Rufformel aynnes Liebhabrstücks' (*B*, p. 123) could perhaps be seen as representing the acoustic aspects of sex.[80] The poem by Paul Wiens that Beatriz sings at Laura's wedding (*B*, p. 337) also has sexual connotations.

---

[79] cf. also Book 2, chapter 10, 'Die letzten beiden Pariser Stücke der Trobadora' (*B*, pp. 68-9).

[80] The mechanical poems bear a close resemblance to Christian Morgenstern's '"Fisches Nachtgesang". Das tiefste deutsche Gedicht'. J.H. Reid (*1990*) notes the connection with morse code, which gives a very different reading.

Love stories in *Beatriz* include Obilot's fairy tale,[81] Valeska's 'Gute Botschaft', Laura's 'Liebeslegende' and the 'Flaschenpostlegende'. Valeska's narrative uses the erotic to express her emotions and thoughts, it is, as Petra Reuffer (1988, p. 417) claims, 'in mehrfacher Hinsicht ein Konzentrat des gesamten Romans'. Her early relationship with Rudolf, for example, is characterised in a short sex scene, a 'turbulenter Abend mit reichlich Liebe' (*B*, p. 422). This, however, is not a celebration, at least not for her: 'Valeska war anpassungsgeübt. Schrie sogar lauter als gewöhnlich. Da sie sich tatsächlich der Liebe nicht erfreuen konnte' (ibid). The sex which Valeska experiences after her metamorphosis is more enjoyable. It questions prejudice through originality and offers new forms of pleasure.

The first time that Valeska, as a man, sleeps with a woman, she realises that 'die erstmals erprobte Apparatur ohne herrschliche Gefühle und Unterwerfungsvorstellungen funktioniert hatte' (*B*, p. 434), obviously not what both women are used to. When she makes love with Wibke, a virgin, she is particularly careful, for she remembers her own experiences. These experiences are depicted not as natural, but as cultural: 'Wer so in die Liebe eingeführt wird, kann die Liebesfähigkeit verlieren, noch ehe sie gewonnen ist. Der Brauch lastet solche Frigidität der Natur an, nicht den Bräuchen' (*B*, p. 440-41). Valeska's unexpected behaviour challenges such traditions and creates utopian images of liberated erotic relationships. Her love story, the opposite of accepted romantic fiction, plays with roles of masculinity and femininity and exposes both as historically determined rather than essentially fixed:

> Da erkannten sie, daß sie notfalls die Bilder entbehren konnten, die sie sich voneinander und die andere gemacht hatten.
> Da wußten sie, daß sie einander liebten. Persönlich – Wunder über Wunder
> (*B*, p. 443).

Love here goes beyond the images and is thus more 'personal'.

Laura's 'Liebeslegende' (*B*, p. 128) contains a particularly detailed, naturalistic description of sex, explicit and yet neither voyeuristic nor sensationalist. There is little poetic beauty here – sex is a fight, a fight with a wet body to which she cannot yet put a name:

> Wir schlugen einander die Zähne in die Lippen und wetzten die Zungen, daß der Speichel uns aus den Mundwinkeln rann, zerrten an den Kleidern dabei, entstiegen ihnen, die Hände spielten auf den Leibern wie auf Instrumenten. [...] Ich warf den Kopf,

---

81 This again has direct connections to the Middle High context of the novel, here to Wolfram von Eschenbach's *Parzival*.

krallte wohl auch rückenabwärts, der Kampf trieb rhythmisch schnell und unerbittlich auf den Schmerz zu. Der traf ein, als ich den Schrei vernahm, und der Mund ging mir über. Ich trug noch lange das Gewicht des feuchten Körpers.

The woman is portrayed as an active partner, the clichés of passivity overcome. Again her perspective is the dominant one. Here too this is emphasised by particularly female asides such as post-sex calculations. Laura's abundant sexual descriptions in *Beatriz* contrast with those of Karla's experiences in *Rumba auf einen Herbst*, which give a perfect example of de Bruyn's 'übliche Lücke': 'Also schlafen. Also erwachen' (*R*, p. 194, *B*, p. 157).

Where Laura's 'Liebeslegende' offers a female account of the male body, the 'Flaschenpostlegende' is a female rewriting of the biblical Jonah and the whale story, a rewriting founded on love. The sexual sins of the temptress Eve are given positive value, becoming positive symbols for the feelings that the writer and Jona share. The body is described as a garden of Eden:

> Sein Leib tat sich auf unter meinen Blicken: dichtes Astwerk. Vögel bewohnten es, Marder, Affen. [...] Blaue Früchte hingen in Fülle, ich lauschte dem Gesang der Zikaden, pflückte eine Frucht, aß (*B*, p. 86).

Religious paradise thus becomes concretely physical, available to everyone. Notions of the sexual as shameful are directly attacked and subverted. A similarly biblical female re-vision is to be found in *Der Schöne und das Tier*. This is 'eine Liebesgeschichte' where the young man Beatriz falls in love with is a figure literally cut from a woman's ribs: 'In Paris muß sich eine Frau gesagt haben: Wenn schon zu dieser uralten Tagesordnung übergehen, dann gründlich. Und schnitt sich einen Mann aus den Rippen' (p. 8). Beauty here loves his beast without inhibition, Beatriz adopts Zeus' role as swan to visit her Leda. Both the fairy tale and the myth are also retold from a female angle. These love stories, as the numerous others in Morgner's work, have a purpose beyond that of mere entertainment. They use the genre in order to move beyond it, to suggest alternative possibilities.

Morgner's message in a bottle, like many of her love stories, blends the aesthetics of mimetic realism with the fantastic, a genre more commonly associated with German Romanticism than with official East German cultural policies. The fantastic undermines dominant definitions of what is real. It is, as Sonja Hilzinger (1985, p. 139) states: 'diejenige Produktivkraft, die es ermöglicht, erwünschte Wirklichkeit zu antizipieren und den Vorschein der Utopie in den Alltag hineinragen zu lassen'. Alison Lewis (1989, p. 245), for example, accords such imagery the status of 'the marginalised or banished *other*' within GDR culture of the 1970s. This description recalls psychoanalytic and feminist theories which write of female desire in similar terms. Julia Kristeva, for example, replaces the imaginary with the 'semiotic' where the pre-Oedipal pulsions, Freud's primary processes, are gathered up in the 'chora'. She states (1986b, p. 131): 'what is obvious is that this experience of the semiotic chora in language produces poetry', thus signalling the link between art and desire. Kristeva herself concentrates on the poetry of the male modernist writers Lautréamont and Mallarmé, chosen, according to Jacqueline Rose (1989, p. 20) 'because of the *sexual* and *linguistic* scandal which they represented for bourgeois moral and literary forms – an excess confined to marginal expression by a repressive culture and state'. Morgner's use of both the sexual, as her use of the fantastic, was similarly scandalous, offering a challenge to repressive socialist realism and to patriarchal moral norms.

In *Beatriz* the fantastic and female desire are epitomized in the figure of the unicorn that Beatriz is searching for, 'the elixir which she hopes will change consciousness and conditions in the GDR by undoing sex roles and eroticizing relations of all kinds' (Martin 1980, p. 71). The phallic connotations of the unicorn are clear. The horn, pulverised, is also a well-known aphrodisiac. Traditionally associated with the Virgin Mary, this fantastic creature is, in addition, a symbol of purity, for it can supposedly only be tamed by a virgin. Laura introduces Anaximander in the context of her sexual 'education':

> Außer einer Mischung von Selbstaufgabe und Ausgeliefertsein, die von Lektüre vorbereitet war, entsinne ich mich nur großer Angst und einiger Blutflecken auf dem Laken. [...] Jedenfalls machte es erwachsen: ambivalent. Also hat mich Anaximander in selbiger Nacht verlassen und ist nie zurückgekehrt (*B*, p. 203).

Thus the loss of virginity is portrayed, from a female point of view, as the loss of something particularly special, a childhood utopia, childhood or female fantasies untouched by masculine sexuality.

When Laura sends Beatriz to find the unicorn she paints a wonderfully utopian picture of the possible effects of such a discovery. Pulverised, the horn could effect true communism, and could free the world from 'Kapitalismus, Kriegen, Hunger und Patriarchat' (*B*, p. 168). Morgner's utopia is thus, here as elsewhere, linked to acknowledging the power of the imaginary. The unicorn Laura describes is from a real tapestry, 'Die Dame mit dem Einhorn', which hangs in the Musée de Cluny in Paris, and represents 'a celebration of female sensibility at its most poetic and tender' (Cardinal 1991, p. 148). The words 'A mon seul désir' are written on the tent that the unicorn and a lion hold open for the lady pictured therein; female desire is clearly linked to the fantastic, through both words and images. It is also linked to the utopia symbolised by the unicorn, for the tapestry offers 'ein sanfteres Ideal weltlicher Harmonie' (*B*, p. 27).

Laura's trip to see this tapestry is placed directly after a short chapter devoted to the female orgasm, described as 'ein notwendiges, jedem höheren Lebewesen eigenes, den Gesamtlebensprozeß harmonisierendes Element' (*B*, p. 399). Here too the ideal of harmony is emphasised. However, according to research, women experience orgasm ten times less than do men. As Melusine notes: 'Diese Bilanz fordert die Änderung des heute beobachteten Zustandes' (ibid).[82] This is a formulation which, once again, depicts sex as productive, and as utopian. The ideal image Laura sees in the museum is thus not just about the emancipation of women, but also the emancipation of repressed desires and longings, including the sexual. It is, therefore, important that Laura is naked when she reads the words 'A mon seul désir', highlighting the role of the body in desire.

The eventual appearance of the unicorn as a small dog does not necessarily mean, as Martin (1980, p. 72) claims, that 'the potentially radical implications of sexual emancipation are confined and domesticated within the reformed bourgeois happy home'. One reading is that Beatriz's search in the capitalist West has, necessarily, been futile. Another is that the common household pet symbolises the presence of the fantastic and the erotic in the everyday. There is, therefore, no need to search beyond that which is known. Similarly, Beatriz's fantastic impulses are then, with her apparent death, integrated into the figure of Laura, integrated but not lost, for Beatriz is later twice reincarnated. That the future can be anticipated in the present is also manifested in the structure of the novel. The chapter in which Beatriz returns with the dog is thus also that in which Laura first reads of the new abortion law. Here again, Laura undresses and 'discovers' her body, 'ihre nicht mehr staatlich verwalteten Barschaft' (*B*, p. 328). Her nakedness points forward to the existence of the 'real' unicorn that she will later see, again when naked.

Whereas Beatriz searches for the fantastic, Wanda's 'Legende' is a love story where the female protagonist actually sleeps with the fantastic, as personified here in the figure of the vividly dressed, multilingual minstrel Rade. The links between this man and the erotic are symbolised too in the images printed in the

---

82 Morgner echoes these words in her interview with Huffzky: 'Die Paarung als physisches Erfolgserlebnis [...] ist ein wichtiges Harmonisierungselement des Lebens, die Paarung mit Orgasmus beider Partner.' The book from which Morgner quotes would seem, judging from the number of reprints, to have had an important effect on both her and on many GDR readers. (Siegfried Schnabl, *Mann und Frau intim. Fragen des gesunden und gestörten Geschlechtslebens*). The 1977 edition was the 9th reprint.

original Eulenspiegelverlag edition of the text (1970). That on the fourth die, which Wanda finds on her stomach after her sexual encounter, is of a woman at a dressing table and the minstrel in a four poster bed (p. 71). The erotic overtones are clear, as is also the case with the second die, which portrays Rade playing at a billiard table, a cue in his hand (p. 39). Wanda discovers this die after the short and precise narration of her notably unerotic night with Hubert:

> Hubert kam zur Nacht. Er löschte das Licht, bevor er sich entkleidete. Halb, Wanda spürte noch Stoff auf Brust und Schultern. Später Knöpfe. Als er eingeschlafen war, holte sie den neuen Würfel aus der Handtasche (*Gl*, p. 39).

Her imaginary partner thus begins to take the place of her real one. Desire is once again embodied in symbolic and fantastic form in *Der Schöne und das Tier*, where Beatriz's young man is called 'Désire, was so viel heißt wie "der Verlangende", "der Sehnende" oder auch "der Erwünschte"' (*DS*, p. 36). Morgner's final novel, then, in this as in other respects, productively continues and reworks the concerns of her earlier art.

Direct links between the fantastic and the erotic also form one of the various fairy tale narrative repetitions which structure Gustav der Weltfahrer's tales. The more that Gustav der Schrofelfahrer hears of these adventures, and the more he begins to believe in them, the more varied and exciting his love life becomes. 'Phantasie wird', according to Scherer (1992, p. 80), 'als eine wichtige Produktivkraft herausgestrichen'. Thus the somewhat sarcastic, but realistic depiction, 'er verbrachte den Abend auf seiner Frau und eine schlaflose Nacht' (*G*, p. 34), after the narration of the first journey becomes, after the second, 'Den Abend verbrachte er auf, neben und unter seiner Frau' (*G*, p. 54) Here the increased physical love results not in a sleepless night, but in dreams. The links to Freud's theories, where dreams present sexually symbolic images of the repressed id, are evident.

An important part of the traveller's 'Verdienste um die Sache der Phantasie' (*G*, p. 133) is that Gustav's wife also becomes an active participant in the couple's sex life, rather than a mere passive observer. After Gustav hears about the third journey:

> Verspielte er [den Abend] mit seiner Frau. Als sie gegen zehn plötzlich ihren Kopf auf den Kissen hin und her wälzte, erschrak er und wollte von ihr ablassen. Sie aber hielt ihn fest mit den Armen und Beinen, so daß er erstaunte und es ihm wohl erging. Träumend schlief er ein (*G*, p. 68).

This description echoes the sexual flights of fantasy portrayed in *Der Schöne und das Tier*, where it is Beatriz's male lover who rolls in the cushions. In both

127

of these examples, female emancipation in the erotic sphere includes the man. This can be contrasted with Gustav's fourth journey, set in a world of purely matriarchal power. The effects of this story are again manifested in the sexual.

After the fifth story Gustav can hardly bear to turn out the light and his dreams are increasingly unusual. After the sixth he:

> pries die grünen Augen seiner Frau und hörte Lob, sein Haar betreffend. Nachdem er seine Frau das drittemal erkannt hatte, legte er die linke Hand auf ihre rechte Brust und bestieg das Traumschiff. Es fuhr ihn mählich durch die Nacht. (*G*, p. 130)

Gustav's final dream is thus also sexual. The biblical language that Morgner uses here emphasises the importance of the episode. The fantastic in this novel is, therefore, not simple escapism through images of travel (a reading that limits the novel to its GDR site of production), but rather a strong indictment of any society which lacks fantasy.

Eva Kaufmann (1984b, p. 1525) argues, then, that Morgner creates 'viele Entwürfe erotischer Kultur' in order to combat 'im Leben und auch in der Literatur auftretende Erscheinungen erotischer Unkultur'. In her opinion these images are 'unverblümt, unmetaphorisch', and 'schön'. Beyond this, however, Morgner's love stories represent a productive and sovereign use of sexuality. Morgner is the East German writer most commonly associated with the dismantling of sexual taboos, from coitus to the pill. Her female characters are also narrators, sexual women who create their own role models. Their reclamation of their subjectivity and their *her*story includes the rediscovery of their sexuality, which becomes a vital factor in the formation of identity and in the development of a vision of erotic harmony. Desire is not merely theme but also style. It is foundational for poetics and is expressly linked to the fantastic, female emancipation and human emancipation.

However, Morgner's sexual constructions offer not just utopian images of the erotic, but also detailed analyses of oppression. Her writing criticises existing sexual morality and uses the possibilities of this theme to both demand and effect change. In her literature Morgner recognised that the erotic was the last male domain, one that had to be attacked, not simply because it was taboo, but because: 'auf allen anderen Gebieten sprechen die Gesetze des Landes Frauen Gleichberechtigung zu' (*B*, p. 112). The author contests feminine roles which rely upon codes of sexuality to produce and establish their meanings. Sexuality is shown not merely as a private realm on which the state has no influence, but an area of public society where the effects of ideological beliefs, politics, traditions and morals can be evidenced particularly clearly. The spheres of the private and the political are, throughout Morgner's writing, inexorably linked:

'Es geht darum, wie die dargestellten Liebesverhältnisse mit den derzeitigen Weltverhältnissen zusammenhängen' (Sprigath 1983, p. 149). Sexuality thus becomes a creative force, used to characterise, criticise and envisage. Embedded in a context which elides fields of discourse from the legal to the medical, the erotic in Morgner's lies at the heart of the novel's operative montage structure, forming one of the many threads that leads through the 'Erzähllabyrinth' (Damm 1975, p. 141).

The analysis of sexual themes and images is a vital first step in redressing the sexual balance and positing women as sexual subjects. However, such 'Images of Women' feminist criticism has certain limitations, for it can lead to concentration on thematic, rather than formal, aspects of a text. As Sigrid Weigel (1987, p. 112) states,

> Wenn man Literatur von Frauen betrachtet, die auf den Körper Bezug nimmt, bleibt zu fragen, ob es sich um die Darstellung körperlicher Erfahrungen handelt, d.h. um ein Schreiben *über* den Körper, ob die Körpersprache als Metapher oder Symbol Bedeutung erhält, oder ob es um eine Schreibweise geht, die eine andere Beziehung zwischen Sprache und menschlichem Körper begründet als die der Benennung, indem etwa Sprach-Körper und Körper-Sprache sich berühren.

Morgner undoubtedly speaks of the body, but her language is not specifically a 'Körper-Sprache'. She uses the body to tackle issues of female subjectivity, but she does not 'write the body'. Many critics have classified the open, montage form of her writing as 'female'. Such a classification relies on stereotypes of femininity and on certain statements by the author. Even where the narrator claims that she is writing 'as a woman' (*B*, p. 170) she emphasisies the social rather than the biological foundation of this female style. On the other hand, Morgner does use language to raise issues relating to the semantics of sexuality. Her list of 'Schimpfworte' includes an entire host of derogatory terms for women, many of which are linked to the sexual sphere: 'Lustgreisin – geile Mumie – Hure – Schnalle – Möse – Fickdrossel – Spagatscheißerin – Schwanzleckerin – Masochisten – Sadisten – Fotze – Nymphomanien...' (*A*, p. 446). Male equivalents of such terms are not part of a phallocentric discourse. Specific vocabulary is chosen by the author to criticise this discourse. The use of 'Gemächt' (*Ho*, p. 79, *B*, p. 129), and 'Herrschaftszepter' (*B*, p. 428) for example, suggests both 'Macht' and male rule. It is, however, to younger writers of the GDR that one must look in order to find a systematic and thorough questioning of language from a feminist stance. In their art this questioning takes place at all levels and includes the role of the sexual within its premises. The work of Gabriele Stötzer-Kachold is particularly notable in this respect, as is outlined in the following chapters.

4. Gabriele Stötzer-Kachold: Reviewing the Reception

Gabriele Stötzer-Kachold became famous as the young woman who appears in Christa Wolf's *Was bleibt*.[83] Wolf provides the reader with the basic facts of her visitor's life and art and with her own responses to the girl's imprisonment. This short description is, as Georgina Paul (1992, p. 126) rightly interprets, 'a tribute [...] to those who did put up resistance to the regime and who were hounded or imprisoned for their outspokenness'. It also offers a memorable piece of characterisation, for 'das Mädchen [...] ist nicht zu halten' (Wolf C. 1992, p. 78). Stötzer-Kachold's writing too cannot be 'contained'. As the programmatic titles of her books clearly convey, her prose breaks barriers, barriers of both form and content. It is upon this prose that a revision of Stötzer-Kachold's contribution to GDR literatures must now concentrate, for it is not only Stötzer-Kachold herself who is important, her writing is also 'gut' (Wolf C. 1992, p. 76).

Gabriele Stötzer-Kachold was born in 1953 in Thüringen. She is one of the young writers Uwe Kolbe identified as being 'hineingeboren' into the GDR. After a year spent in prison over the Biermann affair and having been ex-matriculated from her studies in Erfurt in 1976,[84] the young woman decided to turn to art. Constructing her own self-image (1992, pp. 7-8) she writes:

> ich kam aus ganz egoistischen gründen auf die kunst, [...] ich dachte, ich bin hier mit meiner suche nach originalität, nach individualität, mit einem beträchtlichen lustfaktor genau am richtigen platz.

During the 1980s Stötzer-Kachold also ran a private art gallery until its closure by the state and worked with both political and cultural women's groups. The first of her prose collections, *zügel los*, was edited by Christa Wolf's husband Gerhard and published in the Aufbau 'Außer der Reihe' series just before the *Wende*. Stötzer-Kachold was the fourth author chosen by Wolf, and the only woman.[85] A Luchterhand edition of the work appeared in 1990. The texts

---

83 I refer to the author by both of her names. *zügel los* was published under her married name Kachold. *grenzen los fremd gehen* was published under Stötzer-Kachold. She began to use only her maiden name 'Stötzer' in 1992 and *erfurter roulette* was published under this name. Cf. Ricarda Schmidt (1992a, p. 158): 'Christa Wolf's description of her in *Was Bleibt*, although it did not refer to her by name, made her an author to be reckoned with, and, no doubt, boosted the sales of the 1990 West German edition of *zügel los*'.

84 She was awarded an honarary degree in 1992.

85 The others were Jan Faktor, Bert Papenfuß-Gorek and Rainer Schedlinski.

assembled here were written between 1982 and 1987 and in some cases had already been published 'inofficially' in the *Zeitschriften* and *Lyrikmappen* of the 'underground'.[86] With the sudden post-Wende rush of critical interest in this apparently 'pure' GDR art, Stötzer-Kachold became one of the few women included in anthologies of the 'new' GDR literature.[87] Most of these anthology texts appeared again in Stötzer-Kachold's second collection *grenzen los fremd gehen*, published in 1992, together with a selection of the author's drawings.[88]

In interview with Birgit Dahlke (1993a, p. 258) Stötzer-Kachold complains: 'Ich habe Probleme mit dem Markt, sie stellen mich als Exotikum zur Seite, damit bin ich weg von der Literaturszene'. In terms of literary reception, Gabriele Stötzer-Kachold's 'market' consists mainly of short reviews and portraits, serious criticism is rare, though by no means absent. Dahlke's as yet unpublished Ph.D. thesis (1994) and her various articles offer the most detailed analyses of the author's work to date. Dahlke is one of the critics responsible for the important revision, in terms of gender, of the alternative literary scene in the GDR. Ricarda Schmidt's article 'Im Schatten der Titanen: Minor GDR women writers – Justly neglected, Unrecognised or repressed?' (1992) signals in the title the status of Stötzer-Kachold as far as the literary 'canon' is concerned. In this respect alone, she is an author who seems, at first sight, to have little in common with Irmtraud Morgner. However, if Wolfgang Emmerich's plea for 'eine neue Wahrnehmung' is to be heard, then a consideration of two such apparently different writers could, perhaps, contribute towards the creation of 'neue Kanonen', and thus towards the deconstruction of the single concept as a valid category of study.

The process of effectively ignoring a writer's work by concentrating instead on their life, exotic or otherwise, is one with which the study of GDR literatures is familiar. The defamation of Christa Wolf after the revelations surrounding her *Stasi* connections offer the ideal confirmation of this. Indeed the whole *Literaturstreit* had more to do with artists than with their art, as Wolfgang Emmerich (1994, p. 8) writes: 'Es ist im Grunde, paradoxerweise, von *Literatur selber* kaum je die Rede (von ihren Urhebern um so mehr). Kaum je ging es um die Texte als schließlich auch 'ästhetische Gebilde'. Yet this is not a peculiarly

---

86 Various titles in *UND* 5 (1982), 8 (1983), 12 (1983); *Mikado* 2 and 3 (1984); *Ariadnefabrik* 2 (1986), and 1 (1988); *Koma-Kino* 2 (1987), and 4 (1988), *Kontext* 5 (1989).

87 Her work had also been included in the seminal *Berührung ist nur eine Randerscheinung* (1985).

88 Stötzer-Kachold's most recent collection, *erfurter roulette*, was published after this study was written, in 1995. It continues and reworks many of the sexual and erotic motifs discussed here.

East German phenomenon. In asking 'What is an author?' Michel Foucault (1969) shows how modern Western society has created a cult figure, whose name is not just another element in cultural discourse, but has a specific function in society – one of authenticity, of status, of classification, of limitation and of publicity value. Despite Roland Barthes' famous announcements that the author is dead, the business of recreating him/her would seem to be very much alive.

Furthermore, this business is notably gendered. Focussing upon their personal lives creates an image which keeps female artists within the supposedly private sphere that is traditionally women's own. Anna Kühn has made a strong case for seeing the Christa Wolf controversy in similarly gendered terms. She argues (1994, p. 215) that the journalists' aggression is directed both against 'the East's pre-eminent *writer*', and against 'the writer as *woman*'. Kühn writes of 'vituperative *ad feminam*' (p. 207) attacks on Wolf's person rather than aesthetic attacks of *Was bleibt*. The media constructions of Stötzer-Kachold similarly concentrate on her person, which is then elided with her art and upon her identity as female. Stötzer-Kachold is thus justified in her accusations, the market as a whole reviews 'her' rather than offering readings of her slightly less comprehensible work. Almost every review of either *zügel los* or *grenzen los fremd gehen* begins with the biography of the writer, some even describe her appearance – presumably to allow one to picture the 'protagonist':

> Inzwischen ist Gabi Stötzer schön geworden, etwas Weiblich-Weiches ist in sie hineingekommen, die Wende hat ihr gut getan, die Schultern sind gerade, der Gang ist elastisch – die Zeit und diese Frau stehen gut zueinander (Kleinschmidt 1992, p. 20).

Morgner's parody 'Laudatio für den Dichter Guntram Pomeranke' (*B*, p. 396) finds ironic reflection in such statements.

Birgit Lahann's title 'Laß mich schreibend wieder leben' (1994, p. 17) posits 'leben' as 'schreiben', she simply ignores the texts and concentrates instead on such vital details as:

> In der elften Klasse strahlen sie ein Paar leuchtende Augen an. Damals braucht sie jemanden, der ihre Wohnung tapezieren kann. Er kann. Sie lieben sich, heiraten nach dem Abitur, bekommen Ehekredit, Kühlschrank, Fernseher, Auto.

The word *Ehekredit* makes it clear that this is a typically 'GDR biography', the fact that she cannot decorate her own flat labels the subject a woman. The subtitle 'Autorin aus Erfurt' is superfluous. Tobias Gohlis (1993b, p. 148) also finds it necessary to resort to comments such as 'das Türschloß wäre mit einem Handgriff zu öffnen – kein Problem für die Stasi' in order to place his interviewee. As part of this biographical approach Stötzer-Kachold's imprisonment over the Biermann affair, or – as is often preferred – 'wegen *Staats*verleumdung', is offered as sole explanation for her writing time and time again. Böck again (1990, p. 155), with pathos and even drama, exemplifies this tendency:

> Denn das Erfahrungsseelenexperiment, dem wir hier – voyeuristisch – beiwohnen, ist authentisch und alles andere als ein freiwilliges. Sein Anlaß: ein existentieller Notstand, eine Situation auf Leben und Tod – mit schicksalhaften Folgen: 1976, Gabriele Kachold, Anfang zwanzig, wird wegen "Staatsverleumdung" verhaftet, gerät in Acht und Bann.

Imprisonment is then expanded to become a more general metaphor, representing oppression at all levels, both physical and intellectual.

From the emphasis on the author's *life* story as imprisoned GDR woman, the reviews generally move on to her life *story*, equating writing with living. Elisabeth Wesuls (1991, p. 337), for example, writes: 'dieser Band [*zügel los*] läßt sich vom Leben der Autorin kaum trennen. [...] Gabriele Kachold redet von sich direkt und ohne Umschweife'. The critic feels she gets to know the author personally, just through reading her texts. Stötzer-Kachold's writing is therefore, seemingly automatically, 'DDR-Literatur par excellence' (Böck 1990b, p. 154). Other critics, again emphasising the context in which Stötzer-Kachold's poetry was produced, regard her art merely as an attempt, by an emotional and sensitive female, to stay alive: 'ein Aufbegehren ist ihr *Schreiben*, der Versuch, den Kopf oben zu behalten' (Rausch 1990). Indeed Stötzer-Kachold's own contradictory statements can be used to justify this approach. She tells her audience both that she came to art in order to live out her need for individuality and exhibitionism, and that she writes only in times of desperation. Her editor concentrates on the latter aspect (1992, p. 153). He introduces her work thus: 'Gabriele Kachold [...] hat zu schreiben begonnen, um sich in Texten über sich selbst zu verständigen, [...] um Gefühlen und Gedanken endlich einmal freien Lauf zu lassen, sich von Zwängen und Begrenzungen zu befreien'. This portrayal of a young girl who seems to have to write to survive has, furthermore, led to characterisations of her writing as sensitive, as authentic and as true. Christa Wolf's (1992, p. 76) fictional judgement of the poetry that she is asked to read, 'Es stimme. Jeder Satz sei wahr' is amplified in Gerhard Wolf's (1992, p. 157) introduction to *zügel los*: 'Gabriele Kacholds Texte', he maintains, 'bestechen durch ihre Aufrichtigkeit'.

In her analysis of GDR literatures of the 1980s Karen Leeder (1993, p. 84) notes the prevalence of terms such as 'authenticity', 'self-realisation', 'the search for identity' and 'subjectivity'. She notes too 'the assurance with which critics – particularly from the West – have treated these terms as aesthetic criteria and even, quite baldly, as indexes of literary value'. This process is especially notable in Stötzer-Kachold's case. Wolf's tone is repeated by almost every reviewer: 'Seit dem Erscheinen des Buches *zügel los* [...] muß man – wenn von authentischen Texten die Rede ist – auch Gabriele Stötzer-Kachold nennen', claims, for example, Dorothea von Törne (1992, p. 14). Wesuls (1991, p. 339) writes of 'Radikalität, Offenheit, Authentizität', whilst Annette Meusinger (1992, p. 372) similarly praises 'schonungsloser Authentizität und Wahrhaftigkeit'.

The dictionary definition of the word 'authentic' links it with notions such as 'reliable, trustworthy, of undisputed origin' and 'genuine'. Stötzer-Kachold's writing is seen as genuine because it does not appear to be aesthetically constructed or in any way controlled. Critics stress the immediacy of this diary-like prose. Here again the stance can be traced back to Wolf. In his 'Redaktionelle Bemerkung' to *zügel los* (1990, p. 171) he informs the reader:

> Die Autorin hat [...] über die Jahre hinweg ständig an einem Text geschrieben, der, möglichst unkontrolliert vom nachträglich einsetzenden kritischen Bewußtsein, festhält, was ihr in den Sinn kommt, durch den Kopf geht, sie freut oder verstört.

Wolf is writing here about the cycle 'aus einem fortlaufenden text'. Others, however, extend this characterisation to cover all of Stötzer-Kachold's work, which becomes 'écriture automatique', 'spontan', and 'naiv'. Bolder reviews attribute subversive qualities to the writing, because it is so 'truthful'. In a different extension of the same idea, the texts are described as therapeutic, as psychological rather than political or aesthetic. The most dangerous form of this line of criticism is to be found in the secret police files on the author:

> Die dabei von der K. produzierten lyrischen Werke sind derart entfremdet und unverständlich, daß selbst literarisch geschulte und an westlichen Tendenzen orientierte Personen diese Produkte als unqualifiziert und teilweise psychopathisch bezeichnen (in Stötzer-Kachold 1993, p. 132)

In assessing Stötzer-Kachold's work critics have, then, used either the 'autobiographical' or the 'authentic' critical method. Ricarda Bethke's 'Versuch einer Annäherung an Gabi Kachold' (1991), in the form of letters written to the author, combines both of these approaches in exemplary fashion – the epistolary genre being generally seen as one of the most 'truthful' and also one of the most 'female'. The use of the friendly 'Gabi' and 'Du', together with intertextual quotations, make this an author-centred critique. It is strangely woven together with the critic's own thoughts, reflections and indeed, autobiography – as if the writer 'talking' about 'herself' has given Bethke license to do the same:

> Ich wollte über Dich schreiben, dabei passierte es mir, daß ich Dich lieber abgeschrieben hätte. Versuch' ich es mit Briefen. Ich kann Dir nicht zügellos folgen, denn ich habe mich gezügelt und zügeln lassen (Bethke 1991, p. 205).

The irony of this approach is, however, clear when set in the context of Stötzer-Kachold's reaction to Anna Mudry's request for letters for her book *Autorinnen blicken zurück* (1991, p. 124):

> Ich finde die Idee korrupt, einer alten Form entspringend, als Frauen sich noch nicht trauten, frei zu schreiben, daß heißt auch frei zu leben, sondern ihre Existenz immer an jemand anderen banden [...] Insoweit ist diese Briefkonversation Ersatz.

Silvia Bovenschen (1979, p. 209) characterises the 'Briefroman' as 'eine Dialektik des Ausschlusses'. The letter, she argues, was regarded as a suitable form in which women were allowed to express themselves within a dominant male discourse. It seemed to embody the qualities demanded of the 'natural', emotional and sensitive female. In a letter one wrote the 'truth' of one's own life rather than stories about the lives of others. One wrote without care to aesthetic controls necessary for 'literary' quality. Thus the women's writing was 'authentic' and 'autobiographical' but not necessarily good enough to take seriously. In this respect letters were perhaps, as Stötzer-Kachold states, a substitute for art. In the author's own case her life becomes the substitute quality by which her art is judged.

Stötzer-Kachold fears that the reviews summarised above have the effect of placing her 'weg von der Literaturszene'. Whereas some critics are unreservedly positive,[89] others do indeed reject both the artist and her work. Klaus Ramm (1990, p. 4) states:

> Immerhin tut man diesen Texten Gewalt an, wenn man rein literarische Maßstäbe an sie legt. Literatur schließlich wollten sie gar nicht sein, Anspruch auf Qualität oder Originalität wohl kaum erheben.

Wolfgang Emmerich (1994, p. 172) characterises 'Gaby (sic) Kacholds Prosasplitter' with the words 'Banalität' and 'Konturlosigkeit'. Dieter Gräf (1992) patronisingly begins his review with the claim that a difficult life is not a justification for art. He dismisses *grenzen los fremd gehen* as the ravings of a

---

[89] Kleinschmidt (1992), for example, proclaims that: '*grenzen los* ist ein wunderbares Buch, das aus den Reihen aller Bücher fällt'.

woman who is not only depressed but also frigid. Once again, it is not far from this type of judgement to the reports of the secret police: 'G. Kachold ist bisexuell und hat sehr große Kontaktschwierigkeiten auf sinnlicher Ebene. Es ist möglich, daß es eine Art Kompensation ist, sich schriftlich zu äußern' (in Stötzer-Kachold 1993, p. 132). That the majority of these dismissive comments come from male critics is, perhaps, no coincidence. It is easier for them to reject Stötzer-Kachold's prose on the basis of the author's sex. Such reviews show that if her writing is to be taken seriously as an aesthetic product the parameters of the available criticism need to be widened.

To entirely disregard the notions of autobiography and authenticity would be fatuous. The use of labels such as 'honest' and 'true' to describe Stötzer-Kachold's writing can, in part, be justified, although these are not, as Leeder recognises, valid aesthetic criteria. Many of Stötzer-Kachold's texts are intense, intimate and emotional, thematising pain, anger, fear, hatred and love. However, terms such as 'authentic' have to be relativised. 'Reliable, trustworthy, of undisputed origin' and 'genuine' are terms which cannot unequivocally be applied to edited fiction. To further equate the female body with this authenticity is to ignore the discursive creation of what Dahlke (1994, p. 176) terms the 'vereinfachende Formel Frau = Sinnlichkeit'. Foucault's demonstration of how the body is constructed in modern society has delegitimised the assumption that the anatomy is 'natural'. The female body cannot enjoy an unmediated relationship to nature and neither can literature simply reflect a given 'reality'. Böck's (1990, p. 156) definitive statement that 'diese Texte haben nichts Fiktives, sie sind fixierte Realität' merely exemplifies a form of analysis which fails to take account of the system within which literature is manufactured and received.

Relating Stötzer-Kachold's texts to her biography is also an obvious way to approach writing which seems, literally, to flow from the body, writing in which the word 'ich' dominates, writing which we are told by the editor comes from a diary, writing which does indeed thematise prison experiences, *Stasi* experiences and other events specific to the GDR. Particularly in *grenzen los fremd gehen*, the author states openly and constantly that she is writing her self: 'ich habe nur eine geschichte aufzuschreiben | und die bin ich' (*gl*, p. 94). She repeatedly emphasises the importance of the year spent in prison and to deny this would be to trivialise this stage of her life. As Gerhard Wolf (1992, p. 153) writes, 'sicher war die Gefängnishaft ein Grunderlebnis' but, as he continues, it was one which led the author to reflect on other social experiences: 'über ihre Lage als Frau [...] über ihre Verstrickung zu den Männern, zur Elterngeneration und zu ihrer eigenen Generation'. To take the prison theme, *Mauer* and *Grenze*

137

images, or any others, and make of them all-encompassing metaphors undoubtedly provides possible readings of some of Stötzer-Kachold's texts, but can obscure other meanings.[90]

Characterisation of Stötzer-Kachold's work as mere autobiography is, therefore, too simplistic. In terms of content such a label ignores the wider appeal of her work, the 'grundsätzliche Fragen sogenannter moderner Zivilisation' (Althammer 1990, p. 9). This broad relevance is what Elke Erb (1985, pp. 14-16) stresses for the 'new' GDR literatures in her introduction to the anthology *Berührung ist nur eine Randerscheinung*:

> Die neue Literatur spiegelt ein neues gesellschaftliches Bewußtsein als Bewußtsein einer Jugend, die nicht mehr Objekt der erlebten Zivilisation sein will und kann. Dieses neue Selbstbewußtsein läßt sich nicht bestimmen und begrenzen von dem System, dessen Erbe es antritt. [...] Es ist kein Buch über die DDR, sondern ein Buch aus der DDR.

Stötzer-Kachold's work is similarly not 'über die DDR', but 'aus der DDR'.

Stylistically the category autobiography conventionally suggests a linear narrative involving development of characters to a point whereby they can recount their lives. Although Stötzer-Kachold's prose does certainly possess autobiographical features, there is as a whole no telos to a chronological story, no development of character, no one narrator, no one addressee. Her best texts refuse to situate meaning and remain open, symbolising transition in their form. As Dahlke (1994, pp. 123-25) argues:

> Vom Beginn ihres ich-bezogenen Schreibens an durchbricht Gabriele Stötzer-Kachold die Normen einer traditionell autobiographischen Redeweise. [...] Den Texten ist ein Hin- und Hergerissen zwischen einer vermeintlich 'authentischen', 'subjektiven' Schreibweise und der problematisierten Konstitution einer neuen weiblichen Identität nicht nur auf inhaltlicher, sondern auch auf struktureller Ebene, abzulesen.

In Stötzer-Kachold's work the word 'ich', the foundation of any autobiography, is fragmented, the self is split and ambiguous. Stötzer-Kachold herself (in Meusinger 1992, p. 372) states: 'Das Ich ist eine von mir geschaffene literarische Figur und die Kachold'. Statements by critics which imply that the author merely depicts herself are, therefore, inapplicable to many texts. Much of her prose is concerned with 'diese zerrissenheit meiner innerlichkeit' (*zl*, p. 30), a search for a subject – or subjects, rather than discovery or certainty. This

---

90 Cf. for example, 'an treiben', *zügel los*, or 'ich rufe die geister der gegenwart', *grenzen los fremd gehen* for 'Mauer' imagery and language. Stötzer-Kachold herself writes of 'diesem großen gefängnis ddr' (*gl*, p. 187).

search takes place through language, through analysis of personal experiences, through de-construction of social and cultural images, within the body and within the term 'ich'. As Friederike Eigler (1993, p. 150) contends: 'the identity of the writing subject is not fixed or stable, but rather part of the subject matter of these texts, that is, part of the writing process itself'.

In 'der wecker ist geklungen' (*zl*, pp. 7-9), for example, 'ich' gradually disappears, the grammatical form suggesting increasing physical and mental isolation. The stomach, the hands, the heart, the veins, the feet, the eyes, and above all blood, become the new protagonists of the poem. In addition there is the ambivalent 'es' which lurks, unexplained, behind the subject: 'durch den eingang hats mich gelaufn, eine treppe hoch, an die maschinn im großen saal. einen ganzen auftrag hab ich gemacht. nummer 2824 am ganzen tag' (p. 7). Like the grammar of the piece the human subject is passive and mechanised, running to time with his/her alarm clock. The number 2824, together with the repetition of the harsh 'n', express both the thudding rhythm of the text and the monotony of a factory worker's life. The daily routine described is dependent upon shoes, bedding and coffee and again has nothing to do with other human beings. Dahlke (1993a, p. 250) credits this text with 'ein künstlerisches Eigen-leben', it is not a mere reflection of the writer's life. Stötzer-Kachold herself (ibid, p. 255) has said: 'der Text bezicht sich auf einen alten Mann, der sich umbringen wollte. Er wurde gerettet, und ich mußte ihm, da war ich sechzehn, immer Blut abnchmen. Der ist unter meinen Händen, während ich Blut genommen habe, gestorben'. Dahlke argues that it can be read as the narrative of an abortion. It can also be understood as a suicide attempt. All of these meanings extend the text beyond an autobiographical account.

The subject of 'an treiben' (*zl*, pp. 17-19), hovers between 'mir' and 'dir'. The 'zwei gefangene' could either be two separate prisoners sharing the same fate yet unable to communicate, or mirror images of a divided 'ich' figure:

> zwei gefangene sehen sich, stehen vor einer wand, eine davor, eine dahinter, stellen die gesichter sich vor, [...] ich kenn dich irgendwann, irgendwann bist du ich [...] neben dir liegt keine frau, neben dir liegst immer du (p. 17).

Both the ambiguous subjectivity of this text and the dominance of the *Wand* imagery suggest Bachmann's *Malina* (1971), a novel which demonstrates the impossibility of the female 'I'. As Sigrid Weigel (1987, p. 142) writes: 'Mit dem Roman *Malina* hat Bachmann denn auch die Unmöglichkeit einer weib-lichen Autobiographie gezeigt'.

In Stötzer-Kachold's second collection there is less work on the representation of the subject and it is this that has led Dahlke (1993b, p. 150) to criticise the texts, for 'ohne selbstkritische Reflexion geht der Weg der Emanzipation im Kreis'. Leeder (1993, p. 119), much more strongly, calls *grenzen los fremd gehen* 'self-indulgent'. The long text 'erfurt – mein mittelalter' (*gl*, pp. 16-32), for example, can clearly be analysed with reference to the writer's own past, 'ich' here does seem to mean Stötzer-Kachold. Even Lahann's biographical analysis seems justified when one reads:

> da ich mit freunden eine wohnung zu dritt beziehen konnte brauchte ich jemand zum tapezieren – er half mir und wurde zudringlich leidenschaftlich [...] durch die hochzeit bekamen wir ehekredit [...] kühlschrank waschmaschine fernseher auto (*gl*, p. 20)

This text is, however, of documentary as well as literary value. Its aesthetic importance lies in its imagery. The past becomes a corpse to be dissected, a process which takes place in the cycle of texts entitled 'in der pathologie' (*gl*, pp. 12-16,pp. 92-94, pp. 144-45). Furthermore, where the lyrical subject is clearly defined, the 'ihr' against whom s/he struggles are often ambiguous. This group represents society, the GDR, men, friends or family. Such open possibilities exist even where Stötzer-Kachold's work appears to be closed autobiography.

The most interesting text in the largely autobiographical collection *erfurter roulette* (1995) is one in which the protagonist is not Gabriele Stötzer-Kachold but simply 'die sexfigur' (*er*, pp. 106-107). Inside a dirty room, perhaps behind a glass screen, this prostitute is 'eine frau die zurückgelassen ist' (p. 106). She represents merely 'austauschprinzipien ohne geschichte' (ibid), and as such is an object of male desire in whom no-one is interested. However, in the second paragraph this figure is alone and becomes 'eine frau'. After this caesura the tone of the piece changes, the woman is no longer available for others, she discovers herself: 'sie versucht sich mit sich selbst zu verwandeln zu verwenden sie bricht sich auf. in sich hinein' (p. 107). Yet at the end of the text there is another break. The reader is made aware that s/he has, voyeuristically, been watching this woman masturbate: 'es ist eine frau zu **sehen** mit der hand in sich selbst' (ibid. My emphasis). Thus she was, after all, just a whore and an object. The text functions as a comment upon those autobiographcial texts in the anthology in which the reader has similarly observed the author. What seems private is, then, always viewed. In this sense the autobiographical is always fiction. It is thus notable that the text ends with an I figure:

> eine frau zeigt sich mir eine frau lebt sich mir.
> ich bin immer eine frau wenn ich einsam bin. (ibid)

The prostitute has become an artist, for art is also exchanged and paid for, 'nach Austauschprinzipien'. Here, then, Stötzer-Kachold uses the autobiographical 'ich' in order to reflect more generally upon the nature of art.

Monolithic readings which make Stötzer-Kachold's art into simple biography further ignore those aspects which are concerned with linguistic experimentation. As Alexander von Bormann (1991, p. 210) maintains:

> Alle Texte [sind] deutlich autobiographisch inspiriert, aber doch nicht schlicht als Zeugnisse zu lesen. Zu entschieden gehen sie von der Spracharbeit aus, von der Arbeit am Wort und mit dem Wort, und zugleich von den Formen, die verschiedene Sprechhaltungen begründen.

Dahlke (1994, p. 171) argues along similar lines with respect to critiques founded upon generalised notions of authenticity, for 'Erfahrung wird stets als sprachlich vermittelt ins Gedächtnis gerufen'. In a manner which links writing by this writer with that by others of the Prenzlauer Berg *Szene*, Stötzer-Kachold investigates the possibilities of language, of alliteration, rhyme, orthography, punctuation, repetition, prefixes and suffixes. Her work not only experiments with words, but also with genre, shapes, typeface, and intertextuality. The writing produced is often poetical prose rather than prose or poetry. Stötzer-Kachold writes raps, speeches, monologues, dialogues, parodies, musical scales, dream sequences and simple statements. 'die rose ist keine rose ist keine rose ist keine rose' (*zl*, pp. 110-13) recalls Gertrud Stein, 'undink' (*zl*, pp. 20-21) Ingeborg Bachmann. References to Goethe are frequent, as in 'kennst du das land wo die bananen krumm gebogen werden' (*gl*, p. 181). This variety in her work is reflected in the different artistic genres with which Stötzer-Kachold works; tapestry, film, fashion shows, photography, drawing, dance and performance style theatre. This prose is thus polydimensional, impossible to reduce to biographical details or a genuine 'truth'.

Stötzer-Kachold's art challenges the stagnation of official discourse through playing with its codes. Subversion of mainstream language in these forms represents criticism of language as a discourse of power. German, and not simply the 'Orwellsches Neusprech' (Ramm 1990, p. 4) of the GDR, is one of the author's most favoured subjects for attack. Often this is linked with the concept of guilt. Stötzer-Kachold's poetry aims also to expose the male bias of language. In the cleverly entitled text 'in mich dringt das nichts ein' (*gl*, pp. 67-67), for example, she writes:

> er-sticken bis sie stickt
> er-teilen bis sie teilt
> er-eilen bis sie eilt   [...]

geld ist zählbar
liebe ist erzählbar siezählbar
die sprache wird die sprache wenn sie spricht (p. 67)

Here the man is both the FRG and, ironically, 'das nichts, das in mich eindringt'. Women represent the GDR, a motif which is common to much post-Wende literature. Yet in Stötzer-Kachold's text they are not just 'erstickende Opfer' or 'teilende Mütter', they also control language. This language is not spoken passively, 'sie spricht'. And as it speaks it creates new word constellations, or the new truths with which the text ends:

> spachus domanikus wusstus immer ganzus in spuktus ausus in haltus rebulus ni lausus ahnus in singende fragus ni schlagende sagende hackende schweinus fleischus fressus keimus blutus nirwana hammer sichel verloren geistus sprachus durch maschinamä mäander korpus (p. 67)

In order to create a new language the author resorts to an ancient one, namely latin. Both latin and the hammer and sickle may be lost, but the 'Sprachkörper', oder 'korpus', is still developing.

Such attacks on language can, however, become problematic, for texts ultimately remain bound by the language of their creation. Unlike some of the male poets connected with the 'alternative' GDR literature, Stötzer-Kachold cannot afford to abandon meaning altogether in favour of play-ad-absurdum. As Dahlke (1993c, p. 186) contends, the women of the *Szene* both reject official language and, simultaneously, search for a means of expressing what they understand as particularly female experience. Language for them is, paradoxically, both 'Herrschaftsinstrument' and 'Ausdrucksmittel'. Of Stötzer-Kachold's writing in particular Dahlke (1993c, p. 184) states:

> Auch bei ihr wird das Sprachexperiment nicht zum Ziel. Obwohl sie über weite Strecken sprachkritisch arbeitet, findet sie doch gleichzeitig ein großes Vertrauen in die Assoziationskraft der Sprache, worauf man bei männlichen Autoren kaum stößt.

If these linguistic experiments occasionally exhaust themselves in the act of experimentation, they do at least provoke reactions. Michael Braun (1990, p. 7) writes of 'die Sabotage der grammatischen Regelsysteme' and 'literarischen Grenzüberschreitungen'. Others depict a 'Zaubergemurmel', a 'Hexenamalgam aus Alt- und Mittelhochdeutsch, regionalem Dialekt, Litanei und Abzählreim' (Gohlis 1991, p. 29). Stötzer-Kachold turns dialect into poetry and gives nonsense a musical quality. She creates a new 'wahrheit' of her own by twisting words into rhyme:

sech der wehrheit der wehrfreit
de schildfreit de hildbreit
sech de were were schlage tage tege hege
sech der wehreheit der wehrefreit [...]
sech der wehreheit wehr dich endlich breit (*zl*, pp. 121-23)

In this case truth becomes a fight, language defending itself existing concepts. Generally, however, and paradoxically, Stötzer-Kachold's linguistic experimentation is noted but is in no way seen as contradicting the 'authentic', 'writing to survive' argument with which the critics begin.

Yet there are other senses too in which this argument cannot be upheld. Gabriele Stötzer-Kachold, as she tells us herself, wanted to be a famous writer. Gerhard Wolf (1992, p. 153), on the other hand, believes that it was unimportant 'was mit solchen Texten geschehen sollte'. If this was the case, why should the aspiring artist choose him and his wife to visit, members of the elder generation known for their support, financial and more general, of the younger authors? Stötzer-Kachold (in Dahlke 1993a, p. 246) again answers this question herself:

> Christa Wolf war berühmt, hatte Öffentlichkeit, und ich wollte Schriftstellerin nicht im Elfenbeinturm sein, ich wollte es leben, ich wollte damit anerkannt sein, Lesungen machen können, rumreisen, diskutieren.

If she really had been writing solely in order to survive then why did her prose not remain in desk drawers, as did so much written in the former GDR.

Other statements by the author do seem to support the image of her work as 'genuine'. She argues (in Dahlke 1993a, p. 249), for example, that she has not corrected her work: 'Wenn ich die Texte später gelesen habe, konnte ich sie nicht mehr korrigieren, ich hätte sie von außen korrigiert, das ging nicht'. However, the different versions that exist of certain texts – published early in the 1980s 'inofficially' and in later anthologies 'officially' – present further evidence that not all of her writing is 'écriture automatique'. 'Das Gesetz der Szene', for example, first published in *Kontext* 5, March 1989 (in Metelka 1990, pp. 64-72), was cut by more than half before its inclusion in *grenzen los fremd gehen*, where it is dated 1988 (*gl*, p. 133). The punctuation alone is different, as is the case with 'mein erfurt mein mittelalter' (in Döring/Steinert 1990, pp. 273-88), which would appear to be the second version of 'erfurt – mein mittelalter', which appears in *grenzen los fremd gehen*, again labelled 1988.

The changes made to the texts 'mein einzigster innigster todeswunsch...' and 'meine kriminelle zeit' (in Arnold 1990, pp. 188-91 and *gl*, pp. 86-91), are relatively minor, but do affect the way the text is read. The latter version emphasises flight rather than work, *fliegen* rather than *pflügen*:

> und mich lach ich alles faxen alles arbeit körper knallt auseinander in bildern
> in worten die die münder suchen
> wart nur ich werde mein eigenes pflugpferd zügeln (Arnold, p. 191)

> lach ich alles faxen alles arbeit körper knallt auseinander
> in bildern in worte die die münder suchen
> wart nur ich werde mein eigenes flugpferd zügeln (*gl*, p. 91)

The text 'geschwindigkeit' appeared in *Berliner Lesezeichen* (6/7 (1995), pp. 225-230) and then in *erfurter roulette* (pp. 74-82). The first version has no punctuation and appears to flow, emphasising the themes of memory and speed. It is framed by extracts from *Stasi* files and is immediately understood in this GDR context. The later version of the text is almost the same but consists of full sentences and thus reads more like a conventional narrative. It is better suited to the literary market. This time there is no frame and no interpretation. The text 'Sys' which appeared in *Berührung ist nur eine Randerscheinung* (pp. 113-18) is actually misprinted and should be three separate texts. Even if the author herself did not make the sudden change from the third person Karla to the first person, the editors did, a change which again alters the way in which the writing is understood. One cannot know which version of these and other texts is the supposedly 'authentic' one.

Both textual editing and linguistic experimentation, particularly with the autobiographical 'I', provide evidence of the need to deconstruct some of the terms used within general criticism of Stötzer-Kachold's work. One further category which needs also to be examined is that of 'feminist', a term applied both to the author and to her writing. The stereotypical characterisation of *Frauenliteratur* as both 'autobiographical' and 'authentic' would appear to make such an examination especially relevant. It is also an examination which allows comparisons to be drawn between this author's art and that of Irmtraud Morgner.

A secret police report about Stötzer-Kachold states that:

> Eines ihrer Hauptthemen ist die unterdrückte Frau in der sozialistischen Gesellschaft. [...] Hierbei gerät sie in ihren Auffassungen z.T. an die Grenze normal denkenden Menschenverstandes (in Stötzer-Kachold 1993, p. 133).

Sascha Anderson's description of the prose he reviewed for the *Stasi* as 'literarischer feminismus' (*gl*, p. 157) highlights the same important aspect of the author's work.[91] In the same way that Morgner's writing is 'feminist', Stötzer-Kachold's work too is concerned with the status of women in patriarchal societies, whether socialist or capitalist. Yet in the attempt to portray the oppression of the female her writing often appears as anti-man, 'als konkretes Individuum, als Geschlecht, als Machtsymbol' (Meusinger 1992, p. 369), rather than anti-patriarchy. Individual male figures become embodiments of power and masculinity is reduced to a radical feminist stereotype. It is this which upsets the critics, just as it was this which aroused the hatred and suspicion of the men who wrote the reports for the police files, whose attacks focus, in a dangerous extension of biographical analysis, upon the author herself.[92]

Serious literary critics are less harsh. As part of the biographical interpretations outlined above, Stötzer-Kachold's work is treated as writing by, and about, a woman. Thus Kleinschmidt (1992, p. 20) writes of a 'DENK-KÖRPER-FRAU, die sich in allem geschlechtlich zu erkennen gibt'. To assume that the 'ich' of the prose represents the position of the female author is often justified. The lyrical subject in many of the texts, again particularly those in *grenzen los fremd gehen*, is clearly situated in the female position. Texts ask, for example, 'meine frauenfragen' (*gl*, p. 106) and search for 'fraueneigene inhalte energien und kräfte' (*gl*, p. 138). Stötzer-Kachold tells Dahlke (1993a, p. 248) that she has attempted to create 'eine glaubhafte weibliche Ich-figur'. Other texts are, however, more ambiguous and have meanings beyond those of authorial intention.

Other critics regard Stötzer-Kachold's work not just as that of a woman, but as that of a radical feminist, 'eine feministin zum weghören' (*gl*, p. 193). It is her unusually woman-centred feminism, rather than the humanist androgony connected with the Kirsch/Wolf/Morgner canon, that sets this writer apart. Kleinschmidt (1990, p. 4) writes, then, of the 'männerfeindliche Gestus' of Stötzer-Kachold's texts, Wesuls (1991, p. 339) of a 'weibliches Selbstbewußt-sein [...] eng mit Wut und einer starken Verachtung für Männer verknüpft' and Schmidt (1992, p. 159) of 'the war of the sexes' and 'familiar feminist tracts'. Certain statements by the author, both in interviews and within her texts, can be

---

91 Cf. (*gl*, p. 157): 'später, als ich durch meine texte in der prenzlauer berg-szene bekannt wurde, denunzierte er g.k. als "geistige amokläuferin, die früher oder später das land verlassen wird" ihre literatur als "literarischen feminismus" und "schwarzmalerei der psyche"'.

92 Cf. Stötzer-Kachold (1993, p. 130), 'Wichtig bei der Auswertung meiner Stasi-Akten war, daß alle meiner etwa 25 inoffiziellen Mitarbeiter Männer waren, mit Ausnahme einer Frau.'

taken as justification for these reactions. 'rap 2' (*gl*, p. 75), for example, is dedicated to 'alle männer die mich einmal verraten und betrogen haben' and rages:

> eines tages wird es euch kostenlos geben
> wenn eure 1000jährigen reiche zerbrochen sind
> wenn niemand mehr eure uniformen bügelt
> und die spucke auf stiefeln realitäten sind (*gl*, p. 75)

With similar vehemence part of the 'fortlaufenden text' of *zügel los* (*zl*, pp. 27-53) begins, 'die männer sind von ihrer grundsubstanz her barbaren' (p. 40). At times the force of these demands can overshadow any lyrical content they may have. However, this type of directly political text is only one aspect of Stötzer-Kachold's feminism.

The author is concerned not only to criticise men but also to effect change in the constructions and images of femininity which form female subjectivity. Through her art she becomes, therefore:

> die böse frau, die sich gegen das bild zur wehr setzende frau, die um das bild, gegen das bild kämpfende frau (*zl*, p. 50)

She thus analyses existing role models, from the specifically GDR to the German Gretchen to the 'natural' mother figure. In this respect her work can be linked with that of Morgner. 'eine rede' (*gl*, pp. 101-03), for example, is directed:

> gegen die führungsrolle des mannes
> gegen die führer
> gegen die rollen
> gegen die bilder
> gegen die frauenbilder der letzten 40 jahre (p. 101)

The GDR ideal woman is depicted as the woman who stood at her man's side, the mother of his children. Stötzer-Kachold contrasts 'diese nicht lebbaren scheinbilder' with:

> den scheinbaren lebensbildern eines alltags in der ddr
> die frau arbeitend die frau früh das kind aus dem schlaf
> reißend die frau an den mittleren medizinischen oder bürokratischen
> schlecht bezahlten arbeitsplätzen die frau in den
> kaufschlangen stehend die frau ermüdet abgekämpft mit
> den kindern im bett und der mann fängt an zu trinken (p. 101)

146

If these are Eastern roles, pictures of eros, happiness, love and marriage are Western feminine images also, generalised images of femininity.[93] The washing lines, dishcloths and 'kochplatten der elektroherde der küchen dieser welt' (*gl*, p. 80) are, as the last phrase implies, conventional signifiers of feminine models. Stötzer-Kachold aims to revise these models and it is this well-expressed aim which makes her a feminist.

As such she does not, however, stop with criticism of gendered mainstream cultural images. She puts forward her own canon of alternatives. As she states in the tendentiously entitled text 'in sich blicken' (*gl*, pp. 137-38):

> je mehr ich mein abgelehntes ich nach außen brachte in texte bilder filme und fotos um so mehr kam ich auf andere inhalte im leben auch für frauen außer kinderkriegen und lohnarbeit (*gl*, p. 138)

It is only where this canon becomes as prescriptive as that which it aims to replace that problems arise. At times the author fails to recognise that the categories to which she accords positive meanings are themselves elements of existing discourse, rather than essential 'female' qualities. The more successful pieces show an awareness that, 'aus der permanenten wiederholung der frau ergibt sich nicht der beweis der frau' (*gl*, p. 111). The competing voices of 'die rose' (*zl*, pp. 110-13), for example, seem at first reading to be male and female, yet the repeated message of the text is:

> frauen gibt es nicht
> männer gibt es nicht [...]
> es gibt nichts zu beweisen (p. 113)

There is nothing to prove, nothing beyond the cultural constructions which perpetuate the masculine violence portrayed.

Stötzer-Kachold's visual art, integrated with her prose, is determined by similar concerns. In the autobiographical texts of *erfurter roulette* the author describes the importance of the 'Bild' for her work, linking text and pictorial image as 'experimentelle zustände in bild oder sprache' (*er*, p. 16). She notes in particular that: 'mit dem fotoapparat kam ich wieder anders an die körper heran [...] die ideen kamen wie schmerzgeburten aus mir heraus. sie waren nicht ausdrückbar in worten' (*er*, p. 17). The five photographs which appear in her first collection, *zügel los*, together with the collage depicted on the cover of the Luchterhand edition of the work, take issue with existing cultural definitions of femininity and create new images through the medium of the female physique.

---

93 See Eg. 'von dem erschauern öffentlich genannt zu werden' (*gl*, pp. 67-71).

They portray a naked woman who smears make up on to a glass sheet, possibly a mirror or the camera lens. The effect is one of tears and of blood, two substances which flow through the artist's prose:

in der brust das aufgeschlagene ei auf dem körper läuft
wie sperma der nagellack auf den fingernägeln läuft aus
und wird blut (*gl*, p. 168)

In this particular text, entitled 'die verletzte frau' (*gl*, pp. 168-71) injury is conventionally depicted through blood. In the photographs, on the other hand, blood is used to create energetic patterns of life. The reader is informed by Luchterhand that the model for these pictures is 'Birgit Schönheit', a name which – in the context of these images – ironically undermines the ideal beauty myth. As Eigler (1993, p. 159) argues: 'The image of culturally determined female beautification is contrasted with an injured or distorted mask-like face'. The assortment of sketched figures which accompany the texts of Stötzer's second anthology *grenzen los fremd gehen*, are also naked. Here it is as if one is to read the poetry through these surreal bodies. Anatomy is, then, the foundation of imagery.

Critics have used both the feminism and the aesthetics of Stötzer-Kachold's prose to compare her 'writing by a woman' with the West German *Frauenliteratur* of the 1970s. As Dahlke (1994, p. 120) notes, 'die Texte Stötzer-Kachold's [wurden] des öfteren aufgrund des Stichwortes "Authentizität" in die Nähe zu Verena Stefans *Häutungen* gerückt'. For Schmidt (1992, p. 159), for example, this prose is 'reminiscent' of 1970s Western feminist writing. A similar and particularly negative comparison is implied by Leeder (1993, p. 104), who maintains that the texts 'appear scarcely to go beyond the early feminist experiences of the 1970s'. In the 1970s too it had been the 'truthful' nature of the open and honest reports by women of their experiences in a patriarchal society that was praised by Western reviewers. These then were also seen as 'authentic' 'autobiographical' texts. In the context of the new women's movement it is not surprising that autobiography became so popular, designed to make 'private' lives 'public' and therefore 'political'. As Jutta Kolkenbrock-Netz and Marianne Schuller (1982, p. 154) note:

Das von Frauen häufig emphatisch zum Ausdruck gebrachte Verlangen nach unverstellter Artikulation ihrer *authentischen* Erfahrungen ist eine spontane Reaktion des Widerstandes auf das lange Schweigen, zu dem Frauen in patriarchalischen Gesellschaften verurteilt waren und sind.

The closure of traditional autobiography was also considered necessary if writers were to set themselves up as figures with whom readers could identify. Verena Stefan in particular claimed to be writing on behalf of many other women. Apart from anything else, as Weigel (1987) argues, when women begin to write their own life story is often the only material available to them.

The subjectivity of these texts has, however, been criticised for reinforcing female stereotypes, and doing so in a 'male' dominated genre: 'denn schließlich war autobiografische Literatur ein wichtiges Medium der Konstitution bürgerlicher Subjektivität, der Subjektivität männlicher Bürger allerdings' (Richter-Schröder 1986, p. 11). Many writers argue that traditionally accepted forms of poetry do not allow space for a female 'I' to be articulated. Others, such as Sara Lennox (1981, p. 66), claim that emotional, irrational and receptive writing by women merely adopts categories of femininity constructed by patriarchal discourse. Indeed much of the *Frauenliteratur* of the 1970s does not problematise this discourse in any way. Such texts can, according to Richter-Schröder (1986, p. 131), be characterised by linear narrative structures, the avoidance of changes in perspective, and the use of a simple language which is easily comprehended. In *Häutungen*, however, Stefan does experiment with language and thereby 'gropes towards a new feminist structure' (Lennox 1981, p. 65). Schmidt (1990) clearly details some of these experiments. Like Stötzer-Kachold, Stefan is concerned to create new semantic meanings in order to express female experiences. She separates words to expose latent gender bias therein, dispenses with the hierarchy of capital letters, juxtaposes prose and poetry and thus alienates the reader. However, large passages now read, twenty years on, as unoriginal propaganda or as stereotypical clichés. The work ends 'Der Mensch meines Lebens bin ich' (Stefan 1994, p. 158), thereby closing the text within the subject.

Critique of Stötzer-Kachold's writing often echoes these comments, and yet her work cannot unequivocally be called either 'autobiographical' or 'authentic'. Identification with the divided, aoristic self portrayed by this author is highly problematic. If her texts are indeed therapeutic for her, there is no guarantee that they will be so for the reader, often at a loss as to any possible meaning contained therein. As Dahlke (1994, pp. 119-120) defensively, but correctly, notes, 'die Texte Gabriele Stötzer-Kacholds, [...] bilden nun jedoch nicht einfach eine verspätete Umsetzung dessen, was bereits in der Frühphase der Frauenbewegung von BRD-Autorinnen geleistet worden war, in der DDR'. The East German writer's prose is significant in its own right, not just as a copy of a West German original.

Further apparent similarities between Western *Frauenliteratur* and Stötzer-Kachold's writing include the emphasis given to suffering, which is represented in numerous images of woman as victim. The deprivation of prison became, for example, one important theme by which this suffering could be exemplified. As Weigel (1987, p. 77) maintains:

> Ganz selbstverständlich sprechen ihre Aufzeichnungen von spezifischen weiblichen Erfahrungen im Gefängnis und nehmen damit eine Perspektive ein, aus der sich ihre Versuche zur Überwindung der Trennung zwischen "politischen" und "sozialen" Gefangenen motivieren.

Marianne Herzog's *Nicht den Hunger verlieren* (1980) is an autobiographical report of her own experiences whilst held in various jails on suspicion of terrorist activity with the RAF. Thematically there are obvious links with Stötzer-Kachold's writing, not only through imprisonment but also with the GDR, where the early scenes of the novel are set. Again, however, the form is very different. Despite flashback scenes and the juxtapositioning of Herzog's own memories with reports of other female prisoners' lives, this book still reads as a traditional linear narrative. Although the author writes 'Es ist schwer, von sich zu sprechen' (p. 12), she proceeds to do so with relative ease. Her identification with other novelists invites sympathy and understanding, again very different to the effects of Stötzer-Kachold's prose.

Gabriele Stötzer-Kachold thus writes feminist texts which cannot clearly be defined as *Frauenliteratur*. This becomes particularly clear when these texts are juxtaposed with West German women's writing of the 1970s, writing which forms the discursive context within which the term is first used. Classification of Stötzer-Kachold's work as feminist means that it can be compared with that of Irmtraud Morgner. Such a comparison necessitates, however, a revision of criticism which judges the younger author's art within a framework based upon her identity as East German woman. It necessitates too the deconstruction of notions of authenticity and truth when used to qualify aesthetic products. These points of reference are not entirely invalid, but do not allow a worthwhile assessment of poetic writing. The experimental aspects of Stötzer-Kachold's work mean that it is neither purely autobiographical nor a genuine reflection of her life in the GDR. Her work with language – where successful – endows her literature with further meanings which can offer feminist perspectives. It is this side of her work which makes it radical and sets it apart from that by Morgner. It is this which is of value if Stötzer-Kachold's work is to survive in its own right and not just as the poetry mentioned by Wolf in *Was bleibt*.

An important aspect of Morgner's feminist literature, as has been demonstrated, is the analysis of the sexual offered therein. Stötzer-Kachold's work too can be approached through concentration upon this theme. Her use of the sexual is, for example, a major part of her work with notions of identity. It is also foundational for many experiments with language. Where the lyrical subject of Stötzer-Kachold's prose can be clearly defined as female, this is often due to the use of erotic images and vocabulary. Sexual conventions, one of the most important aspects of patriarchal systems, are challenged in both Stötzer-Kachold's writing and her pictorial art. The following chapter analyses in detail the feminist effects of this author's work with the sexual. This analysis forms the basis for the comparisons, in Chapter Six, between writing by Stötzer-Kachold and other female authors, including Morgner.

5. Gabriele Stötzer-Kachold: Written Constructions of The Sexual and Sexually Constructed Writing

Stötzer-Kachold's name has been connected with those of Anderson, Schedlinski, Papenfuß-Gorek and other poets famed for their 'Prenzlauer Berg connection'. As the androcentric bias of the anthologies of this art has slowly been corrected, her work has been compared with that of other women of the *Szene*, including Barbara Köhler, Annett Gröschner, Katja Lange-Müller, Heike Willingham, Raja Lubinetzki and Kerstin Hensel. Of these writers it is Stötzer-Kachold who uses the sexual most strikingly and resolutely. She does so in the themes of her work (which range from orgasm and masturbation to genital mutilation), in her bodily, physical vocabulary and in the 'female' language she strives to create. As Ricarda Schmidt (1992, p. 159) states: 'what characterises the experiences of this subject is above all their physicality'. Birgit Dahlke (1993b, p. 149) writes of a 'Poetik der Körperlichkeit'. In this sense then, Stötzer-Kachold is, perhaps, a female artist who has learned 'die Produktivkraft Sexualität souverän zu nutzen' – productively forming desire into poetry.

Birgit Dahlke (1993c) identifies three major characteristics of writing by the women connected with 'unofficial' GDR literature: the questioning of language, a critique of female role models and the poetic transformation of the body. In Stötzer-Kachold's work all three of these motifs are clearly present and are linked. This study concentrates upon the latter category of the body and sexuality, through which the relationship of the sexual to language and to images offered to women is then explored. Dahlke further isolates two types of physicality within the texts which she analyses: the female body as an object for analysis – as content, and 'Körperlichkeit als strukturierendes Moment' (p. 187) – as form. Both of these aspects are vital to any study of Stötzer-Kachold's constructions of the sexual.

Other critics have linked the open sexuality of Stötzer-Kachold's writing to ideas of truth and authenticity. If the author's mind is, literally, an open book, then so too is her body. In a modern world where the supposed evils of technology have given rise to a yearning for a return to an idealised and un-sullied 'nature', the biological becomes a metaphor for this utopian refuge. Seemingly devoid of cultural inscriptions, both the body and prose about the body are thus regarded as 'natural'. Ricarda Bethke's third letter (1991, p. 207) is a 'Brief, über den Körper und das Geschlecht' which begins: 'Liebe Gabi! Wenn ich Dich lese, dann les' ich einen Körper', between the body and the page there is nothing but truth. The erotic is also considered part of the radical feminism of Stötzer-Kachold's work. Schmidt (1992, p. 159), for example, argues that her 'autobiographical reflection on her sexuality, her determination and explicitness in making the private public, is new to GDR writing'. The issues with which this writer is concerned are not those of traditional socialism.

Stötzer-Kachold's original use of the sexual is, however, most frequently described in terms of simple taboo flaunting. Here, then, there are further parallels with the reception of Morgner's work. Dorothea von Törne (1992, p. 14), for example, states:

> Gegen die "Männersprache" setzte sie ihre Frauensprache [...], die ideologische und erotische Tabus durchbrach. [...] Genau, minutiös, fast exhibitionistisch schreibt die Autorin u.a. über Sexuelles und Erotisches, ohne Scham, doch niemals schlüpfrig.

Stötzer-Kachold's writing is thus not only 'zügel los' and 'grenzen los', but also 'schamlos';[94] breaking down both linguistic and sexual barriers. Walther Hinck (1990) summarises this particular critical trend with the bold statement that Stötzer-Kachold's 'Prosatexte [unterliefen] alle Tabus der DDR-Literatur', a statement which makes a mockery of Honecker's 1971 declaration.

Certainly Stötzer-Kachold openly explores new and previously tabood sexual themes. Even in comparison with texts such as *Amanda* or Braun's *Hinze-Kunze-Roman* her prose, in this respect, shocks. The author clearly believed that the GDR was a prudish, repressed society which needed new and challenging erotic images. In interview she repeatedly asserts that the oppression of East German citizens also functioned at a sexual level. She claims, for example, in interview with Christel Lautert (1992, p. 9), 'Unsere ganze Gefühlswelt ist ja blockiert und diffamiert, da in der DDR über Sexualität öffentlich nicht gesprochen wurde. [...] In der DDR gab's ja nur politische Identitätsmuster, keine sinnlichen.' Erotic ideas and images are not, however, simply a means of titillation in her work, nor can they be neatly categorised as GDR critique. Like Morgner's this sexual art has a much wider feminist purpose. The images are used to both criticise instances of patriarchy and to suggest utopian alternatives. As Schmidt (1992, p. 160) summarises:

> For Kachold, the antagonism between *Volk* and *Macht* is a given of GDR reality that hardly needs exploring any more. She subverts it by shifting her concerns to the body as a place where repression as well as liberation may be experienced.

---

94 This term is used by both Heim (1991, p. 41) and Kleinschmidt (1992, p. 20). From Gisela Bartens interview (1991) it would appear that *scham los* was to have been the original title of Stötzer-Kachold's second book: 'Demnächst erscheint ihr zweites Buch "scham los".

There is thus specific aim behind this artist's portrayal, in various genres, of 'unanständige sachen' (*gl*, p. 79). If Morgner challenges existing socialist *Sitten* by postulating a 'productive' new morality, Stötzer-Kachold dispenses with morals altogether. For the younger writer too sexuality becomes a 'Produktivkraft'. Some of these 'productive' ideas and themes are analysed in the following sections.

'fangt an zu leben wo ihr seid und praktiziert das system der sinne' (*zl*, p. 86)

Gabriele Stötzer-Kachold's 'system der sinne' is a utopia whereby the sensual is primary. Hers is a vision where 'wir frei ficken frei gehen frei sprechen können ohne opfer zu sein' (*gl*, p. 198). Her prose is dedicated to the recognition of sensuality, 'nicht als anbiederung an die außenwelt, sondern als schutz, kampf, spiel mit der außenwelt' (*zl*, p. 41). It is this element of play that gives her work its momentum. At its best Stötzer-Kachold's relationship with both the world around her and that inside remains ambiguous and her most successful visions arise out of this ambiguity. At its worst the sensual offers merely an essentialised, inner truth, located in the body, in the female anatomy, or in the writer's own self. It is a truth which can be discovered through lust, love, fundamental sexual drives, the anatomy, orgasm or masturbation.

Sinnlichkeit, Impulse, Lust and *Liebe* dominate Stötzer-Kachold's writing. Her love is not, however, 'das herrschende Liebesideal' (Morgner, *A*, p. 494) whereby the woman is silenced by the man. It is to this dominant 'ideal' which Stötzer-Kachold refers when she comments in interview that love is pornographic rather than poetic.[95] In her poetry she describes traditional love in terms of oppression:

daß leute mich zum schweigen bringen und nennen die angelegenheit dann liebe # und daß dabei aber irgendetwas abgewürgt wird in mir # nämlich vielleicht gerade diese liebe (*gl*, p. 78)

The text describing this form of relationship, entitled 'geschlecht - schöpfung - geschlecht' (*gl*, pp. 78-79), is about gender and creation. It ends with new linguistic creations, beginning with rejection of the old and perhaps suggesting an attempt at a new form of love:

kotz rotz scheiß ab hang lung rengere teschsch pfff sau kerra tiss reck ffoo scheck zess ping blalabamm (*gl*, p. 79)

95 See eg. Lautert 1992.

155

This new love is neither 'dingwort' nor 'schablone', it is not part of 'ein pornografischer weg' (*gl*, p. 184). 'Liebe' is, rather, a vision rather than existing reality. In a speech the author thus demands, in bold type:

> die andere art geliebt zu werden meine ganz persönliche art nicht als nummer oder markenartikel sondern ich als mein individuelles unvergleichbares ich
> dazu gehört daß frauen sich öffnen darstellen zeigen wie sie wirklich
> sind (*gl*, p. 103)

It is clear that the role of women in this utopia is primary, as it was for Morgner. Here, however, Stötzer-Kachold posits a female authenticity which can be revealed, unified subjects who create discourse. This facet of her writing – based around the notion of a specific female identity – reoccurs throughout her work. It is a notion which is necessary for feminism and yet, as postmodern feminist debates show, ultimately obscures difference.

Love for this author has, then, two distinct features. On the one hand it is a concept created in order to entrap and silence women. On the other it is erotic, physical and productive, even more so than is the case in Morgner's writing. It is also identified with the aesthetic, both for men and women; it is 'erzählbar' and 'siezählbar' (*gl*, p. 67). Love is a vast resource. Indeed, the very last word of the *grenzen los fremd gehen* collection is 'liebe', presented as a poetic answer to a mutual search:

> poesie sucht eros
> sie sucht er sucht
> das fünfte eck nach der verdoppelung ist die
> liebe (*gl*, p. 220)

The aspirations and utopias identified by Karen Leeder (1991) for the poetry of the younger generation include love in all of its forms. It is in themes such as these that Leeder discovers meaning in their writing. This judgement would seem to be particularly applicable to many of Stötzer-Kachold's texts.

If love is a primarily productive emotion then so is hatred, again bodily rather than purely rational. Where the former is a longing for freedom, 'haß ist, wenn man sich nicht befreien kann [...] ist erkenntnis der verletzbarkeit [...] haß ist körperlich' (*zl*, p. 45). Often both passions are interwoven within Stötzer-Kachold's poetry, giving rise to anger, pain and fear, necessary concomitants to sensuality and lust. All of these sentiments are expressed in the 'los' of Stötzer-Kachold's titles, which refers not only to the desire for liberty, but also to feelings of rage and frustration. The force and the physicality of *los* are evoked

156

also by the word *Trieb*. This too is an idea which is foundational in Stötzer-Kachold's art.

The 'lustprinzip' behind the 'system der sinne' 'geht [...] von den trieben zur liebe' (*zl*, p. 86). Stötzer-Kachold's *liebe* is, then, one dominated by *Triebe*, her *schreiben* is a form of *treiben*. Indeed she describes writing as if it were a sexual act:

> das schreiben ist wie mein sexueller trieb
> bis zum letzten steigern sich beide und dann gehts los (*gl*, p. 157)

Treiben – in all its grammatical forms – is, for this author, an intrinsic concept.[96] Structured by rhyme and rhythm, often without any form of punctuation, often with new punctuation experiments, her poetry aims to be the written expression of these drives. Syntax itself is productive. The sounds and associations of individual words create their own dynamic, which moves beyond recognisable meaning. The author's sexually driven linguistic experiments thus become erotic.

The poetry produced by allowing physical drives to disrupt ordered language is reminiscent of Kristeva's descriptions of the semiotic in art, where the meeting of the semiotic and the symbolic produces open texts. The modernist works Kristeva analyses exist on the margins of accepted art forms. Stötzer-Kachold's prose is also marginal, both in the physical and the literary sense. In psychoanalytic terms it is experience of repression of desire which forms the split between the semiotic and the symbolic orders. Stötzer-Kachold herself suffered political and cultural repression, as did her work, being produced in the alternative scene of 1980s GDR literatures. In both cases, the subconscious and the 'real', the repression leads to a resulting search for the self. This takes place under the 'Law of the Father', whether this be the order of language or the rule of the patriarchal SED. This search can, when expressed artistically, produce poetry.

Emphasising the physical experience of repression, Stötzer-Kachold (in Dahlke 1993a, p. 247) states: 'überzeugt von der Triebstruktur der Frau wurde ich durch die Frauen im Knast'. A number of her literary texts link the isolation of prison and the discovery of sexual drives.[97] Sensual contact acts as a means

96 Cf. Stötzer-Kachold (in Dahlke 1993a, p. 251): 'Das Intellektuelle ist ja auch eine Triebkraft, die ich als sexuelle Triebkraft einsetzen kann, mit deren Hilfe ich lieben lerne'.
97 Cf: 'ich steckte mitten im unterbewußtsein und hatte nicht eine halbe stunde zum verschnaufen > ich steckte in meinem eigenen triebsystem und mußte damit umgehen [...] mein knast war ein eintauchen in ein unterbewußtsein > das mich mit meinen infantilen sehnsüchten konfrontierte (*gl*, p. 71).

of liberation from loneliness, from bodily oppression, and from a situation where narrative identity is threatened. The text 'an treiben' (*zl*, pp. 17-19), for example, combines sexual imagery with a language literally *angetrieben* by female *Triebe* and offers the subject 'die Möglichkeit, in andere Räume der Sprache zu kommen' (Dahlke 1993a, p. 255). The first section of the text is determined by the monotonous rhythm of work: industrial shift work, prison work and everyday routine. Language too is ordered into hours and separated by full stops: 'alles rechnet sich über stunden aus' (*zl*, p. 17). Stifled by this atmosphere of subjection, 'der trieb' becomes 'statthaft unnatürlich' (p. 17).

Like those of 'der wecker ist geklungen', the lyrical subjects of 'an treiben' are alienated from their bodies, their selves, and from one another. The alienation functions through work, through walls, both visible and invisible, through men (entrapped within their own walls) and through a stream of warnings – imperatives that distance the woman from her sexuality:

> heb die hand unter der decke vor, betreibe keine einsamkeit, nimm die hand von dem körper, berührt nicht deine haut, wer sich die triebe gibt, gibt sich auch das leid, nimm die hand von der haut, fühl dich selber nie aus [...] betreibe dich nicht selbst [...] hab keine sehnsucht nach dir selbst (*zl*, p. 18)

Liberation from this lonely drudgery comes with the introduction of the subconscious into the writing. The words used evoke involvement which is both emotional and sensual. The breathless flow of images, separated only by commas, embodies libidinous drives.

The escape from isolation is thus the text itself, the order 'schreib nichts an die wände' (*zl*, p. 18) has been disobeyed, instead there are new orders:

> treib dich endlich aus [...] treib dich selber davon [...] treib den trieb aus [...] rühr dich selber an, mach aus dir eine frau [...] und die triebe machen manchmal aus allen eine frau (*zl*, pp. 18-19)

The text ends with positive statements, 'jede frau hinter einer mauer hat sich selbst erkannt' (*zl*, p. 19), suggesting the potential of liberated female sexuality. The tension present in this text is expressed thematically in the juxtaposition of this utopian element with the negative commands and fear. This is a juxtaposition characteristic of Stötzer-Kachold's best writing. Linguistically it is the vowel shifts of *treib* and *trieb* and the rhymes of *liebe* and *triebe*, or *schreiben* and *treiben*, which convey this tension. The text thus becomes polyvocal, reaching beyond a restrictive GDR interpretation to a wider meaning.

Although Stötzer-Kachold states in interview (Dahlke 1993a, p. 256): 'Ich habe ganz wenig Freud gelesen. Ich habe keine gute Ausbildung in der Hinsicht',[98] her insistence upon the primacy of sexual forces would seem to show a clear debt to Freud's general ideas, rather than any specifics.[99] The frequent contiguity of these drives with death drives reinforces this impression.[100] Stötzer-Kachold links writing with both sex and death in the declaratory text 'das schreiben ist wie mein sexueller trieb' (gl, p. 157):

die höchste noch zu ertragende angst vor der selbstzerstörung
also vor dem tod lieben und schreiben

'frauenknackzeit' (gl, p. 198) also combines these three motifs in a utopian vision:

sex tod und sprache sind drei wege der befreiung von innen nach außen
sex tod und sprache sind möglichkeiten zur ekstase aus dem jammertal der alltäglichkeit

Many of the author's poetic visions also echo Marcuse's (1962) ideals of erotic transcendence or 'libidinal morality' (p. 208), in which, 'the sexual impulses, without losing their erotic energy, transcend their immediate object and eroticise normally non- and anti-erotic relationships between the individuals, and between them and their environment' (p. ix). For Marcuse personal instincts are shaped and ordered by a 'socio-historical world' (p. 12), and it is the 'sex instincts' that 'bear the brunt of the reality principle' (p. 37). The libido is diverted into alienating labour and it is the so-called sexual 'perversions' which represent rebellion against the established order. The body becomes an instrument of pleasure and the monogamic patriarchal family is transformed. Such a transformation is clearly – in the light of Foucault's writing – based upon an understanding of sexual power which functions at a macro- rather than a micro-level. It participates in the 'grand narratives' which postmodernism has questioned and remains vague. Stötzer-Kachold's *Triebe* are, however, not

---

98 Cf: 'als ich 1976 an der ph erfurt die erste unterrichtsstunde in psychologie hatte fragte ich herrn zolner nach freud und er erklärte mir daß freud das unterbewußte erforscht hätte und der sozialismus arbeite mit dem bewußten [...] > von diesem moment an verlor für mich alles an der hochschule vermittelte jegliche form von interesse' (gl, p. 68).

99 References to Freud are occasionally made explicit in the author's work. Cf. 'es gibt dieses unbenannte leben' (gl, p. 160) and 'ich muß über mich schmunzeln' (gl, p. 206).

100 According to Freud, the death drives are inseparable from the sexual. Cf. Stötzer-Kachold (in Kleinschmidt 1989, p. 28): 'Ich weiß: meine guten Texte sind immer dann entstanden, wenn ich todessüchtig angefangen habe'.

always purely abstract. As with the *Sinne*, they too 'entspringen einer sozialen spannung' (*zl*, p. 42).

'mit dem eigenen körper in der hand' (*zl*, p. 27)

Stötzer-Kachold's writing is not only structured by abstract concepts such as love, lust and subconscious drives, but also by concrete bodies and bodily parts. The individual signifiers which she forms into poetry are themselves physical. Similarly, many of the naked figures drawn in *grenzen los fremd gehen* are engaging in some form of sexual practice. Thus the author's art is characterised by 'ein anderes stück leibverantwortung' (*gl*, p. 89). The word *körper* occurs countless times in extremely varied texts and is given primary significance in the writer's visions:

> der körper ein schiff
> der körper eine erde
> der körper ein blatt
> meine vision ein segel (*zl*, p. 27)

Stötzer-Kachold writes, then, against the 'unendlicher krieg der körper' (*zl*, p. 163) – a lack of mutual understanding. Her poetry becomes the solid expression of the physicality which she feels is absent from modern technological societies. Her answer to the accusation 'Berührung ist nur eine Randerscheinung' is 'sich berühren lernen bis man sich spürt' (*zl*, p. 33), her form of communication is artistic and bodily. For Meusinger (1992, p. 367) it is this aspect of Stötzer-Kachold's use of language that sets her apart from her male colleagues:

> Ein wesentliches Moment der Spezifik von Gabriele Kacholds Texten fixiert zugleich den Unterschied zu den Texten männlicher Autoren: Sprachlosigkeit wird bei Gabriele Kachold vor allem überwunden durch die Artikulation über den Körper, vermittels der Sinne.

Despite the fact that this judgement ignores the differences between male writers of the new generation, it does show how important critics consider the physical aspects of Stötzer-Kachold's work to be.

The body is, however, not simply a word in Stötzer-Kachold's prose, it is also page and raw material. Dahlke (1994, p. 157) emphasises this idea throughout her thesis, repeating that: 'die Poetik Gabriele Stötzer-Kacholds geht direkt auf Körpererfahrung zurück, läßt sich allerdings nicht auf ein Schreiben über

160

den Körper [...] reduzieren'. Referring to Weigel (1987, p. 112), Dahlke writes of the 'Körper-Sprache' of Stötzer-Kachold's art, which relies upon establishing a specific relationship between the body and language in order to extend linguistic boundaries. Against the 'kastrierte deutsche sprache' (*gl*, p. 38) the author sets a 'body language', representing the moment:

> wenn die stimme im körper spricht und tanzt und händelaute hat und füßelaute daß körpersprache nicht röcheln oder schreie nur trauer gebiert (*gl*, p. 45)

It is the idea of writing from the body that leads to classifications of this art as authentic. Such classifications imply that the body itself is not understood through encoded representations but as a fixed point of reference.

Language and the anatomy are specifically associated in the almost theatrical dialogue 'als ich auszog meine einsamkeit zu beenden' (*gl*, pp. 40-43), where the body is given a voice of its own. It is personified in the moment of undressing, thus conquering the loneliness of the title. 'Die erste stimme' sees only the superficial:

> das normal entsprechende von oben nach unten
> sich wellende gewohnte sichere notwendige zur funktion zu
> gebrauchende hautfleischknochensystem (p. 40)

'Der körper selbst', on the other hand, sees:

> den willen die kraft die möglichkeit den abstand die zukunft diesen gleichgewohnten körper aufzugeilen aufzustylen verrücktere haltungen eigensinnigere vorgaben der betrachtungsweise (p. 40)

The anonymous voices seem to represent the 'gewohnheitsblick' (p. 40), the body 'embodies', in words, the future. It is the body which talks of love, a concept with which it is inexorably linked. Neither notion is, however, defined or given any specific meaning, for both are myths created within discourse. Thus the relationship of the three voices in this accomplished text is highly ambiguous, as is the position of the 'ich' of the title.

Articulation through the body is also symbolised in countless images of dance. These images determine the rhythm of some of Stötzer-Kachold's most poetic texts. As the author writes:

> der tanz scheint ein adäquates übersetzungsverhältnis von einem komplex körperlicher bewegungs- und sprachmöglichkeiten zu sein tanz ist die schwingung eines körpers mit energieübermittlung zu außenkörpern [...] tanz ist wie schreiben (*gl*, pp. 45-46)

The combination of kinetic and physical energy with writing is one which, as has been shown, is fundamental to Stötzer-Kachold's work. Dance motifs further influence the writer's drawings and her performance art, which is reliant not only on the spoken word, but also on the body. On stage her poetry is almost danced, and this will certainly affect the way in which the erotic elements of the work are understood. As Dahlke (1994, p. 163) notes, 'die Autorin singt und tanzt, flüstert und schreit, juchzt und jammert, stottert und dehnt'. The anatomy is actively brought into the art, the text moves from the page and into physical and vocal expression. In this sense the published work can only be a pale reflection of the live version. The pictures which accompany the text 'spanien - der tanz - der stier' similarly move with the text and reinforce its musicality (*gl*, pp. 43-62). Their sketchiness signals speed and vitality.

The countless allusions to flight employed by the author have a similar function to the dance symbolism of her work. Flight too is bodily and is again, in numerous texts, identified with the sexual and with the artistic. This would seem to offer freedom and, in this respect, is often combined with imagery of madness or schizophrenia. The title of 'zügel los' alone suggests the liberation of flying, which is echoed in the text 'holla die fahrt beginnt' (*zl*, pp. 167-68):

> nimm die zügel spricht das ich zum ich und sei das im jetzt entstandene frühlingsei und hurtig werden die flügel geschlagen hoch fliegt das gebälk alle räume sind mit aufgestanden und ich flieg damit ich ich sei (*zl*, p. 168)

Flight symbolism also recalls French feminist ideas. Hélène Cixous (1976, p. 258), for example, writes that: 'flying is woman's gesture – flying in language and making it fly'. She too links the notion to originality and change.

The emphasis Stötzer-Kachold places upon the body again opens her texts to criticism. Undoubtedly the demand: 'lassen wir einmal den geist zum körper gehen' (*gl*, p. 39) is occasionally taken to essentialist extremes. This is the case in the piece entitled 'diese gestenlosen hände' (*zl*, p. 33), where an embodied and sexual language is reduced to a single verity:

> diese einzige wahrheit der worte ich küsse deine lippen und zeuge dich mit mir in unser beider lust der umschlingung und der wenigen gaben einer ans unendliche erinnernden befriedigung

The body is portrayed as the source of meaning, the mother of words. The religiously entitled text 'ich bin das wort' (*zl*, pp. 136-38) also identifies the self with language, and indeed with Christ. Here the poet has total control, even where the text threatens to escape its boundaries through the use of meaningless words : 'ich bin die grenze ich bin die sprache' (p. 137). The closure of the text with the single concept 'ich' secures this control. However, the corporeal cannot always be relied upon to tell the truth:

steck ich den finger in den mund
bläht sich der bauch und lacht mich zurück
körper wehrt sich gegen mich selbst (*zl*, p. 43)

In this instance the body has acquired an independence and is no longer synonymous with the narrative subject.

Furthermore, whilst concepts such as dance and flight are idealised in Stötzer-Kachold's work they are not always expressed in the poetic form of the texts themselves, which can seem more like a march than a dance. The censure that 'die Grammatikmaschine [scheint] nur noch mechanisch weiterzuarbeiten und in Banalitäten zu enden' (Dahlke 1993b, p. 150) is often voiced by critics, who recognise a contradiction between the desire for the erotic and bland statements which lack any rhythm or sensuality. Certainly this contradiction is often apparent. It is wrong, however, to reject it as solely negative. The alienation that it can produce in the reader's mind exemplifies in poetic form the contradictions and difficulties that women in particular can feel in the attempt to establish a realisable identity. One such conflict is that between the open assertion of female sexuality and the pressures from society that make this assertion dangerous rather than pleasurable. Indeed Dahlke praises other contradictions of Stötzer-Kachold's work, such as that between the auto-biographical 'I' and the breaking up of this unit. She regards this incongruity as more fruitfully and more artistically developed than those of a sexual nature. In an era where patriarchy, notably in the Eastern Germany of the 1990s, is seemingly reasserting its grip, the almost propagandistic style of some of Stötzer-Kachold's later work is, however, necessary. It provides a contrast to the more ambivalent language often used and thus offers a new perspective.

In the attempt to create her own images of women Stötzer-Kachold thus strips the body naked. She repossesses almost every limb and every organ, from the feet upwards. However, within this process the body does not simply function as a site of female pleasure or truth, but also of suffering and disunity. It reflects, then, the problematic and complex connotations of this cultural arte-fact, one 'exploited as an object of knowledge and an element in relations of power' (Foucault 1979, p. 107). Stötzer-Kachold uses her imagery to embody this power struggle – which is both individual and political.

The stomach is the most visible place of reproduction and is thus traditionally linked with female sexuality. In Stötzer-Kachold's writing it is given a central place in the 'new' range of metaphors. No longer merely personal or biological, it becomes the 'home' of social violence and oppression:

> das haus ist mein bauch, ich habe euch den schlüssel dazu gegeben, damit ihr euch die tür öffnen könnt. ihr habt die tür aufgestoßen und die fenster eingetreten, was ihr für brauchbar hieltet habt ihr mitgenommen (*zl*, p. 22)

In this text, entitled 'unbehaust' (*zl*, pp. 22-23), the body does not represent security for a subject with whom it is unified, but rather pain and loss. Hope comes through retreat beyond and outside society, again expressed through bodily imagery and dance:

> meine brüste streicheln die erde vor jedem schritt, bis die lust aufsteigt und die lippen sprengt und die füße spreizt. und die füße tanzen den rhythmus aller zeiten und der geschändete leib ist der brütende leib [...] ich bin die lust, ich bin die frucht (*zl*, p. 23)

The 'ich' of the text is female, she is given breasts and a 'fruitful' womb. The 'ihr' here is defined as masculine through the force of the phallus, which penetrates into the female subject's inner sanctum: 'in den bauch stößt ihr mir euer tanzendes schwert' (*zl*, p. 23). In both cases power is material, in Freudian terms, anatomy is destiny.

A similarly violent penetration was the operation the author underwent in prison due to a wrongly diagnosed extra-uterine pregancy. This experience is also formative in her use of the image of the belly.[101] Pregnancy itself, the expected and conventional connection with the female stomach, is rejected. Stötzer-Kachold's labour pains are those of writing, her texts come from inside her and 'vorgeburtlich' (*gl*, p. 7). The 'bauchschmerzen' which run through the description of the unpublished text 'tag sonnentag' are physically and artistically productive.[102] The poem is a questioning of the feminine ideal which postulates motherhood as normality. The subject, despite her opposing emotions, rejects this role. Connected with pregnancy are images such as the 'nabelschnur' (*zl*, p. 12). The umbilical cord simultaneously evokes both suffering or loss and independence. In the text 'was tut sie' (*zl*, pp. 10-12) the cord is not cut at birth but has to be loosened by the narrator to avoid strangulation. Once more then, this is a particularly suitable icon of conflict.

The *Kind*, whether this be a human child, a lost child or an artistic one, is a central metaphor in Stötzer-Kachold's prose. Often this would seem to represent the author's own childhood, or a more general lost innocence. The dead child, another image which brutally rejects motherhood, suggests abortion.

---

[101] See for example the text 'bauchhöhlenschwangerschaft' (*zl*, pp. 13-14).
[102] See Appendix.

This is a motif which pervades many texts, both as theme and as impetus for language. The text 'an treiben' in *zügel los* (*zl*, pp. 17-19) is echoed in the 'ab treiben' cycle of *grenzen los fremd gehen* (pp. 127-79). The idea of 'ab treiben' becomes a metaphor of 'Abweisung, Nichtannahme durch einen individuellen Mann wie auch durch die DDR-Gesellschaft schlechthin mit ihren verschiedenen Institutionen' (Dahlke 1994, p. 169). Abortion also embodies contradiction, representing both a woman's right to choose – as was emphasised by Morgner – and intrusion into the female body. The meaning of this concept is, in Stötzer-Kachold's prose, highly ambivalent.

If the stomach in Stötzer-Kachold's writing is most obviously the 'Ort des Leidens, Vergewaltigung und Enteignung', then the lips are a powerful 'Symbol der Lust' (Dahlke 1994, p. 159). These two images represent the opposite poles between which the author's prose moves. The mouth is regarded as especially important because it is the immediate source of both speech and the kiss. Morgner uses this icon in order to portray the different characters of Laura and Amanda and to raise issues of how society constructs food, eating and sex in gendered terms. Stötzer-Kachold accords the mouth fundamental symbolic value: 'ich kann mich selbst aus dem mund nehmen und sprechend zeigen' (*gl*, p. 159). It becomes yet another source of a self which is physical, articulate and sexual. Other physical features dwelt upon by the artist include the eyes, the heart, the ears, the nose, the tongue, the feet and the hands. Her writing is determined by 'augenbilder ohrtöne nasengerüche hautgefühle mundgeschmack' (*gl*, p. 193). It is a poetry made sensual by the work of the senses:

Ich gebe meinen ohren händen lider
schlagen zurück mit den lippen
sagen lust
ich hab lust auf mich (Stötzer-Kachold 1989, p. 30)

The cycle of texts entitled 'in der pathologie' (*gl*, pp. 12-16, 92-94, 144-45) literally dissects corpses, the remains of the GDR. In this way the author escapes the confines of state control – *she* now defines the moment 'wenn der körper ein schmerztrauma erlebt' (*gl*, p. 92). In a manner reminiscent of Gottfried Benn's writing every part of the anatomy becomes poetic material, from the bones to the aorta. These texts are the immediate product of Stötzer-Kachold's reaction to the ban of the journal *Sputnik* in the GDR.[103] As with the

---

[103] Cf. Stötzer-Kachold (in Dahlke 1993a, pp. 255-56): 'Das war 1989, als der "Sputnik" verboten wurde. Ich wußte nicht, wie ich reagieren sollte [...] Das war so ein tiefer Schmerz, diese Hilflosigkeit! Dann bin ich in die Pathologie gegangen [...] Da hatte ich

experience of prison it is to the body that she resorts in order to overcome pain. The GDR too becomes a corpse and the meanings of the text thus extend beyond its immediate origins. In 'der wecker ist geklungen' (*zl*, pp. 7-9) it is 'der bauch', 'die hände' and 'das herz' which are the active protagonists of the text. Furthermore, it is *physical* violence that is the answer to the passive subject's 'Sehnsucht': 'Erst die Signale des Körpers führen im Text wieder zu einem direkten Ich-Sagen [...] Der Körper weiß zum Schluß des Textes mehr als das Ich' (Dahlke 1994, pp. 123-24). Similarly, the recognition with which 'an treiben' (*zl*, pp. 17-19) closes comes from hands and eyes which function as the transporters of longing and lust.

The eyes and the heart are words traditionally connected with love and the erotic. The word *Votze*, however, is more often found in a pornographic context, the domain of patriarchal insult. Stötzer-Kachold accords this literary value too, attempting to reclaim all aspects of female sexual language. 'Meine votzen-energie', she states, 'ist ausgangspunkt' ('tag sonnentag'). She (for this is very clearly a female voice), further describes 'meine votzensignale' and 'meine votzenwärme', notions representing a longing for the 'dunklen gedanken der nacht' (ibid). It is the night, particularly the 'unterleib der nacht', that is connected with both the 'cunt' and with truth, female powers *are* the powers of the night, they are auto-erotic and solipsistic, the 'du' addressed by the lyrical subject could represent a lover, but could equally well refer to a part of the self.

However, the parallels constructed between the female genitalia and a natural, powerful entity detract attention from very real problems of rejecting such strong feminine role models as the mother figure. Similar constructions occur in other texts. In 'rap 2' (*gl*, p. 75) genital satisfaction becomes a cipher for a utopian future:

eines tages wird es euch kostenlos geben
wenn das schwanzsein nicht die weltmacht bedeutet
und die votze nicht mit geld befriedigt wird
und die verachtung aus dem bett geworfen ist

In this reverie orgasms hang freely on trees, words dance and love is 'grenzenlos'. The lack of punctuation in the text 'ich möchte dir etwas sagen' (*zl*, pp. 148-50) further suggests that the lyrical subject *is* her vagina:

---

auch in mir zerstückelt, was mich zerstörte [...] Dieser Leichnam DDR... Ich hatte ein eigenes Mittel gefunden, mit der Sache fertig zu werden und darüber schreiben zu können'.

sagt mir der neue körper weich zum harten halten der umklammerung sag mir meine
größe und wer ich bin vagina in jeder festen form abgetastet geliebt geleibt berührt ge-
führt getrügt getragen gesagt ich hab dich lieb und wenn ich wachse dann wächst du
einfach mit (*zl*, p. 150)

Elsewhere the female anatomy is clearly part of nature, a realm which is
Romantically regarded as positive and indeed inspirational:

meine votze der flüssige spalt der die erde auffängt zum
aussenden von fruchtbarkeit
da versackt nichts im gedächtnis meiner rinden
alle überdeckten figuren sind auffindbar
ich vergaß kassandra mein ich anzubieten (*gl*, p. 204)

Such an unquestioning association of the female body and nature is again
problematic. In this text the feminist icon Cassandra appears as a figure who
can be discovered through communion with the vagina. It would seem as if the
female genitalia too can see, even if their message goes unheard.

Although Stötzer-Kachold denies any knowledge of French feminism,[104] the
stylisation of the body, and more specifically, of the vagina, as a source of truth
and self-knowledge does suggest ideas of 'écriture féminine'. In all of Stötzer-
Kachold's work one is constantly reminded of Hélène Cixous's entreaty to
'write your self. Your body must be heard' (1976, p. 250). 'Die sprache ist', for
this writer, not only 'so was zu entwickeln lebendiges' (*gl*, 185), but also 'eine
frau', a sexual woman with whom the author can identify, to the point where
they enjoy a physically sexual relationship:

die sprache ist eine frau
ich streiche an den beinen der frau lang
bis ich ihren spalt berühren kann [...]
ich geh in die frau rein die sprache ist
sage ich zu der frau die gespalten ist [...]
ich bin eine frau mit diesem spalt zwischen den beinen (*gl*, 140)

As Thomas Jung (1995) correctly notes, the female narrator, the female body
and language are here merged into one. However, his assertion that the result is
'die Bestätigung einer individuellen nicht-teilbaren Identität' (p. 22) appears inappropriate, idealising Stötzer-Kachold's own ideal. The choice of the terms
'Spalt', 'Spaltung' and 'gespalten' suggests a split identity, which is reflected,
but not transcended, in the image of the vagina.

104 Cf: 'Hast du Cixous gelesen? Nein, habe ich nicht' (Dahlke 1993a, p. 257).

Moreover, the 'spalt' of the vagina echos the early psychofeminism of Irigaray (1977), where she accords positive significance to woman's 'two lips which embrace continually', and writes: 'in her statements – at least when she dares to speak out – woman retouches herself constantly' (p. 100). Stötzer-Kachold too makes language both female and tactile. She does not, however, problematise this connection in the same way as Irigaray, but rather reduces, thematically and stylistically, the notions of a female aesthetic theorised by French feminist psychoanalytical thought. It is certainly important that women create their own projections. A form of prose too close to biological 'écriture féminine' can, however, become, as in the use of 'Votze', mystical and essentialist. This essentialism may be construed as strategic, but references to 'alte weibliche kräfte und wissenspotentiale' (Stötzer-Kachold 1992, p. 9) serve rather to mystify than to strengthen the feminist message.

Other texts in Gabriele Stötzer-Kachold's work thus use the concept of 'Votze' as a vehicle of critical comment rather than as an essential force of liberation. One of the most successful pieces in *zügel los* is 'die rose ist keine rose ist keine rose ist keine rose' (*zl*, p. 110-13), where opposing speakers create a strangely rhythmic cacophony of clichés, quotations, insults and, almost buried, answers. The term 'Votze' is here used in its more common context and the links with violence are clear:

> die sau gibt es
> die alte votze gibt es [...]
> eine in die fresse gibt es
> ich hau dir eine in die fresse gibt es
> stell dich nicht so an gibt es
> laß mich mal lecken gibt es
> hol mir einen runter gibt es (*zl*, p. 112-13)

If this voice is 'male', the reply is seemingly genderless and detaches the violence evoked from its roots in gender identity: 'es gibt nichts zu beweisen [...] frauen gibt es nicht, männer gibt es nicht' (ibid). In a much more direct and less ambiguous text Stötzer-Kachold opens: 'es kotzt mich an in einer männerwelt voller lieben mädels und bräuten zu leben' (*gl*, p. 98), a world of:

> du alte votze jeden tag wenn ich nach bahnhof nord gehe
> dieses hetzende atmen bevor sie mir an die schulter greifen
> sie wissen es doch
> sie erlauben es sich
> wir erlauben es ihnen (ibid)

In these examples Stötzer-Kachold acknowledges and demonstrates that the foundation of her utopia is also a word full of negative connotations. In her description of 'silvester 92' (*er*, pp. 57-68) on the other hand, 'Votze' is used to comment ironically upon the relations of German reunification:

> ach wir kuscheligen ostmäuschen. meine freundinnen die sich mit meinen freunden trafen und dort am liebsten gleich die erste nacht ihre votzen unter die schwänze hielten um vom köstlichen westsperma etwas abzubekommen (*er*, p. 58).

Elsewhere the 'cunt' is just one in a long list of parts of the body, it appears almost normalised: 'deine schultern an meinem mund dein arsch zwischen meinen fingern dein schwanz in meiner votze' (*er*, p. 9).

In an interview with Birgit Dahlke (1993a, pp. 249-250), Stötzer-Kachold summarises her aims in using expressions such as 'Votzenenergie': 'Es ist so schwer, diese deutsche Männersprache zu benutzen, das versuche ich: als Frau die Sprache zu verändern, bis ich mit ihr leben kann'. Thus, if we are to take her at her word, she is attempting to find a way of positively constructing the female body, and in particular the female sexual organs. As part of this work, Stötzer-Kachold also widens the range of terms available as alternatives to 'Votze'. She writes of 'votzeleien' and uses the adjective 'votzig'. Synonyms for Votze include: 'ritze', 'schoß', 'scheide', 'möse', 'spalt', 'vagina' and even 'schmetterlingslippen'; whereby this last is unusual in its more conventional associations. Graphic images of the vagina reinforce this message. Avoided, however, are any of the more traditional alternatives connected with 'Scham'.

The choice of names for the male sexual organs is less wide, reversing the existing linguistic situation. It includes 'schwanz', 'stock', 'waffe' and 'pimmel'. The traditional Freudian theory which defines woman according to absence, her lack of a penis, is subverted into an ironically phallocentric joke and applied to the ultimate male figure, God himself:

> wenn gott an sich heruntersah hatte er nur einen makel ∞ in seiner mitte war ein loch und das hieß o ∞ gott war unglücklich er war sich schon des männlichen bewußt ∞ [...] herr gott brauchte einen schwanz ∞ also drehte er den pferdeleib um und hatte nun einen schwanz vor sich (*gl*, p. 76)

Indeed, when a woman is given a penis there are no signs of 'envy':

> etwa so war ihr schwanz dick und biegsam und führungslos
> sie hatte keine kontrolle darüber oder wollte es gar nicht ernsthaft (*gl*, 139)

169

Stötzer-Kachold's reappraisal of the female body is thus emphasised through a 'Valeska' style view of the male genitalia – the sex swap is primarily comic.

In its endeavour to reclaim one of the most fundamental aspects of the female body Stötzer-Kachold's writing certainly represents an important contribution to feminist debate, particularly in the GDR of the 1980s. There are, however, difficulties associated with so great an emphasis on an ostensibly biological feature which has been so greatly invested with cultural meanings. Postmodern feminism questions the notion that the body can be encountered outside discursive frames of reference. Judith Butler (1993, p. 2) has convincingly asserted that 'the regulatory norms of 'sex' work in a performative fashion to constitute the materiality of bodies'. She strongly maintains the need to deconstruct not only *gendered* images, but also *sex* itself. If sex cannot remain outside of discursive production, then nor can bodies. The vagina, then, can never exist except where it is materially embodied through discourse. To define women in terms of their sexual attributes may thus simply add to the list of affronts for which there are no readily available male equivalents. Adverse associations do not simply disappear if an abusive term is combined with positive 'energy'. Language is not an independent entity, and words such as 'Votze' cannot simply be 'reclaimed'. As Deborah Cameron (1985, p. 110) has argued, such a process 'can make meanings (and thus cultural beliefs) less monolithic, but it is a continuing struggle'. Stötzer-Kachold's writing forms part of this struggle.

The semantics of sex, as these examples show, are complicated. Stötzer-Kachold also aims to explode 'die alten schamwolken' (*zl*, p. 124) by reclaiming indecent vocabulary for the sexual act, another area of language seemingly dominated by patriarchal bias. Ultimately nothing is sacred, even the church becomes the site of 'rammelei' (*zl*, p. 107). The sparkling range of terms for intercourse concentrates, however, on 'ficken'. The author's 'ficksprache' (*gl*, p. 117) is used in various contexts. She not only postulates a utopia of 'free fucking' (*gl*, p. 198), but also uses the term to represent sex which is dominated by betrayal. Elsewhere 'fickerinnen' (*gl*, p. 73) are definitely female, and a part of human life as normal as eating and drinking.

It is not only the body and its separate parts that are used to create Stötzer-Kachold's physical images. The corporal juices are also vital elements of her descriptions:

> ich hatte nur immer das blut, den zucker, den saft, die tränen. sie fließen aus mir heraus und in mich hinein, sie fließen für mich durch mich und sie löschen alles feuer (*zl*, p. 22)

170

Tears, sperm, urine, 'shit', vomit, sweat and, most predominantly, blood, flow through many of the author's texts, not only those describing her work as a medical assistant.[105] Blood, a specifically female substance when seen in the context of menstruation, is accorded a primary role in both Stötzer-Kachold's prose and her graphic art. Traditionally considered dirty, blood 'drückt gegen meinen körper' (*zl*, p. 30), oozing, in many texts, from inner into outer realities. Here liberation is symbolised in a very different form. It is the release of blood that allows, for example, the subject of 'der wecker' (*zl*, 7-9) to escape the alienation from his/her body. In this case the blood is social, representative not only of personal disorder but also of violence in general.

Violence as exercised by society upon women is thematised through blood in the text 'was tut sie' (*zl*, pp. 10-12). This question and answer dialogue is particularly powerful, the uncharacteristically short sentences build up a tense and frightening scene, reminiscent of that in 'der wecker'. Psychological pressure is translated into the physical:

> immerhin hat sie das messer.
> gottseidank das messer.
> es hilft ihr.
> sie erbricht sich.
> es hängt aus ihrem mund.
> und aus ihren beinen fließt das blut.
> sie mußte sich davon befrein.
> es hat sie gewürgt.
> zu eng, es hat sie erdrückt.
> es hat sie getötet.
> ausgelöscht.
> sie tut sich nichts anderes an, als was ihr schon angetan ist (ibid).

The sudden change, at the end of this text, to the first person and to prose emphasises the fact that this woman could stand for any female. The knife recurs in other texts exploring blood. Self-mutilation, even in the sense of giving oneself bleeding spots, becomes another form of violence portrayed. Pain can be enjoyed because it is bodily. Dahlke (1994, p. 161) compares these masochistic images with those constructed by Elfriede Jelinek. She credits both writers' work with the successful 'Entmystifizierung des weiblichen Körpers' and the 'Inbesitznahme des enteigneten Leibes'. However, whereas Jelinek's work shocks readers through its directness, and thus always remains socially

---

[105] Stötzer-Kachold trained as a 'medizinisch-technische Assistentin' after leaving school and before studying for her Abitur at evening school.

relevant, in many of Stötzer-Kachold's texts female blood is shrouded in mystery, unable to fulfil any political, or indeed artistic, purpose.

The cycle of texts set in Spain, for example, uses bull's blood in order to identify human and animal subject:

> ein getroffenes vieh sinkt stinkt blutet schwitzt pinkelt
> hängt die zunge ich vieh stinke bin ddr gebrannt [...] ich tier triefend mit der vergangen-
> heit gebrannt (*gl*, p. 59)

The blood provokes questions about power, both social control and inner 'Kraft'. In this instance it is, however, a seemingly natural, female force:

> geschlecht götze tod opfer oder so ein mythos von dem blut was den boden befruchtet
> und wenn wir doch bluten ohne zu sterben sind wir doch keine stiere frauen daseinig
> breitbeinig den boden befruchtend (*gl*, p. 62)

The 'myth' of the connections between blood and 'Mother' Earth is emphasised again in the image which accompanies the text 'vor 11 jahren entlassen' (*gl*, p. 94). This shows a woman lying naked with blood flowing from root-like sources in her body through her vagina and into her hand. It appears to illustrate a cycle of life. Once again, the artist does not always offer this as a fictional creation, but often as an eternal truth.

Just as the sexual drives as theme are paralleled in a sexually driven language, so too do the sexual juices produce a flowing style. As Bethke (1991, p. 208), despite some exaggeration and a reliance on authorial intention, notes: 'Ich denke auch, daß Dein Schreiben körperlich ist, weil Du selber sagst, daß Du es zuerst unkontrolliert herausfließen läßt – wie Blut, Tränen und andere Säfte'. She is referring to Stötzer-Kachold's long sentences, the images which dominate the writing and the tangled web of words. This 'brustmilchmeer' (*zl*, p. 132) of female substances again suggests statements by Cixous. In her 'écriture féminine' the woman 'writes in white ink' (1976, p. 251), the white ink of the mother's milk. For both writers blood is as vital a juice as milk, linked to the sexual drives and to the notion of writing as birth. Sexuality, in both cases, is depicted as essential and natural, rather than as a social and cultural construct.

Stötzer-Kachold's writing is, then, motivated by the senses, by a longing for love, by productive sexual forces and by every aspect of the female body. It is also satiated with images of the orgasm. The use of this theme, together with ideas of masturbation and lesbianism, further demonstrates both the possibilities and the more questionable aspects of the author's work. Where Morgner had devoted one chapter to the female orgasm, Stötzer-Kachold devotes her writing to it, the 'harmony' suggested in *Beatriz* becomes celestial. In interview with Meusinger (1992, p. 374) the author emphasises what orgasm means for her, a meaning which is feminist in the widest sense of the word: 'die Frauen müssen um ihren Orgasmus kämpfen. Er ist wichtige Voraussetzung für Kraft und Identität'. Giving women a voice includes release from imposed frigidity, which comes through orgasm. Stötzer-Kachold's is thus a utopia in which 'der orgasmus frei am gabenbaum hängt' (*gl*, p. 75). As Dahlke (1994, p. 167) comments: 'der Orgasmus [wird] zum Symbol der Selbstbefreiung und Selbstannahme schlechthin'.

The text 'reflexion 1' (*zl*, pp. 41-42) opens with an explosive statement, defining this theme and expressing the author's determining presence:

> ich weiß daß, wenn ich mich mit dem orgasmus der frau beschäftige, ich immer meinen orgasmus meine, und mit orgasmus genauer das sich in sich selbst vollkommen freigemachte, die loslösung jeglicher verkrampfung, die synchron läuft mit der lösung äußerer verkrampfungen.

Orgasm is presented as the culminating moment of 'selbsterkennung, selbstübereinstimmung, selbstüberwindung', resulting in 'ichüberwindung durch ichfindung'. The divisions between body and mind are transcended in this spiritual experience. A similar idea is expressed in the text 'als ich auszog meine einsamkeit zu beenden' (*gl*, pp. 40-43) which exhorts female readers to 'live' their orgasms. The text 'kopfschmerzen bereiten neue denkwege vor' (*zl*, pp. 109-10) again analyses the relationship between mind and body through orgasm. In this case the experience is definitely female:

> hat der intellekt was mit orgasmus zu tun
> das werde ich mir als frage aufschreiben
> das werde ich mir als frau aufschreiben.

'in sich blicken' (*gl*, pp. 137-38), almost an essay, discusses with analytical clarity the differences between the vaginal and the clitoral orgasm.[106] The clitoral is an outer orgasm, the vaginal is an inner sensation, an awakening. Here again orgasm is about self-discovery, and writing the self.

---

[106] The anal orgasm is also a theme, this would, on the other hand, appear to be more about violence than truth:
  'erhielten sie schon einmal den analen orgasmus
  warn sie schon mal von vorn und hinten angespießt
  das ist da räumliche fickdreieck
  das oberdeck zum unteren fickdreieck' (*gl*, pp. 190-191).

The title of 'in sich blicken' suggests the connection between orgasm and masturbation, another sexual motif which the author accords essential value and power to transform:

> wenn ich onaniere eröffnet sich mir ein imaginärer raum
> die anatomie eines blütenstengels
> das bild einer mit licht und schalmeien gefüllten unendlichkeit
> der orgasmus eröffnet mir einen imaginären raum
> und die bilder unserer vorvergangenheit sind ahnungen (*zl*, p. 40)

Thus Dahlke (1994, p. 160) claims that Stötzer-Kachold begins to seek salvation 'nicht in der Veränderung der Partnerbeziehung [...] sondern darin, sich selbst sein eigener Maßstab zu werden, sich selbst zu entdecken und anzunehmen'. The 'Sehnsucht nach Lust' does not, as Dahlke further argues, replace the 'Sehnsucht nach Liebe'. It is, however, clear in many texts, particularly those of *grenzen los fremd gehen*, that masturbation becomes the path to, a purer orgasm, infinite escape from fear, where, 'das dasein wird wahrer' and 'erreichbarkeit stöhnt auf' (*gl*, p. 35):

> so leg ich mich noch mal allein ins bett
> zum ruhefassen
> zum ausruhnsehn
> zum wartefassen der unendlichkeit [...]
> den orgasmus habe ich nur mit mir alleine
> die worte sind alle beschissen die mich von der tat wegtragen (ibid).

The pictorial image which shows a woman examining her naked body with a mirror, within which are reflected both her eyes and her vagina, symbolises similar beliefs (*gl*, p. 86).[107] Even Eve has to make do without her partner:

> eva reckt sich ohne adam
> befriedigt sich selbst an diesem morgen (*gl*, p. 219)

Our sacred image of Eve is thus challenged, sexually redrawn to alienate the reader, forcing her/him to re-evaluate personal sexual prejudices. Motifs traditionally considered within the realm of pornography are invested with literary value. The reader is enabled to take such themes seriously, and to do so from a point of view which is constructed as female. Female protagonists do not

---

[107] Mirror imagery in Stötzer-Kachold's writing is generally connected with the problematic search for identity.

function as objects providing sexual pleasure and knowledge for men, but for themselves. Again, this re-vision is undoubtedly of importance if women are to break the silence surrounding their own sexuality – as the author discovers: 'über die orgasmusfrage kam ich schnell im gespräch mit anderen frauen zu ihren problemen' (*gl*, p. 138). However, where this pleasure is presented as an essential value in itself the writing, as has been shown, becomes clichéd. The route to vaginal orgasm would appear, for example, to involve a rejection of rings, (whether these are the chains of prison or of marriage is unclear), and suspension of time:

> bevor ich zum vaginalen orgasmus kam mußte ich die uhr ablegen die ein metallring um meinen linken arm ist (*gl*, p. 131)

Sexuality is, therefore, removed from history. The text 'in sich blicken' (*gl*, p. 137-38) similarly correlates orgasm with truth, with no analysis of what this concept involves:

> mit dem orgasmus wollte ich an eine innere gefühlswelt herankommen die sich nicht mehr belügen läßt also fühllos = belogen   gefühl = wahrheit über wirklich wesentliche zusammenhänge (ibid.)

One cannot, however, reject Stötzer-Kachold's writing with the simple comparison that where Irmtraud Morgner, as a Marxist, continually sets sexuality in a social context, the younger writer fails to do so. Interwoven with generalising texts on the power of the female orgasm or the vagina, are comments and poetry which challenge her own simplified constructions. Truth, for example, is relativised where the author writes 'was ist die beweisbarkeit von wahrheit? andere wahrheiten' (*gl*, p. 124). Through the use of both language and ambivalent imagery a productive contradiction arises between texts which rely on innate meanings and those which deliberately refuse to fix significance. Where issues such as masturbation, orgasm and one's own sexuality are problematised, Stötzer-Kachold's prose is successful.

The state of orgasm is a complex issue and as such is not always easily portrayed. In 'reflexion 1' (*zl*, pp. 41-42), as in other texts, the equally abstract ideas of 'geilheit' and 'brunst' become important elements of the description, hindering simple interpretation. 'geilheit' represents 'wachheit' and 'umwelt-bezogenheit'; 'bis zum spüren des reinsten und organischsten, klarsten orgasmusses' (p. 42). 'brunst' on the other hand is associated with 'verwischung, verwässerung, versumpfung':

> brunst ist die höchste form des sich ständigen verlierenkönnens und hingebenkönnens.
> sie ist vollkommen brutal gegen jegliche außenwelt, setzt sich über vorhandene persön-
> liche und gesellschaftliche konstellationen verantwortungslos hinweg (ibid)

In the text 'nächstes jahr ist wieder frühling' Stötzer-Kachold writes of the
'neu[es] land der brünste' (*zl*, p. 102). The 'new land' suggested in 'reflexion 1'
is not simply an inner vision, but necessarily social. The 'wechsel einer
gruppen-moral-alters-oder traditionsschicht' (*zl*, p. 42) with which the work
closes uses the terminology of the social sciences to create a vision that moves
from the 'inner' to the 'outer' reality. This is a much more subtle and imaginative rendering of the issues than the simple statements of 'in sich blicken'.
Similarly, although Stötzer-Kachold admires the 'tanz mit christina hoyos' for
the freedom expressed therein and once again posits masturbation as vital to
self-knowledge, she recognises too that the dance also constructs a female body
as an object of social display:

> es geht alles über eigenliebe onanie zur kenntnis des eigenen körpers zur sprache des
> eigenen körpers zur lust bis sie es nach außen gibt und damit bild kultur geworden ist
> mit der preisgabe der selbstgewonnenen sexualität ist sie ein gesellschaftliches angebot
> (*gl*, p. 49)

The short piece 'anpassungsorgasmus' (*gl*, p. 79) also combines sexual vision
with appreciation of the real. The author juxtaposes a column of the forms of
orgasm she critically rejects with a utopian column, headed by 'widerstands-
orgasmus' and ending with one word, 'neu':

anpassungsorgasmus	widerstandsorgasmus
hinlegeorgasmus	drauflegeorgasmus
reflexionsorgasmus	futuroorgasmus
mitmachorgasmus	gegenmachorgasmus
abwarteorgasmus	vorlauforgasmus
schreiorgasmus	lachorgasmus
schweigeorgasmus	redeorgasmus
alt	neu

The 'alt' column, deliberately repetitive, sums up the stereotypical sexual
choices on offer for women. The use of words such as 'anpassung', 'mit-
mach(en)' and 'schweige(n)' further suggests that women are expected to
conform to these choices. The 'neu' column offers, in vocabulary and in shape,
an alternative to each form of 'alt' orgasm – widerstand rather than anpassung,
drauflegen rather than the missionary hinlegen, gegenmachen rather than
mitmachen, and reden (and by implication schreiben) rather than schweigen. In

176

a literary context this 'redeorgasmus' is perhaps the most important. The 'alt' side of the orgasm is flat on the page, straight and linear. The repetition of the 'sch' sounds in 'schrei' and 'schweig' emphasizes the boredom of this format. The shape of the second column on the other hand suggests the muscle contractions of climax or the laughter of the more exciting 'lachorgasmus'.

It has been claimed by critics that much of Stötzer's writing exhausts itself in these gestures of fluidity, particularly as the reader, schooled in conventional sentence structure, will subconsciously set his/her own punctuation anyway. In the case of this particular text, however, it seems hardly reasonable to argue, as does Dahlke (1994, p. 167), that the author is guilty of 'stoischen Gleichförmigkeit und mechanischen Aufrechnerei'. This argument discounts the experimentation with layout which is so intrinsic to this piece, which can be read backwards or forwards, horizontally or vertically. A further criticism is that the text reproduces mainstream cultural stereotypes. The first column of the text can be read as 'male', dominant and indeed determining of the 'female' reaction to it. This reaction, the 'neu' column, is utopian and as such is dependent on the Romantic notion of the feminine as a form of human salvation. Whilst this interpretation sheds interesting light upon the passage, it relies upon an imposed split into masculine and feminine which is not necessarily present. The text thematises possible female reactions to orgasm and organizes them into two patterns – the male is only implied. Here then the erotic has become a part of language structure.

The connection between masturbation and orgasm is unsettled, rather than simplified, within the topic of lesbianism, which received relatively little attention in mainstream GDR literatures. Once again Stötzer-Kachold dramatically expands upon the portrayals offered by Morgner, Wolter and others. In the text 'bin ich schwul' (zl, p. 38), for example, the lyrical subject questions her own sexuality:

> bin ich schwul
> weil den ersten wirklichen orgasmus
> habe ich mir selber gemacht
> ohne stock und schwanz eines fremden
> geschlechts

Sex with women is seen as 'unerreichbar', as a reflection of masturbation. The mirror imagery here recalls that of 'an treiben' (zl, pp. 17-19) and again raises issues of identity:

177

bin ich schwul
weil ich die schönen unerreichbaren profile liebe
die sich nie frontal zu mir kehren
und wenn sie es tun
bin ich in der erkenntnis ihrer verdoppelung zurückgestoßen

Sex with men, however, is linked with power, obedience, fear and domination. Men are characterised through their penis, through sperm and the power which this gives them. Women are beautiful but powerless, threatened with 'den drohnenhaften tod auf den abfallhalden der menschheit'. Thus, although the questioning gesture with which each of the three strophes begins can suggest an open attitude to the problems examined, the poem is in fact closed through the reductionalist use of clichés. Beyond the formal shape there is little lyrical work within the language of the text, and the generalisations are therefore allowed to dominate the poetry.

The question 'soll ich meine tochter lesbisch machen um sie im frauenreich zu halten' in the text 'ich tanze auf des messers schneide' (*gl*, pp. 32-33) again works with generalised categories rather than differentiated individuals: 'nach links die frauenseite nach rechts die männerseite'. A later, much more definitive, text would appear to answer this question, lesbian sex too is now identified with power:

ich habe aufgehört lesbisch zu denken
ich kann körper identifizieren
aber ich mache keine machtsprünge mit
von loch zu loch (*gl*, p. 170)

The recognition that power is involved in any relationship is of course necessary, as is the deliberation surrounding reactions to this recognition. Crude imagery and the reliance on generalising phrases such as 'wir frauen' or 'sein machtsystem' (*gl*, p. 198) appear out of place in poetic prose.

A text which more successfully, and more ambiguously, examines the theme of female homosexuality is 'undink' (*zl*, pp. 20-21), a revision of the Undine legends in which Undine rejects the 'schwanzleib': 'sie begegnet sich selbst und ist sich der schwanz im bauch'. Her 'going' thus appears as a form of androgynous self-discovery which is primarily reliant upon the waves of the sea, rather than human subjects. As in the case of Wolf's *Kassandra* it is self-discovery through rejection of the writings about this female figure, creating an unheard of rewriting, as the title suggests. The exclamation 'wenn du gehst undine, dann sag undine, daß du gehst' (p. 21) is the strong and determined answer to Bachmann's rather more melancholy *Undine geht*. A further reference to this text occurs in 'zellentraum' in *grenzen los fremd gehen* (pp. 182-83). The lesbian sex portrayed here takes place 'bei undine' and 'es ist also knast' (p. 182). Stötzer-Kachold's experiences of female prison, where she claims to have discovered female sexuality, include those of lesbian sex. In the text 'mein einzigster innigster todeswunsch' (*gl*, pp. 86-89) she describes these experiences:

> sie kannten sich aus allen knasts der ddr her und sie riefen ihre namen sie tuschelten sich ihre jahresquoten hinter den rücken zu sie liebten sich hinter aufgehängten woll-decken sie liebten sich durch zerschlagenen scheiben hindurch (p. 86)[108]

The text 'an treiben' (*zl*, pp. 17-19) circles around this expression of female sexuality, the writer's own sexuality, and the social taboos connected with lebianism which are fixed in linguistic commands. Through the confusion both of lyrical subjects and of images, the theme of homosexuality remains, in this highly compact and well constructed text, problematic.

If 'undink' plays with literary traditions, 'ich war heute nacht' (*zl*, p. 154) repeats the process with English traditions. As Eve is shown masturbating, so the Queen of England becomes bisexual. The somewhat schizophrenic Elizabeth II appears as a friendly housewife, proud of her pre-War television set and dressed in a grey apron, yet also a sex-crazed granny who tells the writer:

> daß sie jetzt jeden nimmt und jede nimmt
> die zu ihr ins reich kommt um mit ihnen zu schlafen
> weil das die einzige dosis leben ist die sie noch kriegen kann
> die alte königin von england also lesbisch auch

The reference to lesbianism in this grotesque context has the effect of dramatically breaking the taboos voiced in 'an treiben'. The second message of the piece is, once again, the image of sex as life, as a means to discovery, as relief from routine. This is a message that can, in this case, only be revealed in dreams. The writer must leave the garden backwards, the scene closes in the traditional secrecy of the castle. The heirs to the crown, representatives of the future, remain untouchable and, although in bed, 'angezogen' and 'ausge-wachsen' rather than '*er*zogen' or '*er*wachsen'. Routine and taboo, presented here as a deformity, reign.

---

[108] According to Ursula Sillge (1991, p. 19), the discussion of homosexuality within the context of prison experiences, as opposed to 'normal' life, was relatively common in the GDR. In this way lesbianism was clearly portrayed as 'unnatural'. In Stötzer-Kachold's prose, however, the subject occurs in other contexts also.

Prose which challenges sexual taboos as strongly as this was not common in GDR literatures. Stötzer-Kachold's texts entitled 'reflections' thus differentiate between her form of artistic debate with society and that produced in the majority of contemporary women's writing: 'in allen gegenwärtigen frauenliteraturen treffe ich die äußeren formen der frustration, sie sind gesellschaftlich, politisch, traditionsgebunden, geschlechtsbezogen' ('reflexion 1' *zl*, p. 41). Concrete social phenomena, specific cases of female suffering in a patriarchal society, were typical themes in GDR writing by women of the 1970s and 1980s. In this respect Morgner's Laura is a classic protagonist. Stötzer-Kachold too, however, concentrates in places on the negative sides of female sexual experience, deformed by patriarchy as it exists in the present. The visions of 'reflexion 1' and other texts stand in sharp contrast to writing which concentrates upon the inability to communicate, the oppression of women through society's moral codes, direct violence perpetrated against women, male impotence, betrayal and the incestuous quality of the literary scene in the GDR.

The definitively entitled text 'ich suche nicht mehr den orgasmus' (*gl*, pp. 80-81) thus resolutely rejects the idea of self-discovery through the sexual:

> ich suche nicht mehr den orgasmus Δ ich suche verdammt noch mal mein geschlecht Δ das geschlecht der frauen ist hinter bildern der männer über frauen gemacht haben verschwunden (p. 80)

Here the author focuses instead on exposing some of the dominant images created for Western women, images encoded in shopping bags, prams, washing machines and nappies, as well as the unanswered insults of 'auf der straße heh alte'. The facts of the present, rather than the visions of an imagined future, are that:

> mein geschlecht hat seine worte verloren männer raubten sein verständnis Δ mein geschlecht geht den männerbildern nach und wird das auge des mannes treffen [...] mein geschlecht ist so auf ein unwissendes öffentliches jugend und gebäralter reduziert daß den alten die lippen blüten (p. 81)

Sex is reduced, for women, to the work of reproduction rather than pleasure, a notion repeatedly denounced, as for example in 'eine rede' (*gl*, p. 101-103), where after a hard day's toil a woman is still expected to toil again in bed, a task which represents not desire but comfort for the man. The repetition of, and insistence upon, 'my sex' in texts such as this is extremely powerful. The poetry becomes directly feminist and oppositional.

The poetic force of 'die rose' (*zl*, pp. 110-13) also creates a dismal image of society. The constant emphasis upon the negative article rhythmically hammers home the hatred that can dominate in relationships between the sexes and the denial of the female that takes place within phallocentric communities: 'eine frau ist keine frau ist keine frau' (zl, p. 110). In a world in which the woman has been silenced, nothing exists for her, there is no communication and no female orgasm. Here the leitmotif suggests disharmony and aggression:

> es gibt den orgasmus nicht beim ersten mal
> es gibt den orgasmus nicht beim zweiten mal
> der orgasmus der frau kommt nach dem ersten zweiten dritten vierten orgasmus des mannes und den fünften orgasmus gibt es nicht (p. 111)

What do exist are stereotypes and clichés, insults and opinions about women which reaffirm an artificial male superiority. There are also whores, women whom men can buy, despite the fact that in a communist society there is supposedly no private property. The language Stotzer-Kachold uses is again uncompromising, and reflects the real world with which she is dealing in this text, as opposed to the utopia painted in 'reflexion 1'. Crude sexual slang has taken over, the simple respect of 'bitte' and 'danke' 'gibt es nicht'.

Perhaps the most striking criticism of patriarchy occurs in the text 'ich rufe die nachträume' (gl, pp. 130-31), where the clitoris is not connected with orgasm or masturbation, but with genital mutilation. The momentum of this piece comes not only from the dramatic scenes portrayed but also the speed with which the unpunctuated and assonant language tumbles over itself:

> klitoris angeritzt klitoris ausgemerzt schamlippen abgeschnitten und dann zugenäht das kind mit einer kleinen öffnung für urin blut und später schwanz (p. 131)

The harsh sounds provided by the affricates 'zt' and 'tt' evoke the sense of painful cutting. The fact that it is the mother who repeatedly 'lechzt mit der kastrationsscherbe in der hand' (p. 130) makes the depiction yet more powerful. Here then woman carves her child into adult sexual object:

> die mutter schneidet dem kindmädchen das kind ab von jetzt ab erwachen schmerz und erwachsensein das loch zeigt dem penis den muttermund | verdammt und zugenäht (p. 131)

The unusual punctuation here emphasises the sewing together, the closure. The use of vocabulary such as 'ja jah jah jah jah' (ibid) vivdly suggest both the screams of the young girl and the tacit acceptance, the 'yes', of her mother and of society.

The construction woman as object is again criticised through the sexual themes of rape and pornography. Rape is clearly represented as violence in the text 'staatliche gewalt' (*gl*, pp. 148-49), violence which would appear to be sanctioned by the state.[109] Indeed in a play on the words 'gewalt' and 'gewählt' the state representatives become 'gewählten vergewaltigern' (p. 148). The specific examples of this violence given are the death threats to Salman Rushdie and Honecker's policy of shooting to kill at the border. In 'texastraum' (*gl*, pp. 99-100) Stötzer-Kachold describes:

> ein wirkliches pornogeschäft in form einer normalen kneipe und an der wand ständig die heißesten pornofilme sex in allen stellungen außer der anderen frau gibt es keine frauen nur männer (p. 99)

The men are audience, the women the exist only on screen, a role which the writer decisively and visually resists: 'ich bin kein schwanzverlängerungs-mittel' (*gl*, p. 121). The wave of interest in pornographic images in the former GDR after the *Wende* may have influenced the dominance of this theme in Stötzer-Kachold's second collection.[110] She defines the pornographic as an abstract expression of male fear of female sexuality and recognises that there is thus no easy legal answer to the problem. As a writer with personal experience of what censorship can mean she demands the 'abschaffung der pornografie-gesetze unter einhaltung der gesetze der verführung minderjährige betreffend' (*gl*, p. 182). Here her work, which could itself be labelled pornographic, recog-nises the problems of definition of sexual terms.

Stötzer-Kachold's depictions of rape and pornography are often directed at men themselves and can become harsh rather than analytical or poetic. Impotence too is a theme which is often used simply in order to criticise men. The text 'mit den männern' (*zl*, p. 37) is a tirade against men who are not only impotent, but also alcoholics and misogynists. It describes:

> das wenige was sie tun und das viele was sie wollen
> die eine frau die sie nicht befriedigen können und die vielen
> wechselnden an denen sie sich rächen mit impotenz

'Gegen' would seem more of an appropriate preposition for the title in this case. Male impotence is emphasised again and again in Stötzer-Kachold's writings and is associated with the negative ideas of violence, fear and betrayal.

---

[109] For further examples of rape as theme or idea see also 'ischtar - eine persiflage' (*gl*, pp. 84-85) and many texts in *zügel los*.

[110] See especially the 'amsterdamer tagebuch' texts (*gl*, pp. 197-212).

The theme of betrayal runs through all of Stötzer-Kachold's work. It not only occurs in a sexual context but it is also an integral part, for example, of the author's prison texts. It is both personal and social, the lyrical subject is betrayed by 'freundinnen und feindinnen' (*gl*, p. 60), by her former husband, by men in general and by the State, epitomized in the institution of the *Stasi*. Her 'ewige geschichte des betrogenwerdens' (*gl*, p. 61), is experienced through the body and in images of sexuality: 'körperlos gewesen ich im unterleib betrogen Δ ich an meinen brüsten betrogen Δ ich mit deinen lippen denkend zensur' (*gl*, p. 179). Censorship here refers both to cultural policies in the GDR and, more widely, to the oppression of the female in patriarchy. The theme of betrayal is particularly strong in the autobiographical texts of *erfurter roulette* where the reader is confronted with detailed and concrete acts of treachery, usually concerning friends who have reported on the author for the *Stasi* or who have had relationships with her husband. Many of these texts can best be interpreted as an attempt by Stötzer-Kachold to rewrite her identity following the pain of having read her *Stasi* files.

Stötzer-Kachold describes the GDR as a state of terror and treachery. The secret police, the administrators of this terror, existed because of the willingness of collaborators to betray others. Towards such collaborators Stötzer-Kachold is understandably bitter, in interviews and in her earlier prose too, as in 'portrait j.s.' (*gl*, pp. 8-10), 'muttertagbericht' (*gl*, pp. 172-77) or 'auf den gothaer marktplatz' (*gl*, p. 104), where the narrator feels:

eine wut angesichts der internierungspläne der ddr-stasi 1989
angesichts der waffenlederhüllen unterhosengleich in der
männerstasi erfurt abgepenist

In this text the *Stasi* is clearly regarded as a male institution. Betrayal is gendered, as the dedication to the text 'rap 2', 'an alle männer die mich einmal verraten oder betrogen haben' (*gl*, p. 75), also shows. The author (1993, p. 130-31) thus writes of her experiences with the *Stasi* in terms of biology:

Gelang das Kriminalisieren oder das Definieren als politisch staatsfeindlich nicht, begann das Biologisieren. Sosehr sie bei mir nach einem politischen Anlaß zur Verurteilung als Staatshetzerin suchten und sie nicht finden konnten, (post-1977, BVL) sosehr versuchten sie mich als Frau zu sexualisieren und zu idiotisieren.

This particular 'Biologisieren' was made easier for the secret police because of the nature of Stötzer-Kachold's feminist art.

Part of the psychology of the disloyalty of the *Stasi* men is expressed by the writer in explicitly sexual terms. Of Sascha Anderson, for example, she says (in

Lautert 1992, p. 9), 'Man nannte ihn ja nicht umsonst den König des Prenzlauer Bergs; die Frauen dieser Literaten hat er meistens beschlafen, was er irgendwann den Männern erzählt und damit die Beziehungen zerbrochen hat'. More generally she argues that on the one hand the *Stasi* had feared sexuality, yet on the other it had used sex as a means to dominate and destroy. Men were thus allowed to have affairs as part of their 'work', women were not. In Stötzer-Kachold's prose this idea is similarly expressed:

> stasi weiß die fremdgängereien der männer
> ein kleineres delikt
> hauptsache die frauen wissen es nicht
> stasi der kumpan
> frauen wie immer die dummgehaltenen betrogenen (*gl*, p. 106)

Fremdgehen here is not used in the positive, challenging sense of the title grenzen los fremd gehen. In this case it evokes the more traditional sense of lack of fidelity.

The figure and the name of Sascha Anderson denote not only the Stasi but also the Prenzlauer Berg Szene with which he was so famously connected. This too is characterised by Stötzer-Kachold as a sphere not just of literary readings, but mainly of sexual betrayal and incestuous relationships:

> v. schlief mit a. der vorher mit m. geschlafen hatte
> m. schlief mit e. der vorher mit v. geschlafen hatte
> e. schlief mit a. die vorher mit r. geschlafen hatte
> v. schlief mit r. der vorher mit a.g. geschlafen hatte
> g. schlief mit r. der vorher mit a. geschlafen hatte
> a. schlief mit e. der vorher mit m.v. geschlafen hatte
> e. liest öffentlich neben g.
> der stöpsel ist gezogen
> die brühe kann auslaufen (*gl*, p. 132)

Names and personalities are unimportant, reduced to letters in a sexual game. The verb 'schlafen' dominates, 'lesen' is accorded only one line of the poem. This 'public' activity is minor compared to the 'private'. It is no coincidence that the masculine definite article dominates here, as men did in the *Szene*.

The text 'das gesetz der szene' (*gl*, pp. 133-36) also emphasises that the law of this jungle is betrayal, betrayal by 'lochbrüder' and 'schwanzschwester'. The 'scene' here could also represent GDR society or society in general, due to the associative process employed. 'The fruits of fucking' and the 'sexualised linguistic community' (Simpson, p. 10) are two of the major motifs of this text.

The version printed in *Kontext* 5 (March 1989, in Metelka 1990, pp. 64-72), was more openly sexual. Here, for example, 'das gesetz der szene' is also: 'impotent / unter orgasmussuche wird jedes bett niedergemacht [...] sex ist überall' (p. 65). Neologies later rejected include 'astschwänze', 'stock-schwänze', 'schnellschrumpfschwänze' and 'dampferschwänze' (ibid), terms which characterise the phallocentric community by its most important attribute. Even the alphabet, the foundation of language, is a sexual one, from 'a' to 'z' each letter has a 'sexuell' equivalent (pp. 71-72).

The generalising nature of some of Stötzer-Kachold's statements on betrayal have led to the rejection of her work as radically feminist. Power here is often expressed as the monopoly of certain macro-sections of society, rather than as a complex web exercised dynamically in the Foucauldian sense. Stötzer-Kachold's lyrical subject is continually misled, she herself would appear to be totally innocent and powerless. Incisive critique can thus become endless complaint, as for example in the repetition of:

ich bin die betrogene frau
ich bin die belogene frau
ich bin die beklaute frau
ich bin die verhaftete frau
ich bin die exmatrikulierte frau
ich bin die verlassene frau
ich bin die ausgetauschte frau (*gl*, p. 154)

The undisguised message of such pieces begins to appear pointless, even if undoubtedly liberating in the sense of giving women a voice. A possible reading will merely confirm the image of woman as passive victim. Such a portrayal rarely leads to identification and does not aid understanding of the complexity of sexuality. Repetitive complaint is, however, only one aspect of Stötzer-Kachold's writing. Often within the same text a reader is offered more impressive and powerful critique, skilfully juxtaposed with alternative visions of the future. Women are thus also afforded a chance to resist the role of martyr, to claim the status of sexual subject, as the author has done in her prose.

The awareness of the complex relationship between inner and outer realities, between reality and language and beween utopia and critique is especially prominent in Stötzer-Kachold's use of dreams. The author's symbolic *Triebe* are not her only debt to the discourse of psychoanalysis, especially where her dream sequences are of a sexual nature. Here she analyses her conscious experiences through the subconscious, constructing fiction from a form of reality:

B.D: Sind die Träume im selben Buch (*gl*, BVL) reale Träume oder 'konstruierte'?
G.S-K: Wirkliche.
B.D. Du erinnerst dich also so genau an deine Träume?
G.S-K: Ja. Die muß ich morgens aufschreiben, sonst habe ich sie vergessen. (Dahlke, 1993a, p. 256)

The 'real' dreams do, in some cases, correspond to autobiographical events. The short dream depicted in 'erfurt - mein mittelalter' (*gl*, pp. 16-32), for example, is interwoven with an autobiographical account and is clearly related to the sexual anxieties of the lyrical subject:

> ich bin in einem raum eingesperrt habe ein büßerhemd an in der ecke liegt stroh die tür geht auf d. kommt rein er schläft mit mir während er das tut sind an den wänden viereckige kleine löcher sie gehen auf und ich sehe dahinter die gesichter aller seiner verwandten die nicken und gucken ob es auch gut ist (*gl*, p. 21)

Primarily this imagery appears as the internalising of the writer's fears, notably concerning d's mother. It further suggests not only the prison experiences of the author, but the wider feeling of sex as imprisoning when regarded as sin, the traditional view propagated by Christian morality. Set in italics this dream is accorded a specific function in the account, one of explanation and of enlightenment. After this passage the writer gains in confidence and understanding. A similarly autobiographical dream expresses the agony of the operation undergone in prison. In the text 'bauchhöhlenschwangerschaft' (*zl*, pp. 13-14) the nightmares have to be 'absolviert, wie die strafarbeit in der klasse, allein nach dem unterricht' (p. 13). The dreams of boats, water, blood and never-ending journeys contain classic Freudian elements, here representing birth and contrasted with the devouring by dogs.

The dreams recorded in *grenzen los fremd gehen* are almost entirely sexual. They explore the erotic in ambiguous ways, offering no immediately apparent readings or single meanings. Thus 'geisterhandtraum' (*gl*, p. 136) circles around the familiar theme of orgasm, but here the 'visionen des eindringens eines goldenen stroms' are unachievable:

> immer kurz vor dem orgasmus hatte ich das gefühl eines hochsexuellen potenten zustandes der die ersten anfänge eines orgasmusses effektivisierte und gleichhielt und sich nicht mehr steigerte mal zu mal versuchte ich aber es wurde immer wieder kampf keine erlösung

This dream is inspired by Italian buildings. In this sense Stötzer-Kachold's use of dreams functions as a form of escape, an evasion of borders. The escape depicted in 'nachttraum' (*gl*, p. 129) is seemingly animated by sex which is 'das erste mal erfüllend lang und gut'. The text describes coitus with two different partners, both prisoners like the subject. The act is normal and beyond shame, expressing the author's aim in writing about the erotic.

'Texastraum' (*gl*, pp. 99-100) examines, through the motifs of AIDS, pornography and alcohol, the role of conscious will and social indoctrination in sex. The subject, who sleeps with a man who has AIDS, is racked with guilt regarding her irresponsible behaviour. Yet she also feels herself to have been the medium of male thoughts influenced by pornographic films:

> mein wunsch war nur spiegel dessen was sie in mich setzen war ich von anfang an willenlos schon als ich diese stadt betrat
> der traum endet unentschieden (p. 100)

If the raising of pornography, orgasm, masturbation or lesbianism onto literary level represents a breaking of taboos, then perhaps even more radical is the introduction of AIDS into GDR literatures, for this was a subject absent from most cultural and social spheres in the East.[111] In 'texastraum' AIDS appears as a 'gay plague', reflecting this lack of real knowledge about the illness. In the text 'zum allesschreiben' (*gl*, p. 37) both pregnancy and sexual disease are regarded as risks connected with intercourse: 'liebe aber kinder oder aids wie schirmt frau das ab liebe ohne geschlechtsverkehr'. Here the reference to AIDS is more general, the statement appertains to the relationship between sex and love, rather than to America, homosexuality or dreams.

The indecision with which the text 'texastraum' ends is important, as is the apparent paradox of using a subconscious medium to explore the conscious. The multiplicity of sexual demands and discourses is expressed here both directly through the language and imagery chosen and indirectly through the genre.[112] Where successful, Stötzer-Kachold's texts disavow monolithic formulae for utopia and attempt to show the complexity of the sexual. The writer's own definition of 'Sexualität' is one of the best examples of this disavowal:

> sexualität ist überlagerung des wahllos suchenden sex sucht wahllos sex ist anarchistisch sex sucht sorgen liebe liest lippen leib leid laichläßt (*gl*, p. 82)

---

[111] Cf. In a survey carried out by Kurt Starke only 18% of boys in the East and only 9% of girls were worried about AIDS. Starke (1990, p. 168) states: 'Die öffentliche Diskussion über die Krankheit AIDS in all ihren Zusammenhängen war [...] eher gering.'

[112] See also 'ficktraum' (*gl*, pp. 141-420, 'ärztetraum' (*gl*, pp. 143-44), 'kraftfeldtraum' (*gl*, pp. 145-46) and 'zellentraum' (*gl*, pp. 182-83), all of which revolve around sexual themes and imagery. The dream related in interview with Lahann (1994, p. 17) is also sexual, concerning the author's relationship with Sascha Anderson.

The alliteration of the final six words suggests the intertwined nature of various aspects of sexuality: love, cultural constructions, the body, suffering and biological reproduction. If the sexual in Stötzer-Kachold's writing remains ambiguous, rather than essentialised, it fulfils a number of important feminist aims. Woman is given a sexual voice, she becomes sexual subject rather than an object constructed by men, for men. This subjectivity is not, and cannot be, complete nor is it final, as the author, in her best texts, shows. Situated within competing forms of power the female sexual subject is exposed to conflicting demands, expressed where the prose remains enigmatic.

Within this process of offering new female subjectivities stereotypically feminine images are exposed as such and critically rejected. Tabood areas of the erotic are opened up to new, and challenging, ways of thinking. Moral codes which deform sexuality are swept aside. Patriarchal domination of female sexuality is censured and utopian futures are suggested. These are futures where liberated sexuality is primary, evoked by Stötzer-Kachold principally through metaphors of orgasm and masturbation. The orgasm is depicted as the most important of the Freudian drives which structure so much of this writer's prose, both as content and within her language itself. Other driving passions which are used in this way include love and the senses in general. The body and all its parts, both solid and fluid, also act as leitmotif and as linguistic inspiration, often symbolised through dance and flight. The *Votze* is reclaimed as a source of positive energy and blood is allowed to flow freely throughout the works. Occasionally this transformation of the body into language is not successful, but the contradictions thereby produced can prove thought-provoking and challenging. The links with Western feminist theories, in particular those of French feminists, enable the reader to engage with the texts on a further level. The wider role of this erotic feminist writing within both German and East German traditions is considered in the following chapter, where Stötzer-Kachold's art is compared with work by Verena Stefan, Kerstin Hensel and, most importantly, Irmtraud Morgner.

6. Sexuality and Writing by Women

Stötzer-Kachold's constructions of sexuality attempt to posit woman as subject. In this respect her work can be compared with that of other female authors who, through their art, contribute to a tradition of writing by women. This tradition offers a new canon, a gynocritical source of inspiration for future female artists, who must no longer rely solely on a literary history narrated by, and about, men. In this section Stötzer-Kachold's use of sexuality is contrasted with the writing of Verena Stefan, Kerstin Hensel and Irmtraud Morgner. Stefan is a West German writer with whose prose Stötzer-Kachold's work has often been compared. These are comparisons which, although a useful starting point, are only partly valid. Kerstin Hensel is a contemporary of Stötzer-Kachold who uses sexuality in a very different way to her compatriot. Analysis of her writing, in many respects similar to that of Irmtraud Morgner, can help to show some of the alternative routes available to women writers wishing to tackle the theme.

> 'Als ich über empfindungen, erlebnisse, erotik unter frauen schreiben wollte, wurde ich
> vollends sprachlos' (*Häutungen*, p. 34)

It is not only the style of Stötzer-Kachold's art which provokes comparisons with West German *Frauenliteratur*, but also its physicality. Those West German women writing in the 1970s also accorded the female body primary significance, both as theme and within language. The suffering so characteristic of their texts was portrayed primarily within the sexual sphere. The traditional theme of love was replaced by its modern equivalent: sex. The *Spiegel* (20.12.1976, pp. 118-31) feature on West German *Frauenliteratur* is thus entitled, 'Schreibende Frauen: Sagas von Sex und Leben', whereby sex seemingly takes priority over life. Ursula Krechel (1979, p. 104) also emphasises this aspect of the works, she summarises 'die ersten authentischen Texte bewiesen ihren Wagemut auch darin, daß sie den tabuisierten Bereich der Sexualität ins Blickfeld rückten'. Open portrayal of female sexual experience, from a female point of view, was seen as emancipatory and vital to these *Erfahrungsberichte*. Female masturbation, lesbian sex, orgasm, menstruation and giving birth became worthy literary topics. The links with Stötzer-Kachold's work, on a thematic level, are clear. Critics of the East German writer echo the illustrations of taboo-breaking and of a bold new erotic content.

In *Häutungen*, the most famous text of West German *Frauenliteratur,* Stefan highlights the female body, orgasm, bisexuality and lesbian sex. Her narrator asks, for example:

> was ist ein orgasmus? Einmal überall hin atmen können, bis unter die schulterblätter und in die beckenschalen hinein, spüren, warm werden, *sein.* Alle falten des körpers öffnen, nicht mehr zusammenziehen und anspannen müssen.
> Ein ganzer mensch werden. (p. 48)

The italicised *sein* and the isolation of the final line suggest the essential power of this sensation, a force which Stötzer-Kachold exploits to the full. In Stefan's prose too the questioning of the potential of the orgasm goes beyond that of mere sexual enjoyment, suggesting liberation of human sexuality:

> Der orgasmus ist aufgebläht worden. Er hat die sexualität platt gedrückt. Er ist oft das einzige, was von ihr übriggeblieben ist. Alles andere wird darüber vergessen, bis hin zu der frage, was ein orgasmus eigentlich ist und welche bedeutung er für die menschliche verständigung haben könnte. (p. 101)

Passages in *Häutungen* such as 'ich bin mir wichtiger als die vereinigung mit dem penis. Ich bin von mir durchdrungen' (p. 103) also evoke Stötzer-Kachold's utopian sexual motifs. For Stefan hope is discovered in lesbian sex, portrayed much more positively than it is by Stötzer-Kachold. The narrator's encounters with her partner Fenna are exciting, enjoyable and different. Lesbian sex appears fundamentally different to heterosexual intercourse.

The sexual experiences of Stefan's protagonist are used by the author to chart the character's biography. They are, however, not all gratifying, a trait typical of the writing of the time. As Karin Richter-Schröder (1986, p. 130) notes, 'die in heterosexuellen Beziehungen erzwungene Entfremdung vom eigenen Körper wird für viele der schreibenden Frauen zur Metapher für die gesellschaftliche Demütigung der Frau'. Thus the happy endings of romantic fiction were denounced as false by what was seen as the reality of painful loss of virginity, problems with contraception, unfulfilled marriages, separation, sexual violence and lack of communication between man and woman. Stefan's autobiographical narrator first experiences intercourse as 'das problem' (*Häutungen,* p. 42). When she does finally lose her virginity it is connected with pain and blood. Further sexual events in her life include 'die vierzehn buchstaben vergewaltigung' (p. 54). Her relationships with men are disappointing because she is not an equal partner. Sex becomes: 'Ein zu ärmliches unterfangen, um glück zu produzieren, um über die andere person und sich selber etwas zu erfahren, um einander mitteilungen zu machen. Eine verzweiflungstat' (p. 103).

Stötzer-Kachold similarly uses the sexual to portray both lack of meaningful human communication and her subject's development from innocent girl to knowledgeable woman. This is particularly clear in those of her texts which are traditionally autobiographical. In 'erfurt - mein mittelalter' (*gl*, pp. 16-32) details of the first person narrator's education, her family and GDR politics are interwoven with descriptions of her loss of virginity and further sexual maturity. The first sexual experience is unfulfilling, the woman is, grammatically and physically, passive, distanced by the repetition of the prefix 'ent': 'entjungfern ließ ich mich dann mit 18 von einem entfernten bekannten im park – den ich dann noch einmal traf um die entjungferung zu vollenden' (*gl*, p. 18). In the text 'nohmal zurück in de wieg' (*zl*, pp. 123-29), again a coming to terms with the subject's past, Stötzer-Kachold also describes the loss of virginity as an horrific event. Sex continues to be disappointing, at least for the woman. As in much of the author's prose this fact is expressed in terms of orgasm: 'orgasmus bekam ich nie – das war auch kein wort in meinem leben geworden – ich weiß nicht mal ob er einen kriegte' (*gl*, p. 19).

At a later stage in her sexual development the autobiographical subject meets her husband, this relationship too is portrayed through sexual climax:

> in der abstellkammer zwischen leiter und kleistereimer liebten wir uns – er beherrschte die kunst des klitorialen orgasmus [...] wir sprachen nie darüber aber es gefiel mir (*gl*, p. 20)

The theme is still taboo, silenced even where enjoyed. Further development and self-confidence, intellectually as well as physically, brings dissatisfaction. This is also characterised through erotic scenes, here with unusual irony:

> d. hat mir nie einen vaginalen orgasmus gemacht – obwohl er zu kleineren perversionen bereit war – immer wenn ich auf unter seinem schwanz mich bewegte spürte daß es kommt und ihn bat durchzuhalten ging er vorher los er hat dieses beginnende feuer in mir nicht ertragen [...] er konnte meine intellektualität nicht verstehen (*gl*, pp. 21-22)

In both the work of Stefan and that of Stötzer-Kachold these portrayals function most obviously as criticism of traditional sexual stereotypes.

Thus Ricarda Schmidt (1990) argues, in a statement echoed in her later summary of Stötzer-Kachold's work, that Stefan constructs the female body as a site of both political and social oppression and possible change. It was undoubtedly liberating that women were increasingly able to voice their sexuality. *Häutungen* in particular had an important role in consciousness raising and in discussions about female sexuality. There were, however, problems with using the 'feminist picaresque form', which 'adapted itself readily to empty sexual adventurism' (Engels 1979, p. 144), to stimulate this debate. The texts became schematic, the key sexual events stereotypes. Indeed Ros Coward (1986, p. 233) regards such outwardly feminist works as mere equivalents of traditional romantic fiction. She claims that 'speaking about sexuality, a preoccupation with sexuality, is not in and of itself progressive'. Critics such as Kolkenbrock-Netz and Schuller (1982, p. 165) have similarly seen the portrayal of woman as sexual victim as 'die bloße Verdoppelung des Bestehenden', rather than as an effective form of resistance to this role.

These same arguments can be used to criticise Stötzer-Kachold's work. There are, however, important differences between the two writers' use of the sexual, as there are between their writing more generally. Love, in Stefan's text, is 'oft nichts anderes als eine schreckliche reaktion' (*Häutungen*, p. 55), linked by the author with brutality and dependency. 'Liebe ist' she summarises, 'eine tausendfache verwechslung von begehrt sein und vergewaltigt werden' (p. 56). Love for Stötzer-Kachold, on the other hand, is not simply designed to trap women and is not reduced to brutal sex. It is a constant leitmotif, a longing for a distant utopia. Furthermore, autobiographical texts such as 'erfurt - mein mittelalter' are not characteristic of the East German writer's entire oeuvre, which is varied and difficult to label in any form. As Dahlke (1994, p. 169) recognises:

> Den Vorwurf einer 'reduktion der autobiographischen Sujets auf Sexualität', wie er zu Recht so manchen Texten von Autorinnen gemacht wird, kann man/frau Gabriele Stötzer-Kachold kaum machen. In der Schreibweise, die physiologisch-konkrete Bildersprache mit einer experimentellen Sprachstruktur verbindet, wird Privates und Politisches bewußt in Zusammenhang verbracht.[113]

Verena Stefan does not merely write about erotic experiences. She further attempts to depict the semantic difficulties encountered whilst attempting to articulate her 'female' needs in a language she regards as male. Like Stötzer-Kachold she recognises the problem of finding suitable terminology for both the sexual act and the sexual organs. In the introduction to *Häutungen* she notes:

> Beim schreiben dieses buches, dessen inhalt hierzulande überfällig ist, bin ich wort um wort und begriff an der vorhandenen sprache angeeckt. Sicher habe ich das zunächst so kraß empfunden, weil ich über sexualität schreibe. *Alle* gängigen ausdrücke – gesprochene wie geschriebene –, die den koitus betreffen, sind brutal und frauenverachtend. [...] Die sprache versagt, sobald ich über neue erfahrungen berichten will. (p. 33)

---

[113] The quotation is from Kolkenbrock-Netz/Schuller 1982, p. 165.

Stefan's answer to this dilemma is to use the clinical jargon of medicine when depicting heterosexual love, and a flowery, nature-bound diction of 'seen', 'flüsse', 'funkelnden mooshaar' and 'sonnenenergie' (p. 122) to raise her homosexual experiences into the mystical. Statements such as 'der penis tappt blind in die vagina' (p. 101), are contrasted with 'Ich gleite und sinke mit Fenna durch wiesen von lippenblüten' (p. 130).

Whereas Stötzer-Kachold accords positive meaning to the word *Votze*, Stefan does not reclaim terms such as 'möse'.[114] Again her answer lies in nature. She asks, for example: 'Die vagina – ein dunkler schlauch? Was kam danach? Gab es perlen in der tiefe des körpers, korallenriffe?' (p. 47) Similar examples abound in the text and it is this aspect of her writing that has brought her the most criticism. Hiltrud Gnüg (1978, p. 134) bemoans the fact that: 'ein neuer Mythos des Urweiblichen scheint im Entstehen, ein Biologismus, der, wie schon in der bürgerlichen Philosophie, die Frau reduziert als ein Naturwesen begreift'. Marlis Gerhardt (1977, p. 83) employs a similar argument, seeing Stefan's sexual subject purely as a biologically depicted woman and her writing as a mixture of 'abgesunkener Romantik und Naturlyrik bis hin zur erotischen Trivialliteratur'. The style of certain 'Votzenenergie' references in Stötzer-Kachold's work opens it to similar type of censure.

Although in the problematising of sexual language many similarities do again exist between Stötzer-Kachold and Stefan, there are important differences in this respect too. The former does not place the same stress on nature. Where she does appear, in some texts, essentialist, others contradict this appearance. Her use of the word *Votze* is harsher and more demanding on the reader than any of Stefan's proposed alternatives, and yet it is also more liberating, more openly political. As Dahlke (1994, p. 168) argues: 'wo bei Stötzer-Kachold die energie-geladene Textbesessenheit und entfesselte Formulierungssucht überzeugen, behindert bei Stefan der allzu vordergründige Willensakt, der gezwungene Gestus'. Comparison with Verena Stefan thus emphasises Stötzer-Kachold's literary achievements. Comparison with Kerstin Hensel, on the other hand, allows a reappraisal of these achievements. This author's strategies for giving the woman a sexual voice contrast greatly with those employed by Stötzer-Kachold, recalling instead the work of Irmtraud Morgner.

---

[114] Cf. 'Wenn eine frau anfängt, von ihrer 'möse' zu sprechen, hat sie lediglich die ausdrucksweise linker männer übernommen. Der zugang zu ihrer vagina, zu ihrem körper wie zu ihr selbst bleibt für sie verschlossen wie zuvor' (*Häutungen*, p. 33).

Verena Stefan's text *Häutungen* is a product of the early stages of the West German feminist movement. Kerstin Hensel's work, like that of Stötzer-Kachold, was first produced in the GDR of the late 1970s and 1980s.[115] Yet hers is a very different form of literature, whereby the difference is exemplified in her use of language, genre and themes, including the sexual. Hensel's prose does not set out to be specifically 'female', sexual experiences are not raised onto a mythological, essential level. Analysis of gendered relationships is, however, one of the author's major concerns. She portrays a wide range of female protagonists and offers various possibilities for both identification and rejection. The erotic is used in differing forms as part of these portrayals, as an effective method of description and characterisation. As Dahlke (1994, p. 172) comments: 'menschliche Grundbedürfnisse in ihrer sinnlich-körperlichen Dimension bilden auffällig intensiv die Projektionsfläche zur Charakterisierung von Personen und Situationen: Essen und Trinken, Wohnen, Lieben'. Hensel's erotic descriptions possess realistic dimensions, based in the here and now rather than an imaginary future. Hers is a visual approach, the writing is determined by pictures of a sensual and definitive reality; 'bei Hensel [...] gibt es Lust, Sinnlichkeit, Genuß – es wird gefressen, gesoffen, gevögelt, daß es eine Art hat' (Meyer-Gosau 1992, p. 35). Hensel adds distance into her work, a characteristic most often lacking from Stötzer-Kachold's prose. Her narratives tend to centre, for example, around fictional characters rather than an apparently autobiographical subject. They too break taboos, but do so with none of the occasionally forced nature of Stötzer-Kachold's rigid emphasis.

An 'originelle Beschreibung erotischer Szenen' (Dahlke 1994, p. 175) is typical of Hensel's art. This originality is determining in her poetry, where love scenes are often subtley conveyed. The poem 'Wochenend' (1988, p. 21), for example, succinctly expresses the romance of 'der zarte Irrsinn des Alltags':

Vor-Schau bis zur Zerbröselung (Augen Scham Lippen)
Auf!
Auf ein Gläschen. Wir gehen unter
die Decken und wünschen uns eine weißschwanzige
Katze.

---

115 Hensel was born in 1961 in Chemnitz and published both poetry and prose from the late-1970s, both 'officially' and 'unofficially'.

The terms *Schamlippen* and *Schwanz* here acquire a new and highly erotic resonance. It is this positive side of the sensual that is largely absent from Stötzer-Kachold's work. Hensel's nature poems, such as 'Abschiede' (1988, p. 84) or 'Hochmoorsommernachtstraumreise' (1990, p. 10) are also often evocative of love. In 'Garten' (1990, p. 11) the tone of the bountiful description is encapsulated in the last two lines:

Mächtig der Sommer
Knallend von Farben und Lust.

These texts appear much more traditional than Stötzer-Kachold's, immediately recognisable as lyric poetry rather than something inbetween prose and poem. Hensel gives these strict forms 'die Stimme des 20. Jahrhunderts' (Hammer 1991, p. 101). Her originality is in her use of imagery and language, whereby the subject becomes, avoiding the pathos of Stefan, part of the descriptions:

[...] keuchend häng ich
Zwischen den Bäumen. Pappel-
Schnee auf den Lippen
Und die Augen lindig verklebt. (1990, p. 11)

It is this erotic language that recalls Stötzer-Kachold's best and more ambivalent poetic prose. In the poem 'Gänze des Lebens' (1993, p. 42), for example, the poet pictures: 'Das kalte Adreßbuch und des Prinzen Schwopf und Kanz'. The spoonerism cleverly suggests that men think with their *Schwanz* rather than their *Kopf*. Hensel also uses her poetry to comment on the nature of the *Stasi*, but again she achieves this with more subtlety and humour than Stötzer-Kachold:

Schlafe wonniglich beim Strip behangener
Hampelmänner (welche jeden Orgasmus
In meiner Kaderakte vermerken) (1990, p. 13).

The autobiographical here is turned to humour.

It is in Hensel's prose, however, that her use of the sexual is most obvious. In *Hallimasch* (1989) clear and precise language is used to characterise men through their often pornographic acts:

Er streifte die Bettdecke zurück, legte vorsichtig ihre Schenkel auseinander und schob sich sofort hinein. Ihr Gesicht verfinsterte sich, sie stöhnte etwas im Schlaf, schluckte

Speichel und versuchte, die Bettdecke wieder über ihre entblößten Beine zu ziehen. Labuhn deckte sie mit seinem Körper ('Kotterba', p. 117).

Despite the use of the word 'vorsichtig', Labuhn here almost becomes a rapist, his victim obviously suffering. The portrayal recalls Maron's description of Strutzer in *Flugasche*. The disgusting scene of sexual abuse in the fairy tale narrative 'Hallimasch', where the twins Liese and Lotte have to pay for milk by giving the ugly farmer a foot massage, is a similarly effective form of implied critique. In the 'Katzenbericht' Jutta's father Emil Kajunke is depicted as 'der einbeinige Fischhändler, der sonntags immer über ihren Kochtopf und dann über ihre Mutter herfiel' (p. 66). In these examples female reactions to these acts become the focus for attention, and thus also of the reader's sympathy.

The most interesting and most openly erotic story in the East German *Hallimasch* collection is 'Herr Johannes', a historical tale full of references to the former GDR. The central character is a stranger, a Don Juan figure who causes chaos in the State through his ability to physically excite the female population. The main narrator, Leo, functions as voyeur, relating the sexual episodes he spies upon to an imaginary audience, including the reader. The sexual prowess of Herr Johannes is used to show how little pleasure the women have from sex with average men, who are characterised by the use of the adjective 'dumpf' (p. 151). Again, the reader's sympathy is directed towards the female characters and soon the women begin to resist this form of sex that does not satisfy them. The 'Abschied von Don Juan' (1993, pp. 18-27) also concentrates on this figure, distinguished here both through his penis, and through female reactions to this symbolic character.[116] This text, in essay form, is the theoretical explanation of the 'Herr Johannes' story.

Hensel's fascination with the ultimate in male romantic heroism recalls Irmtraud Morgner's portrayal of the same figure in *Amanda* (p. 482).[117] Indeed in interview with Dahlke (1993d, p. 84), Hensel explicitly makes the connection between her writing and that of the older author: 'daß mich die Morgner sehr interessiert hat, ist klar'. She admires her writing for its: 'Lachen, Weisheit, Kraft' and 'Liebe als großes menschliches Gefüge' (Hensel 1993, p. 102). Hensel reviews Morgner's texts,[118] makes her speak at imaginary con-

---

116 'Für seinen Komplex symptomatisch ist die Arbeitsmanie, die er, als Angehöriger der Oberschicht, einzig mit dem Schwanz betreiben kann' (p. 20).

117 Hensel also reworks the story of Adam's first wife Lilith ('Lilit' *Hallimasch*, pp. 7-11) again referred to in Morgner's work (*A*, p. 368).

118 'Trobadora Passé. (Irmtraud Morgner lesen I)', (1993, pp. 100-102) and 'Tanz in gefährdeter Welt (Irmtraud Morgner lesen II)', (1993, pp. 103-108).

ferences,[119] and even structures her novel *Auditorium Panoptikum* (1991) around Morgner's operative montage. She also emphasises (in Dahlke 1994a, p. 93) Morgner's erotic description of men: 'Zum Beispiel bekommt kein Mensch mit, wie erotisch die Morgner die Männer beschreibt, immer wird nur auf ihre Frauenfiguren gesehen'.

Detailed and realistic pictures of male bodies can be found in much of Hensel's own prose. The male body becomes the object of the female gaze. In the short story *Im Schlauch* (1993), for example, it is the erotic profiles of men, from a female viewpoint, which stand out. The man is on sexual display:

> Hauptkommissar Paffrath vollführte zunächst eine halbe Drehung Richtung Ladefront. Die Lampe beschien seine bloße Rückseite. Anneros begutachtete sie eingehend. Dabei zupfte sie zärtlich an den dunklen Haaren, die dicht des Beamten Rücken bedeckten. Sie gurrte, drehte den Mann herum, um ihn anderenorts voll auszuleuchten (p. 21).

The role reversal whereby women are given sexual power is taken to frightening extremes in *Auditorium Panoptikum*, where a group of French girls carry out, in a dramatically convincing dream-like sequence, a gang rape. Although the surreal atmosphere of this episode alienates the reader and hinders immediate interpretation, it is one of the most memorable of the many thought-provoking sexual descriptions in the novel. The reader may be appalled, yet at the same time must recognise that such events, perpetrated by men, do indeed take place.

This use of the erotic to re-view is not limited to a female view of the male body. Men are also scrutinised by a male stare. In *Auditorium Panoptikum* (1991) Egmont admires 'des Freundes helles Stück' (p. 96) and indeed does so for two and a half pages. The exaggeration of this laudatio has a similar effect to Valeska's comic reappraisal of penis envy. Even nature is invoked in this admiration – an ironic comment on writing such as Verena Stefan's. The penis becomes 'mein Berg mit dem rötlich strahlenden Gipfel' and 'die Röhre aller Lebenssäfte', the testes 'birnengroßen Scrotti' (p. 97). Egmont himself is characterised through his inability to fulfill his harem's desires. A useless 'Schlappschwanz' (p. 240), he is thrown out of the artistic commune. Hensel also describes women in intricate sexual detail, again with originality and clarity:

---

119 The *erste Müggelseekonferenz*, described in *Auditorium Panoptikum* (1991). Interestingly, Morgner's paper, like the novel Amanda, is 'ein Hexenbericht' (p. 108).

Die Frau säuberte ihren nabellosen Bauch, spreizte die Beine, seifte mit einem neuen Wulst Rasiercreme ihre Scham, aus welcher die inneren Lippen wie kleine rosa Elefantenohren herausgingen. (p. 38)

The woman portrayed here, a resurrected Walküre, has both the size and stature of Beatriz, as well as her erotic dimension. She even makes similar statements.[120] This use of the sexual to create convincing characters is, then, especially successful in Hensel's writing – as it was in Morgner's – but is a technique which Stötzer-Kachold rarely employs.

Further comparison between the work of Morgner and Hensel can be found in their use of food motifs. For the younger writer too these are often endowed with sexual symbolism. In *Im Schlauch*, for example, sex is inexorably linked to alcohol, be it vodka for Siegfried Kulisch, beer with liqueur for Anneros or beer alone for Natalie. Liese and Lotte indulge themselves with food and drink rather than sexual pleasures, the language here is crafted in order to express the connections:

Vier Stunden lang essen sie, beißen in das knusprige triefende Fleisch, stoßen auf, stippen den Kloß ins Fett, schieben die Bissen im Mund zur gleichen Zeit von links nach rechts, umschließen mit saftigen Lippen die Weingläser. (1989, p. 92)

This lustful scene precedes and prefigures that where the narrator suggests the possible 'Ersticken der Sünde' (p. 94), the girls' erotic discovery of one another. This self-satisfaction can perhaps repress the memory of earlier sexual experiences: 'Die Zwillinge halten sich noch umschlungen, liegen schwer ineinander, atmen, denken vielleicht an Kuczmat, von dem sie keine Milch mehr brauchen...' (p. 94)

Hensel's erotic descriptions are also often humourous, even to the point of being grotesque. Meyer-Gosau (1992, p. 34) writes of the 'Irr-Witz' of the author's stories. Alienating in its effects, the humour forces the reader to reexamine sexual prejudices. In *Im Schlauch*, for example, the juxtaposition of Russian exclamations with mechanical similes creates a picture of the correct 'Genosse' in a somewhat compromising position towards his Russian comrade. Here it is the woman who is in control:

"O ihr Deutschen", flüsterte Duschenka, nahm das lose Schürzenband, schlang es Siegfried um die Handgelenke, knotete es fest und befahl: "Machen ohne Hände! Pronikaja! Pronikaja!" Duschenka hielt Kulischs Hände gefesselt, ohne sie war es aber mühevoll. Kulisch, im Stehen, arbeitete wie eine Fräsmaschine. (pp. 22-23)

---

[120] Cf. 'Eine Geschichte schreibende Frau müsse ähnlich zu leiden haben wie eine Geschichte machende Frau' (p. 108).

Sex between husband and wife on the other hand is deliberately devoid of any sensual element, it only takes place in the dark, according to the orders of comrade Kulisch. The humour here is that of bitter sarcasm, Prussian precision taken to extremes. The atmosphere of the marriage is captured in this scene alone:

> Zwei Knöpfe öffnete er, während er den oberen Hemdknopf in das Knopfloch fügte, so daß Anneros auch das kleinste Brusthaar verborgen blieb. Kulisch drehte Anneros mit dem Gesicht zur Wand. Die Frau öffnete die Augen, sah Tapete und sonst nichts, spürte wie Siegfried ihren Dederon-Schlüpfer ein Stückchen herunterzog, eine Handbreit nur, so daß er gerade eben den Ort erreichen konnte. (p. 49)

Friederike's encounter with Egmont's body in *Auditorium Panoptikum* is another event depicted with humourous ease. As she attempts to massage his front she discovers 'ein mir unbekannter, weicher, milchweißer Nabelfortsatz [...] der sogleich ob seiner lästigen Funktion, nutzlos zu sein, mein Mitleid erregte' (1991, p. 187). She can feel nothing more than pity for this stomach extension. As this scene progresses to orgasm the penis shrinks away into nothing in a grotesque comedy. The title alone of the short text 'VEB Lustzone' (1993, pp. 28-29) is an ironic comment on the GDR's attempted regulation both of speech and of lust. The philosophical arguments against prostitution fall on deaf ears in the new post-*Wende* Berlin.

In Hensel's prose laughter can also function as resistance. Mechthild Labuhn's reaction to being raped by her husband is to laugh, 'sie lachte eine Koloratur' (1989, p. 60). His actions, causing a completely unexpected response, are thus made to appear almost ridiculous. Here again there are parallels with Morgner's writing. The comic was another quality that Hensel (1993, p. 59) admired in the work of her fellow Saxon, '"Ich kann nur leben mit dem Lachen über den Popanz", sagte Irmtraud Morgner, als sie noch lebte. Das ist wohl wahr. Auch sie kam aus Sachsen und ist Beweis dafür, daß dort das Komische, der besondere Blick zu Hause ist'. The humorous aspect of Hensel's sexual art contrasts sharply with the prose of both Stefan and Stötzer-Kachold. In Stötzer-Kachold's texts the term *Lachen* becomes a formula rather than a stylistic device. Her writing merely speaks of laughter, which is portrayed as an integral part of 'Lust', as an idealistic emotion of the future and as a necessary form of rebellion against the present: 'die welt angucken und trotzdem lachen' (*zl*, p. 129).

Dahlke (1993a, p. 252) asks Stötzer-Kachold why there is so little humour in her texts. Her reply, 'für mich ist das die Frage der Lustfindung. Das Lachen bei den Deutschen ist immer das Lachen über andere, ich muß erstmal über mich selbst lachen lernen', expresses a general problem for female authors wishing to write comedies. Prostitution, rape and masochism are not subjects which can easily be laughed about. As Weigel (1987, p. 169) states: 'für Frauen scheint der Eintritt in die Öffentlichkeit, in die Literatur und in die Sprache bis heute ein ausgesprochenes ernsthaftes Vorhaben zu sein'. Particularly where the erotic is concerned, women have traditionally been objects rather than subjects of laughter. To escape this role by mimicry is a difficult and dangerous route. It is, however, one which, if successful, can be liberating. This is perhaps one reason why Morgner's work was so popular in the West, its humour offered an alternative to the style of *Frauenliteratur* of which *Häutungen* is typical. Similarly, the humour of Hensel's prose offers an alternative to the style of writing by Stötzer-Kachold.

Whereas Hensel expresses, both in interview and in her work, a debt to the women's writing represented by Morgner, she finds Stötzer-Kachold's texts 'fremd' (in Dahlke 1993d, p. 95). Stötzer-Kachold herself makes no such statements about a mentor and seems to dismiss the artistic traditions of GDR writing by women that the earlier generation had so remarkably created. Indeed she dismisses not just the art of her parents' generation, but the generation itself. The text 'an die 40jährigen' (*zl*, pp. 79-81) is one of the author's most successful texts, which Schmidt (1992a, p. 159) credits with 'poetic density and political insight'. It skillfully portrays the conflicting emotions of a generation 'hineingeboren' into the GDR, 'die generation zwischen einer generation' (*zl*, p. 81). The rejection by this generation of 'eure ordnung' (p. 79) betrays more than a simple generation gap; it is rebellion against indifference towards a system which seems unchangeable. It is complemented by the acceptance of sexual pleasure, 'eine andere form von hoffnung' (p. 81). Familiar sexual motifs are used in this text in order to distance the subject from the older generation and in doing so, to reaffirm her own identity, her own bodily presence:

> wir sind unser eigenes geschlecht, in jedem geschlecht begegnen wir uns selbst, die lust ist unser faden. uns bindet keine moral, keine mündigkeit, uns trennen nur wir selbst. wir befruchten uns selbst, wir kastrieren uns selbst, wir treiben uns selbst zum orgasmus (p. 81)

Adopting the erotic this text succinctly expresses the emotions which were to be vented in the summer of 1989.

Stötzer-Kachold's attempt to place herself outside any specific East German literary traditions would seem to be characteristic of her female contemporaries in the GDR. As Dahlke (1994b, p. 6) argues:

Von einer "Tradition weiblichen Schreibens in der DDR" zu sprechen, erscheint problematisch [...] Bis auf Kerstin Hensels intensive Bezugnahme auf Werke Irmtraud Morgners lassen die Texte der Jüngeren vorrangig die Ablösung von vorangegangenen Autorinnengenerationen erkennen.[121]

One possible explanation for this attitude is a general scepticism of GDR literature, which was part of a broader rejection of the norms of East German society. Recognised 'offical' writers were regarded, in some cases, as representatives of that society and its values. Stötzer-Kachold's 'mother' figures, if there are any, appear, from the writing itself, to be Ingeborg Bachmann or Gertrud Stein. For Dahlke this is again characteristic. She writes that foreigners, or figures not in the accepted canon became role models.[122] The exception is Elke Erb, whose own writing resembled that of the younger generation in many respects and who greatly supported the artists whose work she edits in the *Berührung ist nur eine Randerscheinung* collection.

Parallels to this phenomenon are to be found in the rejection by contemporary male poets of Volker Braun, who gained almost symbolic value as the personification of another form of literature and another generation.[123] As Kolbe (in Heukenkamp 1979, p. 46) famously stated: 'Meine Generation hat die Hände im Schoß, was engagiertes (!) Handeln betrifft. Kein früher Braun heute.'[124] In his essay 'Rimbaud. Ein Psalm der Aktualität' (1985), Braun takes issue with the ideas, art and lifestyle of the group centred around 'die Erbin, Unsere Flip-out-Elke' (p. 996). The dispute that subsequently developed over this essay showed how the two groups failed to understand one another. Braun, for example, patronisingly writes:

---

[121] Hensel (in Hammer 1991, p. 96) rejects the concept of generation' as a meaningful criterion by which to judge literature, she says: 'Was ist Generation? Was ist Generationsgefühl? Ich kann nicht sagen, daß ich das Gefühl meiner Generation kenne'.

[122] Here again there are similarities with the male poets. Jan Faktor's 'Manifeste der Trivialpoesie', for example, recall Dada manifestos rather than any form of Socialist Realism. Papenfuß-Gorek's poetry has been compared with that of Jandl and the Russian Chlebnikov. Stötzer-Kachold too has been likened to Arp, Schwitters and Jandl.

[123] Leeder (1993) discusses the limitations of this characterisation in her dissertation. It obscures, for example, the continuities that do exist between the work of Braun, Wolf, Morgner etc. and the younger artists.

[124] Cf also Fritz Hendrik Melle: 'Volker Braun? Da kann ich nur sagen, der Junge quält sich' (*Berührung ist nur eine Randerscheinung*, p. 151).

Unsere jungen Dichter, Kinder des administrativen Beamten, suchen auch das Loch in der Mauer. Sie verbrauchen ihre Fantasie an Tunnels und Fesselballons, ihre 'monologe geh'n rechtens 'fremd'. Fluchten wieder, aber auf Hasenpfoten. (p. 983)[125]

An intertextual link with this debate in Stötzer-Kachold's work is to be found in the comments woven into her writing which refer to the title of Braun's collection *Training des aufrechten Ganges*. She writes that: 'untergrund ist nicht den aufrechten gang verlernen' (*gl*, p. 143). Endler, Hilbig, Neumann and Erb became the members of the older generation with whom the younger poets identified. Thus Stötzer-Kachold herself would reject the comparison with an 'official' author such as Irmtraud Morgner. Her use of sexuality does, however, allow certain links to be made between the two groups of texts. Whether or not these comparisons amount to a female 'tradition' is a different question.

'Und immer zügelloser wird die Lust' (*A*, p. 195)

Carol Vance (1992, p. xvi) envisages 'feminism's best fantasy' as a society where women can realize erotic desire and pleasure. Morgner's *Walpurgisnacht* festivities similarly portend a future where women are allowed to celebrate their sexuality; amidst the dancing, the eating and the laughter, lust is allowed free rein. The desire for this freedom is expressed in the titles alone of Stötzer-Kachold's prose; it is a desire which lies at the heart of her work. Both writers offer the reader a vision of erotic pleasure and a new understanding of the concept of love. The difference between these visions is a question of emphasis, and relies on generalisations. It is a question too of contexts of reception, audiences and generations.

Irmtraud Morgner 'dachte 'das Mögliche von übermorgen' – ohne das Unmögliche von heute zu übersehen' (Schwarzer 1990a, p. 66). She remains constantly aware of the material context of the present from which her fantastic future will arise and stresses, therefore, both pleasure and danger in her constructions of sexuality. Her art, although highly imaginary, is founded in historical and political realities. In her later work in particular, sexuality is predominantly portrayed as problematic. This is an important aspect of her utopia, for, as Vance (p. xvii) continues:

125 The reference is to a poem by Sascha Anderson. Cf. also comments by, for example, Christoph Hein (in Elmar Faber 1988, p. 677): 'Mit größter Behutsamkeit und fast ängstlicher Besorgnis aber sollten wir uns den Texten der neuen Generation nähern. Hier trennen uns möglicherweise nicht nur verschiedene Ästhetik, sondern überdies andere Erfahrungen'.

202

any strategy that focuses exclusively or predominantly on one goal while ignoring the other will fail. To encourage a mindless expansion of sexual options, without critiquing the sexist structure in which sexuality is enacted [...] only exposes women to more danger.

The 'moralisch-didaktische Absicht' (Meyer B. 1985, p. 57) of Morgner's writing is clear. Her 'Produktivkraft Sexualität' is something which women have to learn how to use, it is not essentially female. This non-gendering of the concept allows further possibilities of meaning to emerge and plays on Marxist and socialist terminology. Morgner remains critical of the construct of masculinity without directly attacking men. Thus emancipation is, for her, 'kein Frauenproblem, sondern ein Menschheitsproblem und kann nur von der ganzen Gesellschaft gelöst werden' (in Neumann 1978, p. 98). Her feminism is one which believes strongly in androgyny.

Stötzer-Kachold, however, often sets her utopia simply in the context of the female body, the female orgasm or female sexual drives. She frequently genders her sexual and artistic 'Kräfte', which she names as 'fraulich' or 'fraueneigen'. This author's narrative subject is searching for 'die frauenzeit und das frauenwissen' (ts). Her energy comes from the vagina. In contrast to Morgner, Stötzer-Kachold distances her productive forces from Marxist ideas, moving instead towards Freudian, French feminist and postmodern theories. Here her art takes issue with influences prevalent in GDR cultural discussion of the 1980s, particularly amongst the artists connected with the underground *Szene*, where cultural theory was as important as fictional work, as the large number of essays which appeared in the *Zeitschriften* evidence. The younger generation of writers deliberately turned away from products of socialism, unless it was in order to mock that which had, in their eyes, failed.

Stötzer-Kachold's occasionally unambivalent gendering results in expressive hatred of, and anger towards, men themselves. A consideration of the issue of betrayal in her work makes this especially clear. Her analysis thus appears largely personal rather than historical, didactic or moral. The difference between the two writers can, then, be expressed in these terms. As Dahlke (1993c, p. 191) summarises, 'Während Morgner und Wolf von der gesellschaftlichen Utopie her auf physisch-psychisch-soziale Besonderheiten der Frau gestoßen waren, kommt Stötzer-Kachold vom Individuellen, von der eigenen Körpererfahrung her'. This individuality can, as the reception of her work shows, give the impression that Stötzer-Kachold writes solely for her own benefit, whereas Morgner wrote for her readers. Yet these readings are not definitive, for they ignore both the personal aspects of Morgner's work and the wider references to social issues within Stötzer-Kachold's.

Individuality does not deprive the younger author's writing of political relevance. As Eigler (1993, p. 150) recognizes, this prose 'provides challenging perspectives on gender identity and the question of individual responsibility'. Stötzer-Kachold too remains aware that, at present, sexual violence of all forms, physical, subconscious and linguistic, threatens any liberation of female sexuality. This awareness can, in some cases, lead to an over emphasis on the image of woman as sexual victim rather than agent; here there is no utopian vision. Her work also rages against the sexist structures within which female sexuality is often experienced, challenging traditional feminine roles. As well as creating her own images, Stötzer-Kachold becomes 'die um das bild, gegen das bild kämpfende frau' (zl, p. 50). Neither author's vision is, therefore, invalid.

Whereas Morgner's work can be characterised as Marxist-feminist and humanist, Stötzer-Kachold's is generally woman-centred. Thus it has been described as radically feminist. Whether radical or Marxist, for both writers feminism is of importance, as their work with sexual motifs, sexual characters and sexual language manifestly demonstrates. Both aim to give the woman a sexual identity, whilst critiquing patriarchal relations which deprive her of this right. For Morgner, this aim is expressed in the creation of a variety of female characters who experience erotic pleasure and pain, sexual subjectivity and objectification. Their appropriation of nature is sexual as well as historical. Their stories are told by a variety of female narrators, often noticeably physical themselves, whose art combines desire and the fantastic. Psycholgical aspects of the sexual are thus intertwined with realistic events and figures. Sexuality becomes an important mode of characterisation, providing humour as well as more serious comment. Both Images of Women and Authentic Realism styles of criticism can be adopted particularly effectively in Morgner's case, for her characters appear as unified subjects with whom readers can identify.

For Stötzer-Kachold the sexual voice is used to construct a semi-auto-biographical and humourless female figure, split and metamorphic rather than unified. Her emphasis lies not merely in characterisation of this figure, but also in experimentation with a sexual language. In this respect her work can be approached with reference to feminist theories which concentrate upon a specific female language or style of writing. Whereas Morgner defends her open, and modernist, montage style as appropriate to a female lifestyle, Stötzer-Kachold goes further, attempting to create 'eine neue Sprache, in der weibliche Erfahrung Platz hat' (Dahlke 1993c, p. 184). Morgner states (in Huffzky 1975) that women writers must experiment with new forms until they discover 'ihre eigenen':

Der Anfang kann keine strenge geschlossene Form bringen, er braucht die strenge offene Form. Der Anfang ist notwendigerweise experimentell. Die Form muß den Prozeß der Wahrheitsfindung mit zeigen können.

Just as she has learnt, 'die Produktivkraft Sexualität souverän zu nutzen', so too has Stötzer-Kachold taken Morgner's suggestions concerning aesthetics to extremes. In Kristeva's terms it is the dynamic between the semiotic and the symbolic that produces some of this writer's most successful work, where meaning is constantly in process. Deliberately breaking down grammatical order and structured instead by movement, breaks, leaps, musicality, physicality, bodily parts and sexual drives, her best prose thus becomes poetic: 'Zeugnisse eines Übergangs' (Dahlke 1993c, p. 180). Morgner's montages, however, although including poetry, remain prose.

Morgner created, in the figure of Beatriz, a 'Grenzüberschreiterin' (in Kaufmann E. 1984, p. 1498). The author herself also crossed border lines, both of style and of content. Stötzer-Kachold too has become known for her breaking of barriers and taboos, particularly where these taboos were of a sexual nature. In the late 1960s Morgner is already challenging 'die übliche Lücke' lett by other writers. By the 1980s her work covers every thematic aspect of the sexual, regardless of political doctrine or censorship demands. In so doing, novels such as *Beatriz* and *Amanda* must have offered a lead to other artists and it is within this context that Stötzer-Kachold's increased concentration on the themes of homosexuality, masturbation, rape, prostitution, pornography and particularly orgasm must be set. The seminal role which sexual dreams and fantasies play in her writing is also reminiscent of the novels of the older artist. The same 'Phantasiewelle' which influences Helga Königsdorf (1978, p. 61) rolls into Stötzer-Kachold's portrayals, where dreams interact with and comment upon the conscious world, ambiguously questioning unconscious meanings given to sexual difference. Of course, neither Morgner nor Stötzer-Kachold is alone in challenging prejudice by introducing formerly taboo themes into their work, but both stand out as notable iconoclasts. Their iconoclasm is not sensationalist or gratuitous but, for both writers, is politically motivated.

The comparison between the work of Morgner and Stötzer-Kachold can be drawn not only between their writing – its themes and forms – but also in terms of generations, audiences and contexts of reception. Morgner was born in 1933 and her work is clearly inscribed by her experiences of the War and the early GDR. Stötzer-Kachold was born in 1953 and hers is 'das Gedicht einer 30jährigen, ohne strophe, ohne vers, ohne reim, ohne maß' (*zl*, p. 79). Despite similarities of theme there is notable variance in emphasis. Furthermore, although both authors suffered from state intervention and the effects of GDR policies of censorship, there was also, in the early 1980s, undoubtedly a difference in the readings given by the older writer in the USA or Switzerland and those 'performed' by the younger artist in the courtyards of Prenzlauer Berg and elsewhere in the GDR. Where the majority of Morgner's work was published internationally, Stötzer-Kachold's first appeared in limited editions of *Lyrikmappen* privately produced by hand. A specific site of production, and a restricted audience, meant that her writing did not have the same access to the canon as the work of an internationally read and celebrated author such as Morgner. By the end of the decade, however, conditions of reception had changed. The Aufbau and Luchterhand editions of *zügel los*, and avid Western interest in the East German 'avant garde', meant that the work of the younger author too was being noted and critically discussed. Included in a variety of anthologies, it was placed in a new canon of 'alternative' GDR art.

In a reunified Germany the conditions of the free market apply equally to all artists. Women's writing from the GDR can no longer be seen within a framework of alternative versus official art. Ideological demands of the State have given way to the economic demands of publishers which affect every text. Within this new context the works of apparently different writers such as Morgner and Stötzer-Kachold need to be compared on equal terms – which must now function primarily with regard to aesthetic value. A consideration of the authors' work based around the theme of sexuality allows such a comparison, which in turn allows canons to be revised.

Ultimately both Morgner and Stötzer-Kachold, despite the differences in their work, form part of a broad tradition in that they are women writing about their own sexuality. Within fields of disourse traditionally dominated by the male it is vital that women construct their own images, and at the very least attempt to offer alternative role models. As Gnüg (1978, p. 140) states: 'hier müssen die Frauen, ihr eigenes Bewußtsein verändernd, auf Bewußtseins-veränderungen zielen'. Separating one line of tradition from the vast web that is literary history does not, however, assume a specific female aesthetic. Individual writers contribute differently to an artistic field that cannot be delineated solely according to gender. Nor can it, as the comparison between Stötzer-Kachold and Stefan shows, be defined in terms of East or West German. Gender or nation based generalisations can, then, function only as a useful starting point for research. Ideally they eventually become unnecessary, for, as Kristeva (1986, p. 132) states: 'it's a question of subjectivity'. The treatment of sexuality in GDR literatures of the 1970s and 1980s is also 'a question of subjectivity'. Gnüg's (1978, p. 140) assessment of West German women's writing can, then, be fruitfully applied to the texts which have been analysed here: 'neue ästhetische Formen haben sich hier ausgebildet, jedoch keine neue weibliche Ästhetik. Ein geschlechtsspezifischer ästhetischer Blick auf die Welt ist nicht auszumachen'. The tradition of writing by women is not necessarily a female tradition.

Conclusion

In answer to Emmerich's call for 'eine andere Wahrnehmung', the aim of this study has been to reconsider anew literature produced in the former GDR. This reconsideration has been founded upon the theme of sexuality. As a complex cultural construct the sexual participates in, and comments upon, the discourses within which it is created. It is an issue of both artistic and social interest. It is important also as a feminist theme for it can both critique, and offer alternatives to, patriarchal systems of subjugation. The sexual is not 'private' or 'natural', indeed it challenges the boundaries cemented by such concepts. It is public and is a worthy literary topic. In GDR literatures the sexual was not, from the late 1960s onwards, taboo. An increasing number of writers, both male and female, chose to attack 'die letzte Domäne der Männer'. A concentration upon those female writers represents a revision of traditional canons.

Sexual constructions in GDR literatures are challenging and diverse, morally and politically. They contribute to, and take issue with, developments in aesthetic form and content, enriching and democratizing East German culture. In short, lust is 'immer zügelloser' and literature is 'immer zügelloser'. During the 1970s and 1980s the erotic became an accepted literary and artistic theme, in which Honecker's 'no taboos' declaration was effectively put into practice. Within the paradigm of a loving heterosexual partnership, sex was often depicted. Other sexual themes both reinforced and challenged this framework. The sexual was used in order to characterise, to criticise and to envisage alternative moralities. Thus the literature does not simply mimetically reflect a fixed social situation, but forms its own meanings.

Sexual art further represents a dimension of the large and seminal body of writing by women in the GDR, and of feminist writing in the GDR. Irmtraud Morgner and Gabriele Stötzer-Kachold are the two female authors whose work is most prominent in this respect. A comparison of their work recognises their individual achievements whilst emphasising that the feminist struggle for sexual equality can take highly differing forms. Alternatives to, and intersections with, the sexual fictions proposed by Morgner and Stötzer-Kachold can be found in the writing of authors from both East and West Germany. Alongside Kerstin Hensel, other influential East German writers within this field include Helga Königsdorf, Maxie Wander, Christoph Hein, Sarah Kirsch, Günter de Bruyn, Volker Braun, Bert Papenfuß-Gorek, Annett Gröschner, Uwe Saeger, Monika Maron, Gerti Tetzner and Brigitte Reimann.

The choice of two female writers was again concerned with 'eine andere Wahrnehmung'. The canon is, as Karen Jankowsky (1993, p. 102) states 'an institutionalised site of cultural memory at a place in time'. The canons of GDR literatures were written with specific ideological aims in mind and were blinded by specific prejudices. They were often overtly gendered, in terms of authorship and of material considered. The erotic was not, in most cases, a factor in decisions. The traditional canon, as Ricarda Schmidt (1992a) observes, concentrates on the male.[126] The feminist intervention in literary criticism over the past thiry years has recognised and theorised such gendering of knowledge. Feminists have begun to construct alternative gynocritical canons. These canons aim to represent work by women and to offer inspiration to other female artists. As Jankowsky (p. 112) continues, 'we need to continue discussing GDR women writers because of the marginalisation of women in discourses in the formerly socialist countries as well as in the West'.

East German writing by women was, as a category, internationally acknowledged and had its own canon. Indeed Dorothy Rosenberg (1993, p. 13) goes as far as to label the period between 1976 and 1986 'the women's decade in GDR literature'. In the West, however, concentration on Wolf, Morgner, Seghers, Kirsch, Maron, and to a lesser extent Wander, Reimann and Tetzner, tended to obscure the work of more 'minor' female writers. As Eigler (1993, p. 146) has argued, 'we need to critically examine our approaches to this literature and explore works by previously marginalised authors'. The 'canon' of constructions of sexuality in GDR literatures constructed in this study thus includes rather than excludes. It includes 'official' and 'unofficial' work by major and minor authors, men and women. It is still, however, incomplete. There remains much to include that was beyond the scope of this study. Critics also need to differentiate clearly between the work of accepted members of the canon. Neither Wolf nor Morgner produced East German women's writing just because they were women writing in the GDR. As part of this process of differentiation accepted terminology of the reception of work from the GDR must also be redefined and set within new parameters – concepts such as *Frauenliteratur*, feminism, autobiography, authenticity and indeed GDR literature itself.

Here, therefore, sexuality is treated as a literary motif and as an element of form, rather than simply as *Ersatzdiskurs*. Theme, poetic imagery, narrative

---

[126] Schmidt finds, for example, a strong gender specific difference in the number of entries devoted to male and female writers in Emmerich's standard *Kleine Literaturgeschichte der DDR*. Of 25 female writers, 20 are mentioned less than 10 times. Amongst the 25 male writers the lowest number of entries is 17.

stance and the function of language have been analysed. Sex has been posited as a method of literary characterisation. Links have been established between desire and fantasy, and between the body and poetic rhythm. To ask simply what sex in the GDR was like would have been to deny the literary aspects of the texts, seeing them merely as social documents. Sexuality as content, as image, takes issue with the countless gendered representations which structure and resist ideologies of domination. Sexuality as a source of style engages with debates concerning a female aesthetic. It further raises issues of semantics, as patriarchal bias is exposed and new possibilities of signification are suggested. The language of the sexual offers a site where meanings converge and compete for domination. Sexual art can both question and reinforce these meanings.

The validity of this topic as serious academic material, rather than a source of voyeuristic and vicarious pleasure seeking, has been firmly established over the last thirty years. The title of Kate Millett's book *Sexual Politics* makes the political relevance of this subject vividly clear. It is one which is intrinsically linked with the fundamental issues of power, knowledge, responsibility, gender and subjectivity. These are notions which structure the ways in which we understand our world. Yet there are still those who adhere to the view that reseach into sex is frivolous, insignificant and unworthy of scholarly attention. The feminist revision has not always been greeted with enthusiasm. Where subjects of study have traditionally been constituted by a male readership, sexuality and its challenges have therefore, on occasion, been marginalised and even made taboo. Thus the vocabulary of sex remains catalectic. As Ellis (1992, p. 146) argues:

> As a result of blanket definitions, adequate means of writing and portrayal of sexuality have not been developed. [...] There is no discourse which is analytic yet nevertheless engages the subjectivity of the individual uttering that discourse. We are caught between personal confessions and general theoretical systematizations; mutually exclusive modes, each inadequate to the problems addressed.

It is in the context of such prejudices that one reason for the relative lack of detailed analyses of sexuality in GDR literatures may be sought.

Other explanations for this absence can be located in certain dominant methods of literary analysis. Themselves bound by ideology, these methods concentrated upon literature from the GDR which could be regarded as traditionally political and obviously public. David Bathrick (1991, p. 308), for example, notes a 'focus upon theme, politics and history to the exclusion of point of view, narrativity, and imagery'. Literary texts were, he continues:

211

Simply taken at face value, as transparent articulations on the subject of ecology, family, women's experience, gays, or life in the factory, regardless of the narrative strategies or linguistic codes they had employed to communicate such.

Selective practices of reception meant that, in general, Western critics chose texts which allowed a review of socialism as it existed in the GDR, whilst retaining the belief in a left wing utopia. As Patricia Herminghouse (1993, p. 94) recognises, 'in the often unconscious and unreflected projection of our own political agenda onto GDR literature [...] our own critical practices often became caught up in a binary scheme which limited our interpretative horizons'. Correlatively, Eastern critics generally reviewed art which offered an obviously Marxist perspective.

Reunification has destabilised these horizons. Recent critics have urged a reconsideration of GDR literatures from new angles, in order to emphasise relationships to other literatures, other aesthetic traditions and social questions in other parts of the world. In German Studies too, sexuality has become a valid topic of study, one which allows the Western reader to establish connections between East German texts and her own situation. Sexuality is a theme which is not just of interest within the context of the GDR. It is universal and interdisciplinary and as such particularly important within any post-*Wende* revision of East German art, enabling the critic to move beyond the parameters of the site of production. As Emmerich (1994, p. 186) states: 'Bleiben werden Texte, die, konzeptionell und sprachlich, über den bloßen Anlaß DDR und seine offene oder camouflierte (allegorische) Kritik hinausreichen'. Although the portrayal of, for example, homosexuality in literature could possibly be used to 'prove' that there was no open discussion of homosexuality in a repressive GDR society, to claim that Morgner's synthesis of food and sex referred to food shortages in a society where people had a dull sex life would clearly be ridiculous. Successful erotic literature offers a culture of resistance. But this resistance cannot be made to function solely in the context of an outwardly socialist state. The protest against and criticism of patriarchal sexual roles and sexual constructions offered in the work of both Morgner and Stötzer-Kachold represents resistance to effects of instances of patriarchy. Thus it is resistance that is valid in any context where male power denies female sexuality.

A general topic can, therefore, be used to ask questions of a text which are not bound by historical, geographical or political constraints. Where successful, constructions of this topic can contribute to both feminist and more aesthetic, political and social debate beyond the borders of the GDR and beyond the borders of German Studies. The juxtaposing of theoretical writings by Western critical theorists and fiction by Eastern women can offer new perspectives upon both sets of texts. The convergence between the work of Morgner and Stötzer-Kachold and Western critical theories allows this prose to be read from a position which is not bound to terms of reference dependent upon concepts of East German cultural politics. Theoretical arguments have been adopted here in order to justify the consideration of sexuality as construct, providing useful insights also as regards issues of power, utopia and identity. The fiction has shown how fantasy can give expression to theoretical ideas.

Utopian fantasies which dream of a society open to heterogeneous sexuality are necessary not just in the GDR. As one Western commentator writes:

> Attempts to free ourselves from certain forms of experience and self-understanding inherited under conditions of domination and subordination are not enough. We must also continue to struggle for rights, justice and liberties within the constraints of modernity. We must also continue to envision alternative future possibilities (Sawicki 1991, p. 102).

The texts considered here are successful when this demand is fulfilled. They then transcend divisions of East and West German literature. When the forty years of the GDR have become nothing more than a chapter in history books, the concept of 'GDR literatures' will, ultimately, become an anachronism. Looking back, even after only a few years, many texts which appeared challenging and experimental in a particular context do now, as Karen Leeder (1993, p. 242) states, 'seem to exhaust themselves in that gesture'. Her judgement is certainly applicable to some of the art published in the GDR, which exhausts itself in gestures not only of style but also of content. Even Ulrich Greiner's accusations of 'Gesinnungsästhetik' must be applied in a negative sense to some texts, though not necessarily to those selected by Greiner.[127] Such judgements and such accusations must not, however, be extended to all of East German art. Texts which can be rescued must be, for fear that they too may become mere anachronisms.

The wider aim of this study has been to encourage acceptance of sexual variety and to redefine the boundaries of sexual debate. Sexuality is – not only for feminists – a site of struggle. Dichotomies such as good/bad, healthy/sick, moral/immoral contribute very little to any discussion, merely simplifying difficult issues. Broad generalisations lead to proscription and oppression. Recognition of sexual diversity is necessary, for it allows the dismantling of hierarchies. The context and significance of the act for the subjects involved

---

[127] Greiner (1990, p. 214, p. 216) famously wrote that: 'Die Gesinnungsästhetik war das herrschende Merkmal des deutschen Literaturbetriebes, in der DDR sowieso, aber auch in der Bundesrepublik'. This aesthetic is, he continues, 'ein grandioses Mißverständnis'.

213

then becomes important, rather than a classification of the act itself. In deconstructing supposed sexual 'truths' one can begin to comprehend the incredible enigma that sexuality presents us with and to recognise that 'the hallmark of sexuality is its complexity: its multiple meanings, sensations and connections.' (Vance 1992, p. 5). Some of these meanings, sensations and connections have been considered and appraised in this study.

Appendix

Unpublished text by Gabriele Stötzer-Kachold

tag sonnentag es liegt auch noch schnee weiß himmel jauchzt bald
wird noch eine glocke klingeln oder das telefon oder der wecker
eine zeit in diesen winkel stadt einschieben als hätte ich etwas
in ihr zu tun
ich habe bauchschmerzen und schließe die augen
nicht in diesen tag sehen müssen nicht diese wachen gedanken
denken
ich bin allein
irgendwo erinnere ich mich gibt es eine freundin auf die ich
plötzlich neidisch bin weil sie das hat vom leben was sie wollte
oder ist die freundin meine mutter weil sie kinder hat und den
mann dazu die ihr die schritte zur zukunft sagen
die kinder brauchen schuhe und der mann was zu essen die jahre
sind erfüllt auch ich bin deren erfüllung mit dem was ich
brauchte
ich bin neidisch auf meine mutter weil sie mich hat
ich bin verdammt noch mal in deren leben gelandet die von mir
leben ich bin eine bild ihrer zukunft geworden und als ich noch
klein war und sie noch nicht verraten konnte hatten sie mich
lieber als die böse welt aus der immer etwas schlechtes kam
nun bin ich größer und der schlechtigkeit teilhaftiger geworden
jetzt kann ich lügen und ich habe sie belogen jetzt glauben sie
mir nicht mehr so jetzt vertrauen sie mir nicht mehr so und
vielleicht bleiben sie auch gar nicht bei mir
ich kämpfe gegen meine mutter weil sie sich eine welt zusammen-
gelebt hat die immer weitergeht
ich bin ausgestiegen aus dem leben meiner mutter
ich lebe vollkommen sinnlos in den morgen
in diesen besagten weißen tag hinein
ich habe tags sehnsucht nach den dunklen gedanken der nacht
wenn ich diese bauchschmerzen habe wenn ich es sehnsucht nenne
wenn sich da was durchschneidet
ganz zäh und spitz vom hals zum bauch durch das fleisch zieht
sich eine linie schneidet sich was durch meine wünsche
der schmerz am morgen weidet mich aus
noch einige sekunden und dann der schlag gegen den magen und
noch schnell ein würgen an den hals
dieser schöne helle tag fordert seine opfer

er krallt sich in meine luftröhre er drosselt die augen
schmerz der ferne da wo kein platz für mich ist
in der ferne ein gedanke wo sich meine hoffnungen den rücken
brechen
frühs noch im aufstehen das aufbegehren
von etwas das spruch war von etwas das liebe war von einem der
sich mir was sagte und abgewendet hat
früh noch kurz vorm aufstehen da kommt dieses gebet nach dem
glück des tages
im licht liegt alles klar
tags ist realität so ein entsetzlicher platz
wo alles so ist wie anfaßbar wie bleibend wie durchsichtig
tags entblättern sich die rätsel
tags drauf oder tags dran stehe ich auf und mache das was alle
machen und alle denken und spreche mit den worten aller und bin
in einer welt die alle so nennen und in einer straße die alle
verbindet zu der stadt hin deren namen sie auswendig wissen
tags läuft alles drauf zu auf ihr wissen und tags drauf war es
nicht
tags bin ich schwankend aufgestanden stimmt etwas nicht mit mir
tags fehlt mir der unterleib der nacht
tags fehlst du mir meine liebe wenn ich aufstehe und du liegst
in einem anderen bett
ich soll ein schlechtes gewissen haben weil du nicht da bist und
ich will dich und du lebst ein anderes leben und die liebe ist
wieder eine andere zeit und da kriechst du manchmal rein und
dann rennst du wieder weg und meine zeit tickt im liebesrhythmus
der treue die den träumen so nah ist
ich hab ein geheimnis aufgebaut das von der sprache und den
lippen und die haut die darunter zum körper wird und von der
verschmelzung und dem eintauchen in eine andere realität die
sofort die welten wechseln kann visionen offenlegt dich verrückt
und mich entrückt
ich wache am tag auf und habe bauchschmerzen in zehntelsekunden
konstatiere ich daß ich allein bin und daß du woanders liegst daß
ich aus dem alltag meiner mutter ausgestiegen bin und du nicht
aus dem alltag deines vaters
ich bin eine frau ohne kinder und du siehst die frau als die
mutter deiner kinder oder wenigstens die eine frau und das eine
kind
blutsverwandtschaft nennst du das und liebst im inzeß
alles was dir blutig nahe ist
ich wache mit bauchschmerzen auf weil ich schuldig bin einem
anderen glauben anzugehören als eurer tage wahrheit ist
kinder fallen ab wie äpfel aber der baum wächst
diesen apfel aßen adam und eva romeo und julia er war der tod

sie vergifteten sich daran
das lachen der eltern über die gesichter der kinder da können
sie sich völlig sicher sein im sichtbaren sind sie sich so
ähnlich bald werden sie sich ähnlich belügen betrügen bekämpfen
eben so wie menschen sind
ich liege im bett kann nicht aufstehen ein entwürdigung
schneidet sich ein und aus meinem fleisch gedanken wüten in mir
zerwerfen mich matt sprechen anderer gedanken worte
da ist es im dunkel besser da sagen sich die unbeweisbaren
schwüre da haben deine fliehenden worte zeit sich zu mir zu
gesellen
wie soll ich es am tage beweisen was vergangenheit ist wenn du
nicht neben mir liegst
da wo der schwanz sich in die votze schiebt ist es nacht und im dunkel wartet die
wahrheit
wer redet schon von der votzenenergie und deren strahlung
und den worten einer lebendigen unterwelt
es ist nicht jedes liebespaar das sich liebt und treu bleibt
ohne der welt kinder zu schaffen ein mörderpaar
ich bin nicht deine zu verachtende nutte weil ich mir den samen
nicht als lehrmeister einer nächsten generation vereinnahme
ich bin eine forscherin geworden folge der sprache einer unterwelt die nicht aus leichen besteht
außer der zeit ist stets wenn wir uns der unendlichen energie
der liebe anschließen
träumend ineinander leben und verändert in räumen und körpern
spazierengehen
lieben ist eine trance der verwandlung
ich will mit uns das geschaffene wissen behalten was sich der
vergänglichkeit entzieht
meine kastration und verweigerung des alltags zukunft wie es
meine mutter kennt in das nichts der suche zwischen zwei die
anderen geschlechts sind
in der männerwelt und der männerzeit weil nur die männer ein
unabhängiges wissen behalten suche ich die frauenzeit und das
frauenwissen
meine votzenenergie ist ausgangspunkt
immer wenn ich allein erwache mit dem kleinen wissen der
vereinzelten ficks aus denen sich meine hoffnung rekrutiert
diesem größeren wissen einmal nah zu sein
immer wenn sich morgens in meine eingeweide dieser schmerz
schiebt sich deinen wünschen nach einem kindsmutteralltag zu
entziehen
diesem tageswissen das sich rastlos in die zeit schmeißt das
sich weiß und bewiesen hat
bin ich die fremde des tages die ein anderes wissen sucht

alleingelassen von den vätern und den müttern
dieser tag der nichts weiß von meinem wissen
sehne ich mich in die träume der nacht die ein vollständiges
geflecht meiner räume sind
streiten wir uns wenn ich weine oder weine ich nach allem das
ich litt endlich um mich
eines tages aufstehen in ein anderes wissen
du neben mir der küsse zauber auf den lippen
wenn es kein wegrennen gibt in einen anderen alltag als der der
unser nachtwissen mit in den tag hinneinnimmt
nie hörte ich von den kräften der frau es sind die kräfte der nacht
der tag schiebt uns sündig wollen wir unser wissen aufschreiben
unter die haut
das wissen verblödet in irgendeinem geheimniskrämerschrank
da wo das wissen falsch gemünzt wird
da wo die tage geräte der ersatzmaschinen sind
ich liege am morgen eines tages der mein wissen entmachtet
dunkel in meiner votze vegraben das gespür einer fremden welt
fremde kommen und gehen sprechen sprachen die ich nicht hören
kann
aber in mir wärmt sich die verzweiflung anderer welten als
dieser die ihr ausstoßt und mit krieg verteidigt
es gibt die wahl der wahrheit
und es gibt die erkenntnis der geschlechter und es gibt die
einzigartigkeit des wesens mensch und die aufgaben des geistes
aus den geschichten der geister
diese unentdeckten kontinente der sinne
meine votzensignale meine votzenwärme meine energie die wir als
geilheit spüren dieses reservat an strahlung wenn du es mir
zurückgibst am tag was du nachts genommen hast wenn wir das
behalten und nicht der statisten zahlen gehören
komm mund küß mich leck dem schmerz von den lidern

The text is reproduced as sent to me by the author.

Abbreviations

A	*Amanda. Ein Hexenroman*
AE	*'Apropos Eisenbahn'*
B	*Leben und Abenteuer der Trobadora Beatriz nach Zeugnissen ihrer Spielfrau Laura*
DH	*Die Hexe im Landhaus. Gespräch in Solothurn*
DS	*Der Schöne und das Tier*
er	*erfurter roulette*
G	*Die wundersamen Reisen Gustav des Weltfahrers*
Gl	*Gauklerlegende. Eine Spielfrauengeschichte*
Gl	*grenzen los fremd gehen mit Zeichnungen der Autorin*
Ho	*Hochzeit in Konstantinopel*
R	*Rumba auf einen Herbst*
Zl	*zügel los*

BIBLIOGRAPHY

1.1. Primary Literature: Morgner

Morgner, Irmtraud *Das Signal steht auf Fahrt* (Berlin/Weimar: Aufbau, 1959)

Morgner, Irmtraud *Ein Haus am Rande der Stadt* (Berlin/Weimar: Aufbau, 1962)

Morgner, Irmtraud 'Notturno', *Neue Texte. Almanach für deutsche Literatur* (Berlin/Weimar: Aufbau, 1964) pp. 7-36

Morgner, Irmtraud *Hochzeit in Konstantinopel*, (Berlin/Weimar: Aufbau, 1968. Repr.Darmstadt und Neuwied: Luchterhand, 1988)

Morgner, Irmtraud *Gauklerlegende. Eine Spielfrauengeschichte*, (Berlin: Eulenspiegelverlag, 1970. Repr:Darmstadt und Neuwied: Luchterhand, 1982)

Morgner, Irmtraud *Die wundersamen Reisen Gustav des Weltfahrers*, (Frankfurt am Main: Luchterhand, 1981)

Morgner, Irmtraud *Leben und Abenteuer der Trobadora Beatriz nach Zeugnissen ihrer Spielfrau Laura*, (Berlin und Weimar: Aufbau, 1974. Repr. Frankfurt am Main: Luchterhand, 1990)

Morgner, Irmtraud *Amanda*. Ein Hexenroman, (Frankfurt am Main: Luchterhand, 1984)

Morgner, Irmtraud *Die Hexe im Landhaus. Gespräch in Solothurn*, (Zürich & Villingen: Rauhreif Verlag, 1984)

Morgner, Irmtraud *Der Schöne und das Tier*, (Frankfurt am Main: Luchterhand, 1991)

Morgner, Irmtraud *Rumba auf einen Herbst*, (Hamburg: Luchterhand, 1992)

1.2. Primary Literature: Stötzer-Kachold

Kachold, Gabriele 1989 'ich bin hörig', *Temperamente,* 31 (1989), p. 30

Kachold, Gabriele *zügel los* (Frankfurt am Main: Luchterhand, 1990)

Stötzer-Kachold, Gabriele *grenzen los fremd gehen mit Zeichnungen der Autorin* (Berlin: janus press GmbH, 1992)

Stötzer-Kachold, Gabriele 1992 'Die Frauen und die Kunst', *Weibblick,* 9 (1992), 7-9

Stötzer-Kachold, Gabriele 1993 'Frauenszene und Frauen in der Szene' in *Machtspiele. Literatur und Staatssicherheit*, ed. by Peter Böthig and Klaus Michael (Leipzig: Reclam Verlag, 1993), pp. 129-137

Stötzer, Gabriele *erfurter roulette* (München: Peter Kirchheim Verlag, 1995)

1.3. Primary Literature: General

Anderson, Edith (ed.) 1975 *Blitz aus heiterem Himmel* (Rostock: VEB Hinstorff Verlag)

Anderson, Sascha and Erb, Elke (ed.) 1985 *Berührung ist nur eine Randerscheinung. Neue Literatur aus der DDR* (Köln: Kiepenhauer und Witsch)

Apitz, Renate 1984 *Hexenzeit* (Rostock: VEB Hinstorff Verlag)

Arnold, Heinz Ludwig (ed.) 1990 *Die andere Sprache. Neue DDR-Literatur der 80er Jahre. Text und Kritik Sonderband* (Munich: edition text + kritik)

Bartsch, Kurt 1980 *Wadzeck* (Hamburg: rowohlt)

Borst, Meta (ed.) 1988 *Partnerschaften. Wandel in der Liebe* (Halle/Leipzig: Mitteldeutscher Verlag)

Bothig, Peter and Michael, Klaus (ed.) 1993 *Machtspiele. Literatur und Staatssicherheit* (Leipzig: Reclam Verlag)

Braun, Volker 1975 *Unvollendete Geschichte* (BRD: Frankfurt am Main: Suhrkamp, 1977)

Braun, Volker 1979 *Das ungezwungene Leben Kasts* (Berlin: Aufbau. Repr. 1984)

Braun, Volker 1985 'Rimbaud. Ein Psalm der Aktualität', *Sinn und Form*, 5 (1985), 978-98

Braun, Volker 1985 *Hinze-Kunze-Roman* (Repr. Baden-Baden: Suhrkamp, 1988)

Bräunig, Werner1965 'Rummelplatz', *Neue deutsche Literatur,* 10 (1965), 7-29

De Bruyn, Günter 1968 *Buridans Esel* (Halle/Leipzig: Mitteldeutscher Verlag. Repr. Frankfurt am Main: Fischer, 1991)

De Bruyn, Günter 1972 *Preisverleihung* (Repr. Frankfurt am Main: Fischer, 1982)

Döring, Christian and Steinert, Hajo (ed.) 1990 *Schöne Aussichten. Neue Prosa aus der DDR* (Frankfurt am Main: Edition Suhrkamp)

Döring, Stefan 1989 *Heutmorgestern. Gedichte* (Berlin/Weimar: Aufbau Außer der Reihe)

Drawert, Kurt (ed.) 1988 *Die Wärme die Kälte des Körpers des Andern. Liebesgedichte* (Berlin/Weimar: Aufbau)

Faktor, Jan 1989 *Georgs Versuche an einem Gedicht und andere positive Texte aus dem Dichtergarten des Grauens* (Berlin/Weimar: Aufbau Außer der Reihe)

Fühmann, Franz 1988 *Unter den Paranyas. Traum-Erzählungen und -Notate* (Rostock: VEB Hinstorff Verlag)

Görlich, Günter 1982 *Die Chance des Mannes* (Berlin: Verlag Neues Leben)

Grass, Günter 1980 *Kopfgeburten oder Die Deutschen sterben aus* (Darmstadt: Luchterhand Literaturverlag)

Gröschner, Annett 1990 'Maria im Schnee' *Sondeur*, 5 (1990), 48-55

Gröschner, Annett 1990 'Anekdoten', *Sondeur,* 5 (1990), 55-57

Hein, Christoph 1982 *Der fremde Freund* (Berlin/Weimar: Aufbau)

Hein, Christoph 1985 *Horns Ende* (Berlin/Weimar: Aufbau. Repr.Hamburg: Luchterhand Literaturverlag, 1987)

Hein, Christoph 1989 *Der Tangospieler* (Berlin/Weimar: Aufbau. Repr.Hamburg: Luchterhand Literaturverlag, 1991)

Hein, Christoph 1989 'Ich bin ein Schreiber von Chroniken...', *Neues Deutschland*, 2/3.12.1989, p. 11

Hein, Christoph 1989 'Die Vergewaltigung', *Neues Deutschland,* 2/3.12.1989, p. 11. Repr. in *Exekution eines Kalbes und andere Erzählungen*, pp. 131-38.

Hein, Christoph 1990 *Als Kind habe ich Stalin gesehen. Essais und Reden* (Berlin/Weimar; Aufbau)

Hein, Christoph 1993 *Das Napoleonspiel* (Berlin/Weimar: Aufbau)

Hein, Christoph 1994 *Exekution eines Kalbes und andere Erzählungen* (Berlin/Weimar: Aufbau)

Hensel, Kerstin 1988 *Stilleben mit Zukunft. Gedichte* (Halle/Leipzig: Mitteldeutscher Verlag)

Hensel, Kerstin 1989 *Hallimasch. Erzählungen*(Frankfurt am Main: Luchterhand)

Hensel, Kerstin 1990 *Schlaraffenzucht. Gedichte* (Frankfurt am Main: Luchterhand)

Hensel, Kerstin 1991 *Auditorium Panoptikum* (Halle/Leipzig: Mitteldeutscher Verlag)

Hensel, Kerstin 1993a *Angestaut. Aus meinem Sudelbuch* (Halle/Leipzig: Mitteldeutscher Verlag)

Hensel, Kerstin 1993b, *Im Schlauch*, (Frankfurt am Main: edition suhrkamp)

Hensel Kerstin 1993c, 'Trobadora Passé. (Irmtraud Morgner lesen I)', in *Angestaut. Aus meinem Sudelbuch* (Halle: Mitteldeutscher Verlag), pp. 100-102

Hensel Kerstin 1993d, 'Tanz in gefährdeter Welt (Irmtraud Morgner lesen II)', in *Angestaut. Aus meinem Sudelbuch*, pp. 103-108

Herzog, Marianne 1980 *Nicht den Hunger verlieren* (Berlin: Rotbuch Verlag)

Hesse, Egmont (ed.) 1988 *Sprache und Antwort. Stimmen und Texte einer anderen Literatur aus der DDR* (Frankfurt am Main: Fischer)

Jakobs, Karl-Heinz 1973 *Die Interviewer* (Berlin: Verlag Neues Leben. Repr. Frankfurt am Main: Fischer, 1974)

Jendryschik, Manfred 1976 *Ein Sommer mit Wanda. Legenden von der Liebe* (Halle/Leipzig: Mitteldeutscher Verlag)

Kant, Hermann 1965 *Die Aula* (Berlin: Rütten und Loening)

Kautz, Christine 1979 'Sonnabend' *Temperamente*, 4 (1979) p. 158

Kirsch, Sarah 1973 *Die Pantherfrau* (Berlin/Weimar: Aufbau Verlag)

Kirsch, Sarah 1973 *Die ungeheueren bergehohen Wellen auf See. Erzählungen aus der ersten Hälfte meines Landes* (Zürich: Manesse Verlag)

Kirsch, Sarah 1974 *Zaubersprüche* (Munich: Langewiesche-Brandt)

Kirsch, Sarah and Morgner, Irmtraud and Wolf, Christa 1974 *Geschlechtertausch* (Repr. Darmstadt und Neuwied: Luchterhand Literaturverlag, 1980)

Kirsch, Sarah 1978 *Erklärung einiger Dinge (Dokumente und Bilder)* (Ebenhausen bei Munich: Langewiesche-Brandt)

Kolbe, Uwe 1980 *Hineingeboren. Gedichte 1975-79* (Berlin/Weimar: Aufbau. Repr: Frankfurt am Main: Suhrkamp, 1982)

Kolbe, Uwe and Trolle, Lothar and Wagner, Bernd (ed.) 1988 *Mikado oder der Kaiser ist nackt. Selbstverlegte Literatur in der DDR* (Darmstadt: Luchterhand)

Königsdorf, Helga 1978 *Die geschlossenen Türen am Abend* (Berlin/Weimar: Aufbau. Repr.Luchterhand Literaturverlag, 1989)

Königsdorf, Helga 1978 *Meine ungehörigen Träume* (Berlin und Weimar: Aufbau. Repr. 1981)

Königsdorf, Helga 1989 *Ungelegener Befund* (Berlin/Weimar: Aufbau. Repr. Luchterhand Literaturverlag , 1991)

Königsdorf, Helga 1992 *Gleich neben Afrika* (Berlin: Rowohlt)

Kunert, Günter 1972, *Offener Ausgang. Gedichte* (Berlin/Weimar: Aufbau)

Kunert, Günter 1975 *Notizen in Kreide. Gedichte* (Leipzig: Reclam Verlag)

Kunert, Günter 1977 *Unterwegs nach Utopia. Gedichte* (Munich: Carl Hanser Verlag)

Lambrecht, Christine 1986 *Männerbekanntschaften. Freimütige Protokolle* (Halle/Leipzig: Mitteldeutscher Verlag)

Lewin, Waldtraut 1983 *Kuckucksrufe und Ohrfeigen. Erzählungen* (Berlin: Verlag Neues Leben)

Löffler, Hans 1987 *Briefe über ein Modell* (Berlin/Weimar: Aufbau)

Maron, Monika 1981 *Flugasche* (1981 BRD. Berlin: Union Verlag, 1990)

Martin, Brigitte 1977 *Der rote Ballon* (Berlin: Buchverlag Der Morgen)

Merian, Svende 1983 *Der Tod des Märchenprinzen* (Reinbek bei Hamburg: Rowohlt)

Metelka, Torsten (ed.) 1990 *Alles ist im Untergrund Obenauf: Einmannfrei. Ausgewählte Beiträge aus der Zeitschrift KONTEXT 1-7* (Berlin: edition KONTEXT, KONTEXT Verlag)

Michael, Klaus and Wohlfahrt, Thomas 1991 (ed.) *Vogel oder Käfig sein. Kunst und Literatur aus unabhängigen Zeitschriften in der DDR 1979-1989* (Berlin: Druckhaus Galrev)

Müller, Christine 1985 *Männerprotokolle* (Berlin: Buchverlag Der Morgen)

Panitz, Eberhard 1972 *Die sieben Affären der Dona Juanita* (Halle/Leipzig: Mitteldeutscher Verlag)

Papenfuß-Gorek, Bert 1988 *dreizehntanz* (Berlin: Aufbau. Repr: Frankfurt am Main: Luchterhand, 1989)

Plenzdorf, Ulrich 1973 *Die neuen Leiden des jungen W.* (Rostock: VEB Hinstorff Verlag. Repr. Suhrkamp, 1976)

Plenzdorf, Ulrich 1979 *Legende vom Glück ohne Ende* (Rostock: VEB Hinstorff Verlag)

Reimann, Brigitte 1974 *Franziska Linkerhand* (Berlin: Verlag Neues Leben. Repr.Munich: Deutscher Taschenbuch Verlag, 1990)

Saeger, Uwe 1981 *Nöhr* (Rostock: VEB Hinstorff Verlag)

Saeger, Uwe 1981 *Warten auf Schnee* (Rostock: VEB Hinstorff Verlag)

Saeger, Uwe 1983 *Sinon oder die gefällige Lüge* (Berlin: Buchverlag Der Morgen)

Saeger, Uwe 1988 'Unfachliche Notizen', in Borst (ed), pp. 250-87

Saeger, Uwe 1989 *Das Überschreiten einer Grenze bei Nacht* (Halle/Leipzig: Mitteldeutscher Verlag)

Schubert, Helga 1985 *Anna kann Deutsch* (Frankfurt am Main: Luchterhand)

Schubert, Helga 1982 *Das verbotene Zimmer* (Darmstadt und Neuwied: Luchterhand)

Schubert, Helga 1975 *Lauter Leben* (Berlin/Weimar: Aufbau. Repr. 1983)

Schütz, Helga 1980 *Julia oder Erziehung zum Chorgesang* (Berlin/Weimar: Aufbau. Repr. Luchterhand,1988)

Schwaiger, Brigitte 1984 *Wie kommt das Salz ins Meer* (Reinbek bei Hamburg: Rowohlt)

Stefan, Verena 1975 *Häutungen* (Repr. Frankfurt am Main: Fischer, 1994)

Tetzner, Gerti 1974 *Karen W.* (Halle/Leipzig: Mitteldeutscher Verlag)

Wander, Maxie 1977 *Guten Morgen, du Schöne* (Berlin: Buchverlag Der Morgen. Repr.Darmstadt: Luchterhand, 1989)

Wander, Maxie 1983 *Leben wär' eine prima Alternative* (Darmstadt und Neuwied: Luchterhand)

Wolf, Christa 1963 *Der geteilte Himmel* (Halle/Leipzig: Mitteldeutscher Verlag. Repr.Munich: Deutscher Taschenbuch Verlag, 1985)

Wolf, Christa 1968 'Lesen und Schreiben', *Die Dimension des Autors II*, pp. 7-47

Wolf, Christa 1968 *Nachdenken über Christa T.* (Repr. Darmstadt und Neuwied: Luchterhand, 1987)

Wolf, Christa 1976 *Kindheitsmuster* (Repr. Darmstadt und Neuwied: Luchterhand, 1979)

Wolf, Christa 1979 *Kein Ort. Nirgends* (Berlin: Aufbau. Repr. Luchterhand, 1989)

Wolf, Christa 1983 *Kassandra* (Darmstadt: Luchterhand)

Wolf, Christa 1983 *Voraussetzungen einer Erzählungen: Kassandra* (Darmstadt und Neuwied: Luchterhand)

Wolf, Christa 1986 *Die Dimension des Autors* (Berlin und Weimar: Aufbau)

Wolf, Christa 1989 *Sommerstück* (Berlin/Weimar; Aufbau)

Wolf, Christa 1992 *Was bleibt* (Hamburg: Luchterhand)

Wolf, Lutz 1976 (ed.) *Frauen in der DDR, Zwanzig Erzählungen,* (Munich: Deutscher Taschenbuch Verlag. Repr.1990)

Wolter, Christine 1976 *Wie ich meine Unschuld verlor* (Berlin/Weimar: Aufbau)

Zeplin, Rosemarie 1980 *Schattenriß eines Liebhabers. Erzählungen* (Berlin/Weimar: Aufbau. Repr. Frankfurt am Main: Ullstein Buch, 1984)

2. Secondary Literature: General

Achberger, Karen and Achberger, Friedrich 1975 'The Life and Adventures of Trobadora Beatriz as Chronicled by her Minstrel Laura', *New German Critique,* 15 (1975), 121-24

Agde, Günter 1991 *Kahlschlag. Das 11. Plenum des ZK der SED 1965. Studien und Dokumente*, (Berlin: Aufbau Taschenbuch Verlag)

Ahlings, Gabi and Nordmann, Ingeborg 1979 'Arbeiten wie ein Mann und wie eine Frau dazu. Frauen in der DDR', *Ästhetik und Kommunikation,* 37 (1979) 85-95

Allendorf, M. and others 1978 *100 Jahre August Bebel "Die Frau und der Sozialismus" Die Frau in der DDR* (Dresden: Verlag Zeit im Bild)

Althammer, René 1990 'Postmoderne Prosa als Mitteilungsform. Aufbau Verlag: "zügel los" von Gabriele Kachold', *Berliner Zeitung,* Nr.95 24.4.1990, p. 9

Anderson, Edith 1982 'Feministische Utopien' *Sinn und Form,* 2 (1982), 443-455

Anon, 1976 'Schreibende Frauen: Sagas von Sex und Leben', *Der Spiegel,* Nr.52, 20.12.1976, pp. 118-131

Anon, *Filmspiegel,* 26 (1972), p. 18, 3 (1973), p. 18, 5 (1973), p. 18, 6 (1973), p. 18, 7 (1973), p. 18 and 9 (1973), p. 18

Anz, Thomas 1991 *Es geht nicht um Christa Wolf. Der Literaturstreit im vereinten Deutschland* (Munich: edition spangenberg)

Arnold, Heinz Ludwig (ed.) 1991 *Literatur in der DDR. Rückblicke. Text und Kritik Sonderband* (Munich: edition text + kritik)

Auer, Annemarie 1975 'Mythen und Möglichkeiten. Nachwort', in Anderson (ed.), pp. 237-284

Auer, Annemarie 1976 'Trobadora unterwegs oder Schulung in Realismus', in Gerhardt (ed.), pp. 117-49

Böck, Dorothea 1990a '"Ich schreibe, um herauszufinden, warum ich schreiben muß". Frauenliteratur in der DDR zwischen Selbsterfahrung und ästhetischem Experiment', *Feministische Studien,* 1 (1990), 61-74

Böck, Dorothea 1990b 'Fixierte Realität. Gabriele Kachold *zügel los*', *Neue Deutsche Literatur,* 11 (1990), 154-56

Böhme, Waltraud (ed.) 1973 *Kleines Politisches Wörterbuch* (Berlin: Dietz Verlag)

Badia, Gilbert et al 1976 'Pariser Gespräch über die Prosa der DDR', *Sinn und Form,* 8 (1976), 1164-1192

Bammer, Angelika 1990 'Trobadora in Amerika', in Gerhardt (ed.), pp. 196-205

Bartens, Gisela 1991 'Die Machos sind überall', *Kleine Zeitung,* 23.11.1991

Barthes, Roland 1977 *Image, Music, Text* (London: Fontana Press)

Bathrick, David 1991 'The End of the Wall Before the End of the Wall', *German Studies Review,* 2 (1991), 297-311

Batt, Kurt 1975 *Einführung in den Sozialistischen Realismus* (Berlin: Dietz Verlag)

Batt, Kurt 1976a 'Realität und Phantasie. Tendenzen in der Erzählliteratur der DDR', *Neue Deutsche Literatur,* 2 (1976), 10-28

Batt, Kurt 1976b 'Was wir haben - was wir brauchen', *Neue Deutsche Literatur,* 2 (1976), 10-28

Belsey, Catherine 1980 *Critical Practice* (London: Methuen)

Belsey, Catherine and Moore, Jane (ed.) 1989 *The Feminist Reader. Essays in Gender and the Politics of Literary Criticism* (London: Macmillan Education)

Berger, Christel 1977 'Fragen der Moral und die neueste Prosaliteratur der DDR', *Deutsche Zeitschrift für Philosophie,* 8 (1977), 984-93

Berger, Christel 1983 'Amanda', *Sonntag,* 29.5.1983

Berger, Doris 1988 'Vom Optimismus der Aufbruchszeit zu Alltagsproblemen und Magie. Die Entwicklung der Frauenliteratur in der DDR', in Hildebrandt (ed.) 1988, pp. 123-136

Berger, John 1972 *Ways of Seeing* (London: Penguin Books, 1972)

Bethke, Ricarda 1991 'Versuch einer Annäherung an Gabi Kachold. Gabriele Kachold: *zügel los,* prosatexte, 1989', *Sinn und Form,* 1 (1991), 204-210

Boa, Elizabeth and Wharton Janet (ed.) 1994 *Women and the Wende: Social Effects and Cultural Reflections of the German Unification Process. German Monitor* 31, (Amsterdam: Rodopi)

Bovenschen, Silvia 1976 'Über die Frage: Gibt es eine "weibliche" Ästhetik?' *Ästhetik und Kommunikation,* 25 (1976), 60-75

Bovenschen, Silvia 1979 *Die imaginierte Weiblichkeit. Exemplarische Untersuchungen zu kulturgeschichtlichen und literarischen Präsentations- formen des Weiblichen* (Frankfurt am Main: Suhrkamp)

Braatz, Ilse 1980 *Zu zweit allein - oder mehr? Liebe und Gesellschaft in der modernen Literatur* (Münster: Verlag Frauenpolitik)

Brandes, Ute 1992 *Zwischen gestern und morgen. Schriftstellerinnen der DDR aus amerikanischer Sicht* (Berlin: Peter Lang)

Braun, Michael 1990 'Entfesselungsversuche. Gabriele Kacholds Prosadebüt zügel los', *Frankfurter Rundschau,* 4.10.1990, p. 7

Brinkler-Gabler, Gisela (ed.) 1988 *Deutsche Literatur von Frauen* (Munich: Beck)

Burmeister, Brigitte 1985 'Weibliches Schreiben. Zu einigen Aspekten französischer Frauentexte der 70er Jahre', *Weimarer Beiträge,* 31, 1630-50

Bussmann, Rudolf 1992 'Die Utopie schlägt den Takt. Rumba auf einen Herbst und seine Geschichte. Ein Nachwort', in Morgner, *Rumba auf einen Herbst*, pp. 331-345

Butler, Judith 1990 *Gender Trouble. Feminism and the Subversion of Identity* (London: Routledge)

Cameron, Deborah 1985 *Feminism and Linguistic Theory* (Hampshire: Macmillan. Second Edition 1992)

Cardinal, Agnès 1991 'Be realistic: Demand the Impossible. On Irmtraud Morgner's Salman Trilogy', in Kane (ed.) 1991, pp. 147-159

Castein, Hanne 1987 'Scherz, Satire, Ironie und tiefere Bedeutung: Zur Thematik der Frauenlyrik in der DDR', in Flood (ed.) 1987), 99-119

Childs, David 1983 *The GDR. Moscow's German Ally* (London: Allen & Unwin)

Cixous, Hélène 1975 'Sorties', in Marks/de Courtivron (1981), pp. 90-98

Cixous, Hélène 1976 'The laugh of the Medusa', in Marx/de Courtivron (1981), pp. 245-264

Cixous, Hélène 1977 *Die unendliche Zirkulation des Begehrens* (Berlin: Merve Verlag Gmbh)

Clason, Synnöve 1984 'Auf den Zauberbergen der Zukunft. Die Sehnsüchte der Irmtraud Morgner', *Text und Kontext*, 2 (1984), 370-86

Clason, Synnöve 1985 'Uwe und Ilsebill. Zur Darstellung des anderen Geschlechts bei Morgner und Grass', in *Frauensprache - Frauenliteratur? Für und Wider einer Psychoanalyse literarischer Werke. Akten des VII Internationalen Germanisten-Kongresses.* Band 6 1985, ed. by Inge Stephan and Carl Pietzcker, (Tübingen: Max Niemeyer Verlag, 1986), pp. 104-07

Clason, Synnöve 1990 'Mit dieser Handschrift wünschte sie in die Historie einzutreten. Aspekte der Erberezeption in Irmtraud Morgner's Roman [...] Beatriz', *Weimarer Beiträge*, 7 (1990), 1128-45

Cocalis, Susan and Goodman, Kay (ed.) 1982 *Beyond the Eternal Feminine. Critical Essays on Women and German Literature* (Stuttgart: Akademischer Verlag H.D.Heinz)

Cosentino, Christine 1985 'Gedanken zur jüngsten DDR-Lyrik: Uwe Kolbe, Sascha Anderson and Lutz Rathenow', *The Gremanic Review*, 3 (1985), 82-90

Coward, Rosalind 1984 *Female Desire. Women's Sexuality Today,* (London: Paladin Grafton Books)

Coward, Rosalind 1986 'Are Women's Novels Feminist Novels?' in Showalter (cd.) 1986, pp. 225-239

Cramer, Sibylle 1973 'Gustavs Weltfahren mit Hulda. Irmtraud Morgners Lügenroman', *Frankfurter Rundschau*, 8.12.1973

Cramer, Sibylle 1979 'Eine unendliche Geschichte des Widerstands' in *Christa Wolf Materialenbuch*, ed. by Klaus Sauer (Darmstadt und Neuwied: Luchterhand, 1979/1983), pp. 121-142

Culler, Jonathan 1983 *On Deconstruction. Theory and Criticism after Structuralism* (Suffolk: Routledge. Repr.1987)

Dölling, Irene 1980 'Zur kulturtheoretischen Analyse von Geschlechterbeziehungen', *Weimarer Beiträge*, 26 (1980), 59-88

Dahlke, Birgit 1992 'Die Chancen haben sich verschanzt. Die inoffizielle Literatur-Szene der DDR', in *Mauer-Show. Das Ende der DDR, die deutsche Einheit und die Medien*, ed. by Rainer Bohn and others (Berlin: Sigma Medienwissenschaft, 1992), pp. 227-242

Dahlke, Birgit 1993a 'Eine glaubhafte weibliche Ich-Figur kommt von einer glaubhaften weiblichen Identität. Gespräch mit Gabriele Stötzer-Kachold', *Deutsche Bücher*, 4 (1993), 243-58

Dahlke, Birgit 1993b 'ein stück leibverantwortung. Gabriele Stötzer-Kachold: *grenzen los fremd gehen*', *Neue deutsche Literatur*, 6 (1993), 148-50

Dahlke, Birgit 1993c 'Im Brunnen vor dem Tore. Autorinnen in inoffiziellen Zeitschriften der DDR 1979-90', in *Neue Generation - Neues Erzählen. Deutsche Prosa-Literatur der achtziger Jahre*, ed. by W. Delabar and W. Jung and I. Pergande (Opladen: Westdeutscher Verlag GmbH, 1993), pp. 177-193

Dahlke, Birgit 1993d 'Gespräch mit Kerstin Hensel', Deutsche Bücher, 2 (1993), 81-99

Dahlke, Birgit 1994 *Die romantischen Bilder blättern ab. Produktionsbedingungen, Schreibweisen und Traditionen von Autorinnen in inoffiziell publizierten Zeitschriften der DDR 1979-90*, (doctoral thesis. Berlin)

Dahlke, Birgit 1994b *Thesen zur Dissertation* (Unpublished. Berlin)

Dahlke, Birgit 1995 'Kanon und Norm. Zur literarischen/kulturellen Kommunikation in der SBZ/DDR', *Zeitschrift für Germanistik*, 1 (1995) 74-81

Damm, Sigrid 1975 'Irmtraud Morgner. Leben und Abenteuer der Trobadora Beatriz', W*eimarer Beiträge*, 9 (1975), 138-48

Damm, Sigrid and Engler, Jürgen 1975 'Notate des Zwiespalts und Allegorien der Vollendung', *Weimarer Beiträge*, 7 (1975), 37-69

De Beauvoir, Simone 1949 *The Second Sex* (London: Picador, 1988)

De Stefano, Christine 1990 'Dilemmas of Difference: Feminism, Modernity and Postmodernism', in Nicholson (ed.), pp. 63-82

Deiritz, Karl and Krauss, Hannes (ed.) 1991 *Der deutsch-deutsche Literaturstreit oder "Freunde, es spricht sich schlecht mit gebundener Zunge" Analysen und Materialien* (Hamburg: Luchterhand Literaturverlag)

Deiritz, Karl and Krauss, Hannes (ed.) 1993 *Verrat an der Kunst? Rückblicke auf die DDR-Literatur* (Berlin: Aufbau Taschenbuch Verlag)

Dieckmann, Friedrich 1992 'Christoph Hein, Thomas Mann und der Tangospieler', in Hammer (ed.), pp. 153-58

Doerry, Martin and Hage, Volker 1994 'Ich hab' ein freies Herz. Monika Maron über Autoren in der Politik und die Zukunft des VS. Spiegel-Gespräch', *Der Spiegel*, 17 (1994), 185-192

Drescher, Angela (ed.) 1989 *Christa Wolf. Ein Arbeitsbuch* (Berlin: Aufbau)

Easthope, Anthony and McGowan, Kate (ed.) 1992 *A Critical and Cultural Theory Reader* (Buckingham: Open University Press)

Eberhardt, Karl-Heinz (ed.) 1989 *Familiengesetzbuch* (Berlin: Staatsverlag DDR)

Eigler, Friederike 1993 'At the Margins of East Berlin's Counter-Culture: Elke Erb's *Winkelzüge* and Gabriele Kachold's *zügel los*', *Women in German Yearbook*, 9 (1993), 145-61

Eigler, Friederike and Pfeiffer, Peter (ed.) 1993 *Cultural Transformations in the New Germany: American and German Perspectives* (Columbia: Camden House)

Ellis, John 1992 'On Pornography', in Merck (ed.) 1992, pp. 146-70

Emmerich, Wolfgang 1980 'Nachwort', in Christa Wolf and Irmtraud Morgner and Sarah Kirsch, *Geschlechtertausch*, pp. 101-26

Emmerich, Wolfgang 1989 *Kleine Literaturgeschichte der DDR* (Frankfurt am Main: Luchterhand. Fifth edition)

Emmerich Wolfgang, 1992 'Für eine andere Wahrnehmung der DDR-Literatur: Neue Kontexte, neue Paradigmen, ein neuer Kanon', Goodbody/ Tate (ed.) 1992, pp. 7-22

Emmerich, Wolfgang 1993 'Do We Need to Rewrite German Literary History Since 1945? A German Perspective', in Eigler/Pfeiffer (ed.), pp. 117-31

Emmerich, Wolfgang 1994 *Die andere deutsche Literatur: Aufsätze zur Literatur aus der DDR* (Opladen: Westdeutscher Verlag GmbH)

Endler, Adolf 1971 'Im Zeichen der Inkonsequenz. Über Hans Richters Aufsatzsammlung "Verse Dichter Wirklichkeiten"', *Sinn und Form*, 6 (1971), 1358-66

Endler, Adolf 1975 'Sarah Kirsch und ihre Kritiker', *Sinn und Form*, 1, 142-170

Engel, Stephanie 1979 'The legacy of devotion', Socialist Review, 46, 143-51

Engels, Friedrich 'Die Entwicklung des Sozialismus von der Utopie zur Wissenschaft' *Werke*. Band 19. pp. 189-228

Engels, Friedrich 1892 'Die Familie', *Der Ursprung der Familie, des Privateigentums und des Staats* 4.Auflage. Stuttgart 1892. Marx/Engels Gesamtausgabe Band 29, (Berlin: Dietz Verlag, 1990), pp. 150-94

Engler, Jürgen 1983 'Die wahre Lüge der Kunst. Irmtraud Morgner: Amanda', *Neue deutsche Literatur*, 7 (1983), 135-44

'fb' 1992 'Die DDR war der Bauch des Wolfes. Gabriele Stötzer-Kachold las auf Einladung des "Dritten Programms" im Haus Erlen',*Glarner Nachrichten*, Nr.65 18.3.1992

Faber, Elmar 1988 'Christoph Hein. Ein Briefwechsel', *Sinn und Form*, 3 (1988), 672-78

Feyl, Renate 1984 'Amanda', *Neue Deutsche Literatur*, 1 (1984), 77-84

Fischer, Erica and Lux, Petra 1990 *Ohne uns ist kein Staat zu machen* (Köln: Kiepenheuer & Witsch)

Flax, Jane 1990 'Postmodernism and Gender Relations in Nicholson (1990), pp. 39-62

Flood, John (ed.) 1987 *Ein Moment des erfahrenen Lebens. Zur Lyrik der DDR. GDR Monitor*, 5 (1987) (Amsterdam: Rodopi)

Foucault, Michel 1966 *The Order of Things. An Archaeology of the Human Sciences* (London: Routledge, 1992. First published in French, 1966)

Foucault, Michel 1969 'What is an author?', in *Modern Criticism and Theory*, ed. by David Lodge (New York: Longman, 1988), pp. 197-210

Foucault, Michel 1979 *The History of Sexuality. Volume One, An Introduction* (London: Allen Lane)

Franke, Konrad 1969 'Im Bett über die Spree. *Hochzeit in Konstantinopel* von Irmtraud Morgner', *FAZ*, 6.9.69

Freud, Sigmund 1982 *Trauer und Melancholie. Essays* (Berlin: Volk und Welt)

Freud, Sigmund 1988 *Essays 2*, ed. by Dietrich Simon (Berlin: Volk und Welt)

Fries, Fritz Rudolf 1990 'Emanzipierte Frauen sind alle potentielle Dissidenten. Zu den Texten von und über Irmtraud Morgner', *Neues Deutschland*, 28.8.90

Funke, Christoph 1976 'Leben einer Spielfrau', *Kritik, 1975* (Halle/Leipzig: Mitteldeutscher Verlag, 1976), 122-23

Göhler, Helmut and others 1990, 'Leseland DDR: Ein Mythos und was davon bleiben wird', *Media Perspektiven*, 7 (1990), 438-54

Gabler, Wolfgang 1987 'Moralintensität und Geschlechterbeziehungen', *Weimarer Beiträge*, 33 (1987), 727-748

Gamman, Lorraine and Makinen, Merja 1994 *Female Fetishism: A New Look*. (London: Lawrence and Wishart)

Gerhardt, Marlis (ed.) 1990 *Irmtraud Morgner. Texte, Daten, Bilder* (Frankfurt am Main: Luchterhand)

Gerhardt, Marlis 1977 'Wohin geht Nora? Auf der Suche nach der verlorenen Frau' *Kursbuch,* 47 (1977), 77-89

Gerhardt, Marlis 1986 *Stimmen und Rhythmen. Weibliche Ästhetik und Avantgarde* (Darmstadt und Neuwied: Luchterhand)

Gilbert, Sandra 1980 'What do Feminist Critics Want? A Postcard from the Volcano', in Showalter (ed.) 1986, pp. 29-45

Gill, A.A. 1994 'Rude Food', *The Sunday Times Style Magazine,* 2.10.1994, p. 8

Girnus, Wilhelm 1983 'Wer baute das siebentorige Theben', *Sinn und Form,* 35/2 (1983), 439-447

Gnüg, Hiltrud 1978 'Gibt es eine weibliche Ästhetik', *Kurbiskern,* 1, 131-40

Gohlis, Tobias 1991 'Wo das Unverbrauchte ist. Ein Besuch bei der Dichterin Gabriele Kachold', *Stuttgarter Zeitung,* Nr.25, 30.1.1991, p. 29

Goodbody, Axel and Tate, Dennis (ed.) 1992 *German Monitor. Geist und Macht: Writers and the state in the GDR* (Amsterdam: Atlanta)

Gräf, Dieter 1992 'Gabriele Stötzer-Kachold's zweites Buch. lochbrüder? schwanzschwestern?', *Basler Zeitung,* 18.12.1992

Greiner, Ulrich 1990 'Die deutsche Gesinnungsästhetik', in Anz, pp. 208-16

Grobbel, Michaela 1987 'Kreativität und Revision in den Werken Irmtraud Morgners von 1968 bis 1972', *New Germanic Review,* 3 (1987), 1-16

Grotewohl, Otto 1951 'Die Kunst im Kampf für Deutschlands Zukunft' (August 1951), in Schubbe (ed.), pp. 205-09

Grunenberg, Antonia 1986 'Träumen und Fliegen. Neue Identitätsbilder in der Frauenliteratur der DDR', *Jahrbuch zur Literatur in der DDR,* 5, pp. 157-84

Grunenberg, Antonia 1990a *Aufbruch der inneren Mauer. Politik und Kultur in der DDR 1971-90* (Bremen: Edition Temmen)

Grunenberg, Antonia 1990b 'Unordentliche Vermutungen. Zur Debatte über Macht und Ohnmacht der Schriftsteller in der DDR', *Kommune,* 9 (1990), 61-65

Grunenberg, Antonia 1990c 'Das Ende der Macht ist der Anfang der Literatur. Zum Streit um die SchriftstellerInnen in der DDR', *Aus Politik und Zeitgeschichte,* 44 (1990), 17-26

Hähnel, Ingrid and Kaufmann, Hans 1985 'Eine Literatur der achtziger Jahre? Prosawerke der DDR am Beginn des Jahrzehnts', *Zeitschrift für Germanistik,* 1 (1985), 18-34

Hager, Kurt 1972 'Zu Fragen der Kulturpolitik der SED' (July 1972), in Rüß (ed.), pp. 493-528

Hammer, Klaus (ed.) 1992 *Chronist ohne Botschaft. Christoph Hein. Ein Arbeitsbuch. Materialien, Auskünfte, Bibliographie* (Berlin/Weimar: Aufbau)

Hammer, Klaus 1991 'Gespräch mit Kerstin Hensel', Weimarer Beiträge, 37 (1991), 93-110

Hanke, Irma 1982 'Debütantinnen. Neuere Frauenliteratur aus der DDR, *Deutschland Archiv,* 4 (1982), 420-30

Hanke, Irma 1986 'Lebensweise im Sozialismus, Literatur und Realität, Probleme einer sozialwissenschaftlichen Analyse der DDR-Literatur', *GDR Monitor,* 16 (1986/87), 141-167

Harding, Sandra 1990 'Feminism, Science and the Anti-Enlightenment Critiques', in Nicholson (ed.), pp. 83-106

Hartinger, Christel and Walfried 1984 'Does Women's Literature deal exclusively with problems of women? Women's liberation and the relation of the sexes in the GDR literature of the 1970s', *Journal of Popular Culture,* Vol.18, 3 (1984), 53-69

Hartinger, Walfried and Diersch, Manfred 1976 *Literatur und Geschichtsbewußtsein - Entwicklungstendenzen der DDR-Literatur in den 60er und 70er Jahren* (Berlin/Weimar: Aufbau)

Hartmann, Anneli 1988 'Schreiben in der Tradition der Avantgarde: Neue Lyrik in der DDR', in Labroisse/ Cosentino/Ertl (ed.) 1988, pp. 1-37

Heim, Uta-Maria 1991 'Mißtrauen gegen deutsche Ordnung. Gabriele Kachold im Stuttgarter Schriftstellerhaus', *Stuttgarter Zeitung,* Nr.208, 7.9.1991, p. 41

Herminghouse, Patricia 1979 'Die Frau und das Phantastische in der neueren DDR-Literatur. Der Fall Irmtraud Morgner', in *Die Frau als Heldin und Autorin. Neue kritische Ansätze zur deutschen Literatur,* ed. by Wolfgang Paulsen, (Bern: Francke Verlag, 1979), pp. 248-66

Herminghouse, Patricia 1983 'Wunschbild, Vorbild oder Porträt? Zur Darstellung der Frau im Roman der DDR', in Hohendahl and Herminghouse (ed.) 1983, pp. 281-328

Herminghouse, Patricia 1985 'Der Autor nämlich ist ein wichtiger Mensch. Zur Prosa', *Schreibende Frauen. Frauen Literatur Geschichte,* ed. by Hiltrud Gnüg and Renate Möhrmann (Stuttgart: Suhrkamp, 1985), pp. 338-353

Herminghouse, Patricia 1993 'New Contexts For GDR Literature: An American Perspective', in Eigler and Pfeiffer (ed.), pp. 93-101

Heukenkamp, Ursula 1979 'Ohne den Leser geht es nicht'. Im Gespräch mit Gerd Adloff, Gabriele Eckart, Uwe Kolbe, Bernd Wagner' *Weimarer Beiträge,* 25 (1979), 41-52

Heukenkamp, Ursula 1984 'Gegen das unheimliche Einverständnis mit dem Untergang. Über die Bewältigung von Angst in Werken der DDR-Literatur. 1982/83', *Weimarer Beiträge,* 4 (1984), 557-74

Heukenkamp, Ursula 1985 'Frauen in der Literatur der DDR und die Frauenliteratur', *Germanische Mitteilungen,* 21 (1985), 37-45

Heukenkamp, Ursula 1993 'Reiner Geist der frühen 60er Jahre. Irmtraud Morgner "Rumba auf einen Herbst"', *Neue Deutsche Literatur,* 3 (1993), 142-46

Heukenkamp, Ursula 1995 '*Eine* Geschichte oder *viele* Geschichten der deutschen Literatur seit 1945? Gründe und Gegengründe.' *Zeitschrift für Germanistik,* 1 (1995), 22-37

Hildebrandt, Christel (ed.) 1988 *Liebes- und andere Erklärungen. Texte von und über DDR-Autorinnen* (Bonn: Verlag Kleine Schritte)

Hildebrandt, Christel 1984 *Zwölf schreibende Frauen in der DDR. Zu den Schreibbedingungen von Schriftstellerinnen in der DDR in den 70er Jahren* (Hamburg: Frauenbuch-vertrieb)

Hillich, Richard and Klatt, Gudrun and Pergande, Ingrid 1989 'DDR Literatur in der nationalen und internationalen Literaturgeschichtsschreibung', *Zeitschrift für Germanistik,* 1 (1989), 45-70

Hilzinger, Sonja 1985 *Als ganzer Mensch zu leben, Emanzipatorische Tendenzen in der neueren Frauenliteratur der DDR* (Frankfurt am Main: Peter Lang)

Hinck, Walter 1990 'Vielliebchen bäumt sich auf. Zwischen Adorno und Alarmmeldung: Prosaische Lyrik, lyrische Prosa', *Frankfurter Allgemeine Zeitung,* 21.7.1990

Hirdina, Karin 1972 'Das Phänomen Liebe: Liebesproblematik in unserer Gegenwartsliteratur', in *Sonntag,* 44 (1972)

Hirdina, Karin 1981 'Die Schwierigkeit, ich zu sagen', *Sonntag,* 45 (1981), p. 4

Hirdina, Karin 1983 *Günter de Bruyn. Sein Leben und Werk* (Berlin: Verlag das europäische Buch)

Hirsch, Helmut 1973 'Scherz und Ironie ohne tiefere Bedeutung', *Neue deutsche Literatur,* 8 (1973), 140-43

Hohendahl, Peter and Herminghouse, Patricia (ed.) 1976 *Literatur und Literaturtheorie in der DDR* (Frankfurt am Main: Suhrkamp)

Hohendahl, Peter and Herminghouse, Patricia (ed.) 1983 *Literatur der DDR in den 70er Jahren* (Frankfurt am Main: Suhrkamp, 1983)

Hohmann, Joachim (ed.) 1991 *Sexuologie in der DDR* (Berlin: Dietz Verlag)

Honecker, Erich 1965 'Bericht des Politbüros an das 11. Plenum des ZK der SED' (Dec. 1965), in Schubbe (ed.), pp. 1076-81

Honecker, Erich 1971 'Schlußwort auf der 4. Tagung des ZK der SED Dezember 1971', in Rüß (1976), pp. 287-88

Huffzky, Karin 1975 'Produktivkraft Sexualität souverän nutzen. Ein Gespräch mit der DDR-Schriftstellerin Irmtraud Morgner', *Frankfurter Rundschau*, 16.8.75.

Humble, Malcolm 1992 'Pandora's Box: The rehabilitation of the siren and the witch in Irmtraud Morgner's Amanda', *Forum for Modern Language Studies*, 28 (1992), 335-48

Irigaray, Luce 1977 'Ce sexe qui n'en est pas un', in Marx and de Courtivron (ed.), pp. 99-106

Jachimczak, Krzyztof 1988 'Gespräch mit Christoph Hein', *Sinn und Form,* 2 (1988), 342-59

Jacobus, Mary 1989 'The Difference of View', in Belsey/Moore (ed.), pp. 49-62

Jahnsen, Doris 1992 'Eingeklebt aus Ernst und Spaß und Übermut. Der Bezug von *Rumba auf einen Herbst* zu den späteren Romanen Irmtraud Morgners', in *Rumba auf einen Herbst,* pp. 351-69

Jahnsen, Doris and Meier, Monika 1993 'Spiel-Räume der Phantasie. Irmtraud Morgner: Leben und Abenteuer der Trobadora Beatriz nach Zeugnissen ihrer Spielfrau Laura', in Deiritz and Krauss (1991), pp. 209-14

Jankowsky, Karen 1993 'Canons Crumble Just Like Walls: Discovering the Works of GDR Women Writers', in Eigler and Pfeiffer (1993), pp. 102-16

Jarmatz, Klaus 1973 'Die wundersamen Reisen Gustav des Weltfahrers', *Sonntag,* 6.5.73

Jauß, Hans Robert 1970 *Literaturgeschichte als Provokation* (Frankfurt am Main: Suhrkamp Verlag)

Jessen, Jens 1973 'Nachwort', in Kirsch *Die ungeheueren bergehohen Wellen auf See. Erzählungen aus der ersten Hälfte meines Landes* (1973), pp. 91-100

Johnson, Sheila 1984 'A new Irmtraud Morgner: Humour, Fantasy, Structures and Ideas in Amanda. Ein Hexenroman', in *Studies in GDR Culture and Society, 4*, ed. by Margy Gerber (U.S.A: University Press of America, 1984), pp. 45-64

Kübler, Gunhild 1991 'Erotischer Höhenflug. Ein Text aus dem Nachlass von Irmtraud Morgner', *Neue Züricher Zeitung,* 18.5.1991, p. 25

Kahlau, Claudia (ed.) 1990 *Aufbruch! Frauenbewegung in der DDR* (Munich: Verlag Frauenoffensive)

Kane, Martin (ed.) 1991 *Socialism and the Literary Imagination. Essays on East German Writers* (Oxford: Berg)

Kant, Hermann 1988 'Rede auf dem X.Schriftstellerkongreß der DDR', *Neue deutsche Literatur*, 2 (1988), 5-35

Karasek, Hellmuth 1973 'Im Suppenkraut der Phantasie. Irmtraud Morgners Wundersame Reisen Gustav des Weltfahrers', *Süddeutsche Zeitung*, 4.4.73

Kaufmann, Eva 1982 'Die Frauenfrage in der Literatur der DDR. Konferenz am 5. und 6. Mai 1981 in Perugia', *Zeitschrift für Germanistik*, 2 (1982), 210-212

Kaufmann, Eva 1984a 'Interview mit Irmtraud Morgner', *Weimarer Beiträge*, 9 (1984), 1494-1514

Kaufmann, Eva 1984b 'Der Hölle die Zunge rausstrecken... Der Weg der Erzählerin Irmtraud Morgner', *Weimarer Beiträge*, 9 (1984), 1515-32 (Also in Gerhardt 1990, pp. 172-195)

Kaufmann, Eva 1986 'Für und wider das Dokumentarische in der DDR-Literatur', *Weimarer Beiträge*, 32 (1986), 684-689

Kaufmann, Eva 1991 'Irmtraud Morgner, Christa Wolf und andere. Feminismus in der DDR-Literatur', in Arnold (1991), pp. 109-116

Kaufmann, Hans 1976 *Erwartung und Angebot. Studien zum gegenwärtigen Verhältnis von Literatur und Gesellschaft in der DDR* (Berlin: Akademie Verlag)

Kaufmann, Hans 1986 *Über DDR-Literatur. Beiträge aus 25 Jahren* (Berlin/Weimar: Aufbau, 1986)

Kebir, Sabine 1993 'Weil ich zuhören wollte. Maxie Wander: Guten Morgen, du Schöne', in Deiritz/Krauss (ed.) 1993, pp. 141-45

Kersten, Heinz 1981 'Nackedeis in "wilden Betten". Das Filmjahr 1981 in der DDR', *Deutschland Archiv*, 3 (1981), 232-34

Klässner, Bärbel 1990 'Beobachtungen im Zusammenhang mit einem Wort' in Kahlau (ed.) 1990, pp. 44-47

Kleinschmidt, Claudia 1989 'Gespräch mit Gabriele Kachold. Kunst ist ein Rhythmus, in dem frau leben kann',*Temperamente*, 3 (1989), 21-28

Kleinschmidt, Claudia 1990 'Spannungszustände. Porträt Gabriele Kachold', *Sonntag*, 2 (1990), p. 4

Kleinschmidt, Claudia 1992 'ich wollte nicht eure ordnung. Gabriele Stötzer - für wahnsinnig, hexisch, lästig erklärt', *Wochenpost*, 10.10.92, p. 20

Kolkenbrock-Netz, Jutta and Schuller, Marianne 1982 'Frau im Spiegel. Zum Verhältnis von autobiographischer Schreibweise und feministischer Praxis', in *Entwürfe von Frauen in der Literatur des zwanzigsten Jahrhunderts*, ed. by Irmela Von der Lühe (Berlin: Argument-Verlag GmbH), pp. 154-74

'Konkret-Interview. Frauenstaat', *Konkret*, 10 (1984), 54-61

Krechel, Ursula 1976 'Das eine tun und das andere nicht lassen', *Konkret*, 8 (1976), 43-45

Krechel, Ursula 1976 'Die täglichen Zerstückelungen. Gespräch mit Irmtraud Morgner', in Gerhardt 1990, pp. 24-33

Kristeva, Julia 1986a 'Revolution in Poetic Language', in Moi (ed.), pp. 90-136

Kristeva, Julia 1986b 'A question of Subjectivity - An Interview', *Women's Review,* No.12. Repr. in Rice and Waugh (ed.) 1989, pp. 128-34

Kuczynski, Jürgen 1980 'Jurgen Kuczynski an Herman Kant', *Neue Deutsche Literatur,* 10 (1980), 156-165

Kuhn, Anna 1994 'Eine Königin köpfen ist effektiver als einen König köpfen: The Gender Politics of the Christa Wolf Controversy', in Boa and Wharton (ed.) 1994, pp. 200-15

Löffler, Anneliese 1978 'Der Anspruch und die wirkliche Leistung. Literatur der Debütanten', *Neue Deutsche Literatur,* 9 (1978), 130-40

Labroisse, Gerd and Cosentino, Christine and Ertl, Wolfgang (ed.) 1988 *DDR-Lyrik im Kontext. Amsterdamer Beiträge zur neueren Germanistik Band 26* (Amsterdam: Rodopi)

Lahann, Birgit 1994 'Laß mich schreibend wieder leben', Gabriele Kachold, Autorin aus Erfurt', *Süddeutsche Zeitung,* Nr.144, 25/26.6.1994, p. VI/17

Lange, Inge 1987 *Ausgewählte Reden und Aufsätze* (Berlin: Dietz Verlag)

Lautert, Christel 1992 'Denn wir haben uns doch nur bekämpft und verletzt. Gespräch mit der Erfurter Schriftstellerin Gabriele Stötzer-Kachold über den Fall Sascha Anderson', *Freitag,* 3.1.1992, Nr.2, p. 9

Leeder, Karen 1991 'Poesie ist eine Gegensprache: Young GDR Poets in Search of a Political Identity', in Arthur Williams and Stuart Parkes and Roland Smith (ed.), pp. 413-27

Leeder, Karen 1993 'Hineingeboren: A new generation of poets in the GDR. 1979-89' (doctoral thesis, University of Oxford)

Lennox Sara 1981, 'Trends in literary theory. The female aesthetic', *German Quarterly,* 54 (1981), 63-75

Lennox, Sara 1983 'Nun ja! Das nächste Leben geht aber heute an', in Hohendahl/Herminghouse (ed.) 1983, pp. 224-58

Lewis, Alison 1989 'Fantasy and Romance. A feminist poetics of subversion and the Case of Irmtraud Morgner', *Southern Review,* 22 (1989), 244-255

Lewis, Alison 1995, *Subverting Patriarchy. Feminism and Fantasy in the works of Irmtraud Morgner* (Oxford: Berg)

Liersch, Werner (ed.) 1979 *Im Querschnitt. Günter de Bruyn* (Halle/Leipzig: Mitteldeutscher Verlag)

Lindner, Gabriele 1988 'Weibliches Schreiben. Annäherung an ein Problem', in *DDR-Literatur 1987. Im Gespräch,* ed. by Siegfried Rönisch, (Berlin/Weimar: Aufbau, 1988), pp. 58-75

Lindner, Gabriele 1990, 'zügel los von Gabriele Kachold. Selbsterkundung als eine Überlebensstrategie', Neues Deutschland, 27.7.1990, p. 7

Lodge, David (ed.) 1988 Modern Criticism and Theory. A Reader (London: Longman)

Lukens, Nancy and Rosenberg, Dorothy 1993 Daughters of Eve. Women's Writing from the German Democratic Republic (Lincoln: University of Nebraska Press)

Macclancy, Jeremy 1992 Consuming Culture (London: Chapmans)

Madea, Andrzej 1990 'Das ES gegen das ICH. Neue Texte von Kerstin Hensel und Gabriele Kachold', Freitag, 21.12.1990, p. 21

Mair, Lucy 1969 Witchcraft, (London: World University Library)

Marcuse, Herbert 1962 Eros and Civilisation. A philosophical Enquiry into Freud (New York: Vintage Books)

Margolis, Karen 1991 Der springende Spiegel. Begegnungen mit Frauen zwischen Oder und Elbe (Frankfurt am Main: Luchterhand)

Markgraf, Nikolaus 1975 'Die Feministin der DDR', in Gerhardt (ed.) 1990, pp. 150-155

Martin, Biddy 1979 'Irmtraud Morgner's Leben und Abenteuer der Trobadora Beatriz', in Cocalis and Goodman, (ed.) 1982, pp. 421-39

Martin, Biddy 1980 'Socialist Patriarchy and the Limits of Reform: A Reading of Irmtraud Morgner's "Leben und Abenteuer der Trobadora Beatriz nach Zeugnissen ihrer Spielfrau Laura", Studies in Twentieth Century Literature, 1 (1980), 59-74

Martin, Biddy 1982 'Feminism, Criticism and Foucault', in New German Critique, 27 (1982), 3-30

Marx, Elaine and de Courtivron, Isabelle (ed.) 1981 New French Feminisms. An Anthology (Hertfordshire: The Harvester Press)

Marx, Karl 'Das Elend der Philosophie', Werke. Band 4. (Berlin: Dietz Verlag, 1969), pp. 63-182

Marx, Karl 1844 'Ökonomisch-philosophische Manuskripte aus dem Jahre 1844', Werke. Ergänzungsband 1. Schriften bis 1844, pp. 465-588

Marx, Reiner and Wild, Reiner 1984 'Psychoanalyse und Literaturwissenschaft. Skizze einer komplizierten Beziehungsgeschichte', Zeitschrift für Literaturwissenschaft und Linguistik, 53/54 (1984), 166-93

McNay, Lois 1992 Foucault and Feminism: Power, Gender and the Self (Oxford: Polity Press)

Merck, Mandy (ed.) 1992 The Sexual Subject. A Screen Reader in Sexuality (London: Routledge)

Merkel, Ina 1991 'Keine Zeit. Niemals', in Von Soden (ed.), pp. 66-72

Meusinger, Annette 1992 'Verordnete Sprachlosigkeit und die Artikulation außerhalb des offiziellen Diskurses. *zügel los.* Texte von Gabriele Kachold' in *Lebensweise und gesellschaftlicher Umbruch in Ostdeutschland* ed. by G. Meyer and G. Riege and D. Strützel (Erlangen: Palm und Enke, 1992), pp. 365-71

Meusinger, Annette 1992 'Von der Notwendigkeit ständiger Grenzüberschreitung. Gespräch mit Gabriele Kachold' in *Lebensweise und gesellschaftlicher Umbruch in Ostdeutschland* ed. by G. Meyer and G. Riege and D. Strützel (Erlangen: Palm und Enke, 1992), pp. 371-78

Meyer, Barbara 1983 'Ein Hexenroman. Zu Irmtraud Morgners *Amanda*', *Schweizer Monatshefte,* 9 (1983), 756-58

Meyer, Barbara 1985 *Satire und politische Bedeutung. Die literarische Satire in der DDR. Eine Untersuchung zum Prosaschaffen der 70er Jahre* (Bonn: Bouvier Verlag Herbert Grundmann)

Meyer-Gosau, Frauke 1992 'Aus den Wahnwelten der Normalität. Über Brigitte Kronauer, Elfriede Jelinek und Kerstin Hensel', in *Vom gegenwärtigen Zustand der deutschen Literatur*, ed. by Heinz Ludwig Arnold (Munich: edition text + kritik, 1992), pp. 26-37

Millard, Elaine 1989 'French Feminisms', in Mills (1989), pp. 154-185

Millett, Kate 1969 *Sexual Politics* (London: Rupert Hart-Davis Ltd. Repr.1971)

Mills, Sara and others (ed.) 1989 *Feminist Readings, Feminists Reading* (Hertfordshire: Harvester Wheatsheaf)

Mitchell, Juliet 1974 *Psychoanalysis and Feminism* (Suffolk: Penguin)

Mittenzwei, Werner 1987 'Das Brechtverständnis in beiden deutschen Staaten', *Sinn und Form,* 39 (1987), 1265-1303

Moi, Toril (ed.) 1986 *The Kristeva Reader* (Oxford: Blackwell. Repr. 1992)

Moi, Toril 1985 *Sexual/Textual Politics. Feminist Literary Theory* (London and New York: Routledge)

Morgner, Irmtraud 1973 'Apropos Eisenbahn', in Gerhardt 1990, pp. 17-23

Mudry, Anna (ed.) 1991 *Gute Nacht, Du Schöne. Autorinnen blicken zurück* (Frankfurt am Main: Luchterhand)

Nägele, Rainer 1983 'Trauer, Tropen und Phantasmen: Ver-rückte Geschichten aus der DDR', in Hohendahl/Herminghouse (ed.) 1983, pp. 193-223

Nagelschmidt, Ilse 1989 'Sozialistische Frauenliteratur. Überlegungen zu einem Phänomen der DDR-Literatur in den Siebziger und Achtziger Jahren', *Weimarer Beiträge,* 35 (1989), 450-471

Nagelschmidt, Ilse 1991 'Nachdenken über Sätze. Schriftstellerinnen in der DDR', in Von Soden (1991), pp. 26-34

Neubert, Werner 1969 'Zwischen Phantasie und Gespenst. Irmtraud Morgner: Hochzeit in Konstantinopel', *Neues Deutschland*, 15.1.1969

Neubert, Werner 1974 'Aus einem Gutachten', *Neue deutsche Literatur*, 8 (1974), 103-05

Neumann, Nicholas 1976 'Ein Ritterfräulein hat die Männer satt', *Stern*, 24.6.76

Neumann, Oskar 1978 'Weltspitze sein und sich wundern, was noch nicht ist', *Kürbiskern*, 1 (1978), 95-99

Nicholson, Linda (ed.) 1990 *Feminism/Postmodernism* (New York and London: Routledge)

Nordmann, Ingeborg 1981 'Die halbierte Geschichtsfähigkeit der Frau. Zu Irmtraud Morgners "Leben und Abenteuer der Trobadora Beatriz", in *DDR-Roman und Gesellschaft. Amsterdamer Beiträge*, ed. by Gerd Labroisse Bd.11/12 (Amsterdam: Rodopi), pp. 419-462

Nowak, Erika 1978 'Aber die großen Veränderungen beginnen leise. Irmtraud Morgner gibt Auskunft', *Für Dich*, 21 (1978), 18-20

Oakley, Ann 1972 *Sex, Gender and Society* (London: Temple Smith)

Obermüller, Klara 1980 'Irmtraud Morgner', in Puknus (ed.) 1980, pp. 178-85

Püschel, Ursula 1980 *Mit allen Sinnen. Frauen in der Literatur. Essays* (Halle/Leipzig: Mitteldeutscher Verlag)

Panitz, Eberhard 1978, 'Frauensprache, Frauenliteratur', *Neue deutsche Literatur*, 2 (1978), 70-74

Paul, Georgina 1992 'Text und Kontext - *Was bleibt* 1979-89', in Goodbody and Tate (ed), pp. 117-28

Paul, Georgina 1994 'Über Verschwiegenes sprechen. Female Homosexuality and the Public Sphere in the GDR before and after the Wende.' in Boa/Wharton (ed.), pp. 226-237

Pearce, Lynne and Mills, Sara 1989 'Marxist Feminism', in Mills, pp. 187-228

Pergande, Ingrid 1991 'Volker Braun? Da kann ich nur sagen, der Junge quält sich...' New Voices in the GDR Lyric of the 1980s', in Martin Kane (ed.) 1991, pp. 229-46

Pieper, Rüdiger 1986 'Official policy and the attitudes of GDR youth towards marriage and the opposite sex as reflected in the column Unter 4 Augen' in *Studies in GDR culture and society* 6, ed. by Margy Gerber (U.S.A: University Press of America, 1986), pp. 109-21

Plavius, Heinz 1968 'Gegenwart im Roman: Gespräch mit Günter de Bruyn', *Neue Deutsche Literatur*, 6 (1968), 9-13

Pleßke, Gabriele 1986 'Das ferne Maß der Harmonie. Kulturkritisches von Irmtraud Morgner, Christa Wolf und Inge von Wangenheim', in Richter (ed.) 1986, pp. 210-41

Pollock, Griselda 1992 'What's Wrong with 'Images of Women'?', in Merck (ed.) 1992, pp. 135-45

Prokop, Ulrike 1976 *Weiblicher Lebenszusammenhang. Von der Beschränktheit der Strategien und der Unangemessenheit der Wünsche* (Frankfurt am Main: Suhrkamp. Repr. 1980)

Puknus, Heinz (ed.) 1980 *Neue Literatur der Frauen* (Munich: Beck)

Rönisch, Siegfried (ed.) *DDR-Literatur im Gespräch* (Berlin/Weimar: Aufbau, various editions)

Rönisch, Siegfried 1979 'Notizen über eine neue Autorengeneration', *Weimarer Beiträge,* 25 (1979), 5-10

Rüß, Gisela (ed.) 1976 *Dokumente zur Kunst-, Literatur- und Kulturpolitik der SED. 1971-1974* (Stuttgart: Seewald Verlag)

Rabinow, Paul (ed.) 1991 *The Foucault Reader* (London: Penguin)

Raddatz, Fritz 1972 *Zur deutschen Literatur der Zeit. Traditionen und Tendenzen* (Frankfurt am Main: Suhrkamp. Repr: Reinbek bei Hamburg: Rowohlt, 1987)

Raddatz, Fritz 1973 'Fortbewegung aus der Realität. Irmtraud Morgners *Die wundersamen Reisen Gustav des Weltfahrers'*, *FAZ,* 9.4.1973

Raddatz, Fritz 1976 'Marx-Sisters statt Marx. Neue Bücher von Morgner, Schlesinger, Köhler', *Die Zeit,* 21.5.76

Ramm, Klaus 1990 'Revolte gegen eine erdrosselte Sprache. Gabriele Kacholds Prosatexte "Zügel los"',*Der Tagesspiegel*, 2.10.1990, p. 4

Rausch, Hans 1990 'Gabriele Kachold: zügel los', *Wespennest,* 79 (1990)

Reich, Wilhelm 1951 *The Sexual Revolution. Toward a Self-Governing Character Structure* (London: Vision Press Ltd. Repr.1969)

Reid, J.H. 1984 'Literature without taboos: writers in East Germany since 1971', *GDR Monitor*, Special Series 2, (1984), 101-12

Reid, J.H. 1990 *Writing without Taboos* (Oxford: Berg)

Reinig, Christa 1976 'Das weibliche Ich', *alternative,* 108/109, 19 (1976), 19-20

Reuffer, Petra 1988 *Die unwahrscheinlichen Gewänder der anderen Wahrheit. Zur Wiederentdeckung des Wunderbaren bei Günter Grass und Irmtraud Morgner* (Essen: Verlag Die blaue Eule)

Rice, Philip and Waugh, Patricia (ed.) 1989 *Modern Literary Theory. A Reader* (Kent: Edward Arnold)

Richter, Hans (ed.) 1986 *Generationen, Temperamente, Schreibweisen. DDR-Literatur in neuer Sicht* (Halle/Leipzig: Mitteldeutscher Verlag)

Richter-Schröder, Karin 1986 *Frauenliteratur und weibliche Identität. Theoretische Ansätze zu einer weiblichen Ästhetik und zur Entwicklung der neuen deutschen Frauenliteratur* (Frankfurt am Main: Verlag Anton Hain)

Robbins, R.H. 1959 *The Encyclopedia of Witchcraft and Demonology* (London: Spring Books)

Rose, Jacqueline 1989 'Julia Kristeva: Take Two', in *Coming to Terms. Feminism, Theory, Politics*, ed. by Elizabeth Weed (London: Routledge, 1989), pp. 17-33

Rosenberg, Dorothy 1983 'On Beyond Superwoman: The Conflict between Work and Family Roles in GDR Literature', in *Studies in GDR Culture and Society, 3* (1983), pp. 87-100

Rosenberg, Dorothy 1988 'GDR Women Writers: The Post-War Generations Bibliography of Narrative Prose. June 1987', *Women in German Yearbook. Feminist Studies and German Culture,* 4 (1988), 233-40

Rosenberg, Dorothy 1992 'Neudefinierung des Öffentlichen und des Privaten: Schriftstellerinnen in der DDR', in Brandes (ed.), pp. 17-41

Rosenberg, Dorothy 1993 'Introduction: Women, Social Policy and Literature in the German Democratic Republic', in Lukens and Rosenberg (ed.) 1993, pp. 1-22

Rosenberg, Rainer 1995 'Was war DDR-Literatur? Die Diskussion um den Gegenstand in der Literaturwissenschaft der Bundesrepublik Deutschland', *Zeitschrift für Germanistik,* 1 (1995), 9-21

Rubin, Gayle 1992 'Thinking Sex: Notes for a Radical Theory of the Politics of Sexuality', in Vance (ed.) 1992, pp. 267-319

Russell, Jeffrey 1980 *A History of Witchcraft, Sorcerers, Heretics and Pagans* (London: Thames and Hudson)

Ruthven, K.K. 1984 *Feminist Literary Studies, An Introduction*, (Cambridge: Cambridge University Press)

Salzinger, Helmut 1973 'Die Schöpferkraft der Machtlosen. Ein lügenhafter Roman von Irmtraud Morgner', *Stuttgarter Zeitung,* 22.12.73

Sandford, John 1984 'The Press in the GDR: Principles and Practice', *GDR Monitor*, Special Series 2 (1984), 27-36

Sauer, Klaus (ed.) 1979 *Christa Wolf Materialenbuch* (Darmstadt und Neuwied: Luchterhand. Repr. 1983)

Sawicki, Jana 1991 *Disciplining Foucault. Feminism, Power and the Body* (London/New York: Routledge)

Schütz, Helga 1991 'Once I lived near the wall...', in Mudry (ed.) 1991, pp. 15-29

Scherer, Gabriele 1992 *Zwischen "Bitterfeld" und "Orplid". Zum literarischen Werk Irmtraud Morgners* (Bern: Peter Lang)

Schlenstedt, Dieter 1976 'Prozeß der Selbstverständigung. Aspekte der Funktionsbestimmmung in unserer neueren Literatur', *Weimarer Beiträge*, 12 (1976), 5-37

Schlenstedt, Dieter 1988 'Entwicklungslinien der neueren Literatur in der DDR', in Chiarloni (ed.) 1988, pp. 29-54

Schlenstedt, Silvia 1989 'Fragen der Nachgeborenen. Aspekte gegenwärtiger Lyrik in der DDR', in *Studies in GDR Culture and Society 9,* ed. by Margy Gerber (U.S.A: University Press of America, 1989), pp. 85-99

Schmidt, Ricarda 1990 *Westdeutsche Frauenliteratur in den 70er Jahren* (Frankfurt am Main: Rita G. Fischer Verlag)

Schmidt, Ricarda 1992a 'Im Schatten der Titanen: Minor GDR women writers - Justly neglected, Unrecognised or repressed?', in Goodbody/Tate (ed.), pp. 151-162

Schmidt, Ricarda 1992b 'Utopia and its loss: Women's Writing in the GDR', in *Women: A Cultural Review* 3 (1992), (Oxford: Oxford University Press, 1992), pp. 249-58

Schmitt, Hans-Jürgen and Schramm, Gerhard (ed.) 1974 *Dokumente zum 1. Allunionskongreß der Sowjetschriftsteller* (Frankfurt am Main: Suhrkamp)

Schmitz, Dorothea 1983 *Weibliche Selbstentwürfe und männliche Bilder. Zur Darstellung der Frau in DDR-Romanen der 70er Jahre* (Frankfurt am Main: Peter Lang)

Schmitz-Köster, Dorothea 1986 'DDR-Frauenliteratur der 70er und 80er Jahre. Wenn wir zu hoffen aufhören, kommt, was wir fürchten, bestimmt!', *Feministische Studien,* 1 (1986), 159-165

Schmitz-Köster, Dorothea 1989 *Trobadora und Kassandra und... Weibliches Schreiben in der DDR* (Köln: Phal-Rugenstein Verlag)

Schnabl, Siegfried 1969 *Mann und Frau intim. Fragen des gesunden und des gestörten Geschlechtslebens* (Berlin: VEB Verlag Volk und Gesundheit. Repr. 1977)

Schubbe, Elimar (ed.) 1972 *Dokumente zur Kunst-, Literatur- und Kulturpolitik der SED. 1946-70* (Stuttgart: Seewald Verlag)

Schulz, Genia 1988 'Kein Chorgesang. Neue Schreibweisen bei Autorinnen (aus) der DDR', in *Bestandsaufnahme Gegenwartsliteratur Text + Kritik Sonderband* ed. by Heinz Ludwig Arnold (Munich: edition text + kritik, 1988), pp. 212-25

Schwarz, Gislinde 1990 'Aufbruch der Hexen. Die Revolution der Frauen in der DDR', in Kahlau (ed.) 1990, pp. 8-24

Schwarzer, Alice 1976 'Auch Genossen sind nicht automatisch Brüder', *Konkret,* 9 (1976), 57-58

Schwarzer, Alice 1990a 'Eine Aufwieglerin', *Neue Deutsche Literatur,* 8 (1990), 64-66

Schwarzer, Alice 1990b 'Jetzt oder nie! Die Frauen sind die Hälfte des Volkes!' *Emma,* 2 (1990), 32-39

Secci, Lia 1988 'Von der realen zur romantischen Utopie. Zeitgenössische Entwicklungen in der Erzählprosa der DDR', in Brinkler-Gabler (ed.) 1988, pp. 417-31

Serke, Jürgen 1979 *Frauen Schreiben. Ein Neues Kapitel deutschsprachiger Literatur* (Hamburg: Stern)

Showalter, Elaine (ed.) 1986 *The New Feminist Criticism, Essays on Women, Literature and Theory* (London:Virago Press. Repr.1992)

Showalter, Elaine 1986a 'Toward a Feminist Poetics', in Showalter (ed.), pp. 125-143

Showalter, Elaine 1986b 'Feminist Criticism in the Wilderness', in Showalter (ed.), pp. 243-270

Sichtermann, Barbara 1989 *Weiblichkeit. Texte aus dem zweiten Jahrzehnt der Frauenbewegung* (Frankfurt am Main: Büchergilde Gutenberg)

Sillge, Ursula 1991 *Un-Sichtbare Frauen. Lesben und ihre Emanzipation in der DDR* (Berlin: Linksdruck Verlag)

Silverman, Kaja 1992 'Histoire d'O. The construction of a female subject', in Vance (ed.) 1992, pp. 320-49

Simons, Elizabeth 1979 'Über Ruth Werner', *Weimarer Beiträge,* 9 (1979), 129-140

Simons, Elizabeth 1979 'Interview mit Ruth Werner', *Weimarer Beiträge,* 9 (1979), 117-128

Sperling, Ute 1991 'Erzpoetische Ansichten und die neue Frauenbewegung. Zur Morgner-Rezeption im Westen', in Von Soden (ed.), pp. 48-54

Sprigath, Gabriele 1983 'Frauen und Männer und die Wirklichkeit der Kunst', *Kürbiskern,* 4 (1983), 147-54

Starke, Kurt and Friedrich, Walter 1984 *Liebe und Sexualität bis 30* (Berlin: VEB Verlag der Wissenschaften)

Starke, Kurt 1990 'Trauscheinehe Ost oder 'wilde' Ehe West. Lebenslaufplanung, Partnerschaft und Sexualität von Studierenden', in *Jugend im deutsch-deutschen Vergleich. Die Lebenslage der jungen*

Generation im Jahr der Vereinigung, ed. by Georg Neubauer and others (Frankfurt am Main: Luchterhand), pp. 141-77

Starke, Kurt and Weller, Konrad 1990 *Differences in sexual conduct between East and West German Adolescents before unification* (Unpublished: Leipzig)

Stawström, Anneliese 1991 'Das Ende war der Anfang meiner größten Illusion. Zu Irmtraud Morgners Trobadora Beatriz und Amanda', *Schriften des deutschen Instituts. Universität Stockholm* 21, (1991), 7-24

Swiderski, Gabriele 1983 'Der Planet braucht Hexen. Interview mit Irmtraud Morgner', *Rote Blätter,* 4 (1983), 65-67

Tate, Dennis 1984 *The East German Novel* (Bath: Bath University Press)

Thulin, Michael 1990 'Sprache und Sprachkritik. Die Literatur des Prenzlauer Bergs in Berlin\DDR', in Arnold (ed.) 1990, pp. 234-242

Vance, Carol (ed.) 1992 *Pleasure and Danger. Exploring Female Sexuality* (London: Pandora)

Voigtländer Annie (ed.) 1972 *Liebes- und andere Erklärungen. Schriftsteller über Schriftsteller* (Berlin/Weimar: Aufbau)

Von Bormann, Alexander 1991 'Unbehauste Texte', *Deutschland Archiv. Zeitschrift für das vereinigte Deutschland,* 24 (1991), 209-211

Von Soden, Kristine (ed.) 1991 *Irmtraud Morgners Hexische Weltfahrt. Eine Zeitmontage* (Berlin: Elefantenpress)

Von Törne, Dorothea 1992 'Eine Obduktion der Verhältnisse. Gabriele Stötzer-Kachold schreibt gegen die Zerstörung der Persönlichkeit', *Neue Zeit,* 15.12.1992, p. 14

Walther, Joachim 1973 *Meinetwegen Schmetterlinge. Gespräche mit Schriftstellern* (Berlin: Der Morgen Verlag)

Waugh, Patricia (ed.) 1992 *Postmodernism. A Reader* (London: Edward Arnold)

Waugh, Patricia 1989 *Feminine Fictions. Revisiting The Postmodern* (London: Routledge)

Waugh, Patricia 1992 'Modernism, Postmodernism, Feminism: Gender and Autonomy Theory', in Waugh (ed.) 1992, pp. 189-204

Weedon, Chris (ed.) 1988 *Die Frau in der DDR. An Anthology of Women's Writing from the German Democratic Republic* (Oxford: Blackwell)

Weedon, Chris 1987 *Feminist Practice and Poststructuralist Theory* (Oxford: Blackwell)

Weeks, Jeffrey 1986 *Sexuality* (Chichester: Ellis Horwood Ltd)

Weigel, Sigrid 1984a 'Woman begins relating to herself. (Part One) Contemporary German Women's Literature', *New German Critique*, 31 (1984), 53-94

Weigel, Sigrid 1984b 'Overcoming Absence: Contemporary German Women's Literature (Part 2)', *New German Critique*, 32 (1984), 3-22

Weigel, Sigrid 1987 *Die Stimme der Medusa. Schreibweisen in der Gegenwartsliteratur von Frauen.* (Dülmen-Hiddingsel: tende)

Weigel, Sigrid 1992 'Blut ist im Schuh. Die Bedeutung der Körper in Christa Wolfs Prosa', in *Christa Wolf in feministischer Sicht,* ed. by Michel Vanhelleputte (Frankfurt am Main: Peter Lang, 1992), pp. 145-57

Weigel, Sigrid and Venske, Regula 1992 'Frauenliteratur - Literatur von Frauen', in *Gegenwartsliteratur seit 1968. Hansers Sozialgeschichte der deutschen Literatur Band 12,* ed. by Klaus Briegleb and Sigrid Weigel (Munich: Carl Hanser Verlag, 1992), pp. 245-76

Weisbrod, Peter 1980 *Literarischer Wandel in der DDR* (Heidelberg: Groos)

Westphal, Anke 1991 'Das es mich nicht gratis gibt', *Virginia,* 10 (1991)

Westphal, Anke 1993a 'Das Ich ist eine Sie. Gabriele Stötzer-Kachold: *grenzen los fremd gehen*', *Virginia,* 14 (1993)

Westphal, Anke 1993b 'Mehr Sprache wagen. Zur Lesung von Gabriele Stötzer und Heike Willingham', *Neue Zeit,* 17.2.1993

Wesuls, Elisabeth 1991 'zügellos, ehrlich und radikal', *Die Weltbühne,* 12.3.1991, Band 12, 337-39

Whitford, Margaret (ed.) 1991 *The Irigaray Reader* (Oxford: Blackwell)

Wiesner, Herbert (ed.) 1991 *Zensur in der DDR. Geschichte, Praxis und "Ästhetik" der Behinderung von Literatur. Ausstellungsbuch* (Berlin: Literaturhaus)

Williams, Arthur and Parkes, Stuart and Smith, Roland (ed.) 1991 *German Literature At A Time Of Change 1989-1990. German Unity and German Identity in Literary Perspective* (Bern: Peter Lang)

Wolf, Christa 1986 'Projektionsraum Romantik. Gespräch mit Frauke Meyer-Gosau', in *Die Dimension des Autors II* (Berlin /Weimar: Aufbau, 1986), pp. 422-39

Wolf, Christa 1990 'Der Mensch ist in zwei Formen ausgebildet. Zum Tode von Irmtraud Morgner', *Die Zeit,* 11.5.90

Wolf, Gerhard 1975 'Abschied von der Harmonie', *Sinn und Form,* 4 (1975) 840-46

Wolf, Gerhard 1988 'Wortlaut Wortbruch Wortlust. Zu einem Aspekt neuer Lyrik in der DDR', in *Bestandsaufnahme Gegenwartsliteratur Text | Kritik*

Sonderband, ed. by Heinz Ludwig Arnold (Munich: edition text + kritik, 1988), pp. 226-54

Wolf, Gerhard 1990 'Worte zum Abschied', *Neue Deutsche Literatur,* 8 (1990), 58-64

Wolf, Gerhard 1992 'Gabriele Kachold: "zügel los"', in Wolf G. 1992, pp. 153-58

Wolf, Gerhard 1992 *Sprachblätter. Wortwechsel. Im Dialog mit Dichtern* (Leipzig: Reclam)

Zdanov, Andrej 1936 'Die Sowjetliteratur, die ideenreichste und fortschrittlichste Literatur der Welt', in Schmitt and Schramm (ed.) 1974